The
Grammar

The Grammar Starter

지은이 Nexus Contents Development Team
펴낸이 임상진
펴낸곳 (주)넥서스

출판신고 1992년 4월 3일 제311-2002-2호 2-11
10880 경기도 파주시 지목로 5
Tel (02)330-5500 Fax (02)330-5555

ISBN 979-11-5752-012-1 54740
       979-11-5752-011-4 (SET)

가격은 뒤표지에 있습니다.
잘못 만들어진 책은 구입처에서 바꾸어 드립니다.

www.nexusEDU.kr
NEXUS Edu는 넥서스의 초·중·고 학습물 전문 브랜드입니다.

The Grammar

Nexus Contents Development Team

Starter

NEXUS Edu

Concise and Core
Grammar Points!

The Grammar Series

Sentence Expansion
기초 문법을 기반으로 문장을 완성,
확장해 가는 학습 방법 적용

Grammar Summary
배운 학습 내용을 차트 및 표로 정리하여
쉽게 암기할 수 있도록 구성

A Variety of Question Types
문법 포인트 확인 ➡ 기초 문법 문제 ➡ 응용 문제 ➡
리뷰 테스트 ➡ 문법 확장 문제 ➡ 종합 문제

Preparation for School Tests
다양한 문제 유형을 통해 내신 대비는 물론
말하기 및 쓰기 실력 향상

Workbook
내신 대비 및 서술형 평가 대비를 위한
충분한 분량의 문제가 수록된 워크북 제공

Concise & Core Grammar
불필요하고 잘 사용하지 않는 문법은 배제하고
핵심적인 부분만을 간결하고 정확하게
예문 중심으로 이해할 수 있도록 구성

Features

Concept Note
기본 핵심 포인트의 개념을 간단하게 정의하였습니다.

Grammar Point
문법 포인트를 간단 명료하게 정리하였고, 문장의 예문 패턴을 집중적으로 학습할 수 있도록 한글 설명과 영문 예문을 분리하였습니다.

Quick Test
배운 내용의 개념과 규칙 등을 확인할 수 있도록 간단한 연습 문제를 마련하였습니다.

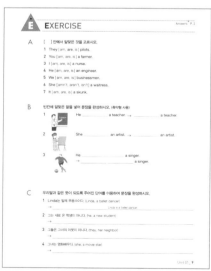

Exercise
단어 · 어구 · 문장을 고르거나 완성하는 연습문제를 통해 실질적으로 학습한 문법 포인트를 익힐 수 있도록 구성하였습니다.

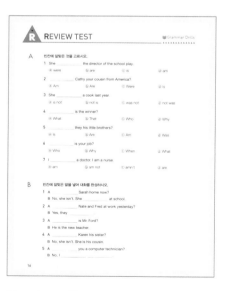

Review Test
각 Unit에서 배운 내용을 총 정리하는 장으로 각각의 문법 포인트를 통합적으로 구성한 문제 풀이를 통해 부족한 부분을 진단할 수 있습니다.

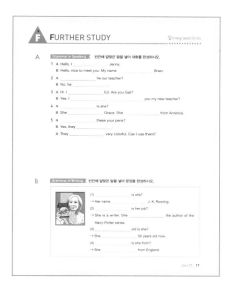

Further Study

각 단원에서 배운 문법 포인트를 대화문과 실용문을 통해 연습해 볼 수 있도록 구성하여 문법 실력뿐만 아니라 말하기/쓰기 실력을 동시에 향상시킬 수 있습니다.

Wrap-up Test

내신형 문제를 통해 앞에서 배운 문법 포인트를 종합적으로 정리할 수 있으며, 학교에서 많이 출제되는 주관식 및 서술형 문제로 구성되어 있어 내신 대비를 완벽하게 할 수 있습니다.

Workbook

기초 문법 확인 문제 외에도 내신 완벽 대비를 위한 객관식, 서술형 문제를 유닛별로 구성하여 자기주도학습을 할 수 있도록 하였습니다.

Answers

간결하고 명확한 설명을 통해 다양한 연습문제에 대한 정답을 확인할 수 있습니다.

Contents

The
Grammar

Starter

be동사,
Wh-의문문

Unit 01

be동사의 현재형

be동사(be verbs) ┌ am → I am a singer.
                 ├ are → You are my friend. We are friends.
                 └ is → He is a doctor.

1 단수형: am, are, is

	주어	동사	예문
1인칭	I	am	I am Lisa.
2인칭	You	are	You are kind.
3인칭	He She It	is	He is a teacher. She is a student. It is a dog.

1
be동사는 주어 뒤에 쓰여
'~이다, ~있다'의 의미로 쓰인다.

축약형
I'm Lisa.
You're kind.
He's a teacher.
She's a student.
It's a dog.

2 복수형: are

	주어	동사	예문
1인칭	We		We are friends.
2인칭	You	are	You are my friends.
3인칭	They		They are doctors.

2
축약형
We're friends.
You're my friends.
They're doctors.

*You are은 단/복수 동시에 쓰인다.
뒤에 따라오는 명사로 구분한다.

3 부정문: be동사+not

		긍정문	부정문
단수	1인칭	I am a girl.	I am not a boy.
	2인칭	You are a student.	You are not a teacher.
	3인칭	He is a dancer.	He is not a singer.
복수	-	They are nurses.	They are not doctors.

3
축약형
I'm not a boy.
I amn't a boy. (X)

You're not a teacher.
You aren't a teacher.

He's not a singer.
He isn't a singer.

They're not doctors.
They aren't doctors.

Quick Test
Answers ▲ P. 2

1. She _is_ an actress. → She's an actress.
2. I ___ a strong man. → I'_ a strong man.
3. Tom ___ a movie star. → Tom'_ a movie star.
4. I ___ Kim. → I'_ Kim.
5. They ___ doctors. → They'_ doctors.
6. You ___ students. → You'_ students.
7. He ___ a waiter. → He'_ a waiter.
8. Jason ___ a good boy. → Jason'_ a good boy.

8

EXERCISE

A [　] 안에서 알맞은 것을 고르시오.

1 They [am, **are**, is] pilots.

2 You [am, **are**, is] a farmer.

3 I [**am**, are, is] a nurse.

4 He [am, are, **is**] an engineer.

5 We [am, **are**, is] businessmen.

6 She [amn't, aren't, **isn't**] a waitress.

7 It [am, are, **is**] a skunk.

B 빈칸에 알맞은 말을 넣어 문장을 완성하시오. (축약형 사용)

1 He _____ a teacher. → _____ a teacher.

2 She _____ an artist. → _____ an artist.

3 He _____ _____ a singer.
   → _____ _____ a singer.

C 우리말과 같은 뜻이 되도록 주어진 단어를 이용하여 문장을 완성하시오.

1 Linda는 발레 무용수이다. (Linda, a ballet dancer)

   → _____ *Linda is a ballet dancer.* _____

2 그는 새로 온 학생이 아니다. (he, a new student)

   → _____

3 그들은 그녀의 이웃이 아니다. (they, her neighbor)

   → _____

4 그녀는 영화배우다. (she, a movie star)

   → _____

Unit 01

2 Unit be동사의 과거형

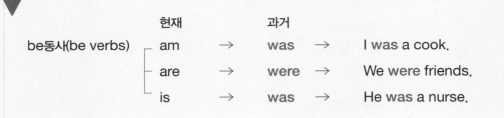

	현재		과거	
be동사(be verbs)	am	→	was	→	I was a cook.
	are	→	were	→	We were friends.
	is	→	was	→	He was a nurse.

1 단수형: was, were

	현재	과거
1인칭	I am tall.	I was short before.
2인칭	You are a man.	You were a boy then.
3인칭	He is a teacher. She is a trainer. It is a chicken.	He was a student 3 years ago. She was a trainee last year. It was an egg a week ago.

1

과거를 나타내는 표현
before: 이전에
yesterday: 어제
last month: 지난 달에
last year: 지난 해에
~ ago: ~전에
then(=at that time): 그때

2 복수형: were

	현재	과거
1인칭	We are teachers.	We were students last year.
2인칭	You are in Paris.	You were in Seoul 5 years ago.
3인칭	They are cats.	They were kittens before.

3 부정문: be동사+not

		현재	과거
단수	1인칭	I am not smart.	I was not smart.
	2인칭	You are not fat.	You were not fat.
	3인칭	He is not a dancer.	He was not a dancer.
복수	-	They are not tall.	They were not tall.

3

축약형
I was not smart.
→ I wasn't smart.

You were not fat.
→ You weren't fat.

He was not a dancer.
→ He wasn't a dancer.

They were not tall.
→ They weren't tall.

Quick Test

Answers ▲ P. 2

1. She is a student. → She ___was___ a student. → She ___wasn't___ a student.

2. My parents are doctors. → My parents _____ doctors. → My parents _____ doctors.

3. You are nice people. → You _____ nice people. → You _____ nice people.

4. I am a cook. → I _____ a cook. → I _____ a cook.

EXERCISE

A [　] 안에서 알맞은 것을 고르시오.

1 We [was, were] police officers two years ago.

2 He [was not, were not] a teacher then.

3 They [was, were] busy last month.

4 She [wasn't, weren't] my friend at that time.

5 Mr. Lee [was, were] a waiter last year.

6 You [weren't, wasn't] home then.

7 It [wasn't, weren't] my fault.

B 빈칸에 알맞은 말을 넣어 문장을 완성하시오. (축약형 사용)

1 My friend _____*is*_____ tall now. → My friend _____*wasn't*_____ tall then.

2 He _____ a golfer now. → He _____ a golfer before.

3 I _____ a singer now. → I _____ a singer before.

4 They _____ smart now. → They _____ smart before.

5 She _____ famous now. → She _____ famous before.

6 You _____ big now. → You _____ big before.

C 우리말과 같은 뜻이 되도록 주어진 단어를 이용하여 문장을 완성하시오.

1 그녀는 작가가 아니었다. (she, a writer)

→ _____*She was not [wasn't] a writer.*_____

2 그들은 변호사였다. (they, lawyers)

→ _____

3 그것은 실수였다. (it, a mistake)

→ _____

4 나는 사진작가가 아니다. (I, a photographer)

→ _____

5 그는 행복하지 않았다. (he, happy)

→ _____

3 be동사의 일반 의문문

He is a cook.

→ Is he a cook?

⌐ Yes, he is (a cook).

└ No, he is not (a cook).

I am a teacher.

→ Are you a teacher?

⌐ Yes, I am.

└ No, I'm not.

1 질문하고 답하기

He is a lawyer. → A Is he a lawyer?

B Yes, he is.

No, he is not.

It is true. → A Is it true?

B Yes, it is.

No, it is not.

They are cooks. → A Are they cooks?

B Yes, they are.

No, they are not.

2 대화에서 주의해야 할 사항

I am a writer. → A Are you a writer?

B Yes, I am.

No, I am not.

You are right. → A Am I right?

B Yes, you are.

No, you are not.

1

부정의 대답은 줄여서 대답할 수도 있다.
No, he is not.
= No, he's not. [he isn't]
No, it is not.
= No, it's not. [it isn't]
No, they are not.
= No, they're not. [they aren't]

긍정의 대답은 줄여 대답하지 않는다.
Yes, I'm. (X)
Yes, I am (O)

2

I로 물으면 you로,
you로 물으면 I로 대답한다.

Quick Test

Answers P. 2

1. He is a wrestler. → __Is__ _____ a wrestler?

2. We are tennis players. → _____ _____ tennis players?

3. This is your dog. → _____ _____ your dog?

4. Jim and Harry are scientists. → _____ _____ scientists?

5. She was tall. → _____ _____ tall?

6. They are nurses. → _____ _____ nurses?

7. That is a spider. → _____ _____ a spider?

EXERCISE

Answers P. 2

A   [ ] 안에서 알맞은 것을 고르시오.

1 [Am, Are, Is] he a cook?   Yes, he [am, are, is].

2 [Am, Are, Is] she honest?   No, she [am not, aren't, isn't].

3 [Am, Are, Is] you writers?   Yes, we [am, are, is].

4 [Am, Are, Is] they visitors?   Yes, they [am, are, is].

5 [Am, Are, Is] you an actor?   No, I [am not, aren't, isn't].

6 [Am, Are, Is] it your dog?   Yes, it [am, are, is].

7 [Am, Are, Is] they happy?   No, they [am not, aren't, isn't].

B   빈칸에 알맞은 말을 넣어 대화를 완성하시오.

1   _____ Mike a singer?

Yes, he _____. _____ _____ a singer.

2   _____ your mother a pianist?

No, _____ _____. _____ _____ a dancer.

3   _____ they painters?

_____, _____ _____. _____ _____ soccer players.

C   우리말과 같은 뜻이 되도록 주어진 단어를 이용하여 문장을 완성하시오.

1 그들은 의사이다. (they, doctors)   →   *They are doctors.*

그들은 의사입니까?   → _____

네, 그렇습니다.   → _____

아니오, 그렇지 않습니다.   → _____

2 나는 경찰관입니다. (I, a police officer)   → _____

당신은 경찰관입니까?   → _____

네, 그렇습니다.   → _____

아니오, 그렇지 않습니다.   → _____

Unit 01
4 be동사의 의문사 의문문

Who are you?	→	I'm <u>Joe</u>. I am <u>a new student</u>.
What is this?	→	It is <u>a bag</u>.
When is the party?	→	It is <u>at 8:30</u>.
Where is it?	→	It's <u>in the bag</u>.
How are you?	→	I am <u>fine</u>.

1 Who: '누구, 누가'

A Who is she?
B She is Christine.

A Who are you?
B I am a new student.

2 What: '무엇이, 무엇을, 무슨'

A What is this?
B It is her bag.

A What is your name?
B My name is Sarah.

> **2**
> What의 기타 용법
> A: <u>What time</u> is it now?
> B: It's 3:30.
>
> A: <u>What day</u> is it today?
> B: It's Thursday.

3 When: '언제'

A When is the concert?
B It's at 7:30.

A When is the history class?
B It's at 9 in the morning.

4 Where: '어디서'

A Where is the theater?
B It's on Maple Street.

A Where is the teacher?
B She is in the classroom.

> **4**
> who, what, when, where
> 이외에 이유를 묻는 'why'가 있다.
> A: Why are you happy?
> B: I passed the test.

5 How: '어떻게, 얼마나'

A How are you?
B I'm fine.

A How was the dinner?
B It was great!

> **5**
> How의 기타 용법
> A: <u>How old</u> are you?
> B: I am 13 years old.
>
> A: <u>How tall</u> is he?
> B: He's 1.85 meters tall.

Quick Test
Answers P. 2

1. _____Who_____ are they? → They are my parents.
2. _____ is Mary? → She is at school.
3. _____ old is she? → She is 65 years old.
4. _____ is the meeting? → It's at 4 o'clock.
5. _____ day is it tomorrow? → It will be Friday.

14

EXERCISE

A [   ] 안에서 알맞은 것을 고르시오.

1 [What, Who] [is, are] it? → It is my textbook.

2 [What, Who] [is, are] that? → He is my cousin.

3 [What, What day] [is, are] it today? → It is Tuesday.

4 [Who, Where] [is, are] the kittens? → They are in the kitchen.

5 [Where, When] [is, am] the meeting? → The meeting is in the evening.

6 [How, Where] [am, is] your brother? → He is fine.

7 [How, How old] [are, am] they? → They are 70 years old.

B 빈칸에 알맞은 말을 넣어 문장을 완성하시오.

1 _What_ _are_ they? → They are socks.

2 _____ _____ _____ it? → It is 5:50.

3 _____ _____ she? → She is my grandmother.

4 _____ _____ the eggs? → They are in the basket.

C 우리말과 같은 뜻이 되도록 주어진 단어를 이용하여 문장을 완성하시오.

1 저 사람들은 누구입니까? (they)
→ _Who are they?_

그들은 나의 부모님입니다. (my parents)
→ _____

2 당신은 얼마나 키가 큽니까? (tall)
→ _____

나는 1.5미터입니다. (1.5 meters tall)
→ _____

3 저것은 무엇입니까? (that)
→ _____

저것은 내 모자입니다. (it, my hat)
→ _____

A 빈칸에 알맞은 것을 고르시오.

1 She _____ the director of the school play.

ⓐ were   ⓑ are   ⓒ is   ⓓ am

2 _____ Cathy your cousin from America?

ⓐ Am   ⓑ Are   ⓒ Were   ⓓ Is

3 She _____ a cook last year.

ⓐ is not   ⓑ not is   ⓒ was not   ⓓ not was

4 _____ is the winner?

ⓐ What   ⓑ That   ⓒ Who   ⓓ Why

5 _____ they his little brothers?

ⓐ Is   ⓑ Are   ⓒ Am   ⓓ Was

6 _____ is your job?

ⓐ Who   ⓑ Why   ⓒ When   ⓓ What

7 I _____ a doctor. I am a nurse.

ⓐ am   ⓑ am not   ⓒ amn't   ⓓ are

B 빈칸에 알맞은 말을 넣어 대화를 완성하시오.

1 **A** _____ Sarah home now?

  B No, she isn't. She _____ at school.

2 **A** _____ Nate and Fred at work yesterday?

  B Yes, they _____.

3 **A** _____ is Mr. Ford?

  B He is the new teacher.

4 **A** _____ Karen his sister?

  B No, she isn't. She is his cousin.

5 **A** _____ you a computer technician?

  B No, I _____ _____.

A   Grammar in Speaking   빈칸에 알맞은 말을 넣어 대화를 완성하시오.

1 **A** Hello. I _____ Jenny.

   B Hello, nice to meet you. My name _____ Brian.

2 **A** _____ he our teacher?

   B No, he _____ .

3 **A** Hi. I _____ Ed. Are you Gail?

   B Yes, I _____ . _____ you my new teacher?

4 **A** _____ is she?

   B She _____ Grace. She _____ from America.

5 **A** _____ these your pens?

   B Yes, they _____ .

   A They _____ very colorful. Can I use them?

B   Grammar in Writing   빈칸에 알맞은 말을 넣어 문장을 완성하시오.

(1) _____ is she?

→ Her name _____ J. K. Rowling.

(2) _____ is her job?

→ She is a writer. She _____ the author of the *Harry Potter* series.

(3) _____ old is she?

→ She _____ 50 years old now.

(4) _____ is she from?

→ She _____ from England.

1 다음 빈칸에 알맞은 말을 고르시오.

> _____ are very happy.

ⓐ He   ⓑ They
ⓒ I   ⓓ She

2 다음 밑줄 친 부분을 바르게 고친 것을 고르시오.

> A <u>Where</u> is that woman?
> B She is my aunt, Ann.

ⓐ What   ⓑ When
ⓒ Who   ⓓ How

3 다음 문장에서 not이 들어갈 알맞은 곳을 고르시오.

Mack and Mike ⓐ were ⓑ farmers ⓒ before ⓓ.

4 다음 중 축약형이 바르지 않은 것을 고르시오.

ⓐ They're strong.
ⓑ He'sn't a baseball player.
ⓒ It wasn't my mistake.
ⓓ I'm not a student.

5 다음 질문에 대한 대답으로 알맞은 것을 고르시오.

> A Was Bill a singer?
> B _____

ⓐ Yes, he was.
ⓑ No, he isn't.
ⓒ Yes, he wasn't.
ⓓ No, he is.

6 다음 빈칸에 들어갈 수 <u>없는</u> 것을 고르시오.

> I was an elementary school student
> _____.

ⓐ now   ⓑ then
ⓒ two years ago ⓓ last month

7 다음 어법상 옳지 <u>않은</u> 문장을 고르시오.

ⓐ Mark is not a pilot.
ⓑ They are at the zoo yesterday.
ⓒ How was the movie last night?
ⓓ Is she a baker?

8 다음 중 짝지어진 대화가 바르지 <u>않은</u> 것을 고르시오.

ⓐ What are these?
  → They are my books.
ⓑ Where were you last Sunday?
  → I was at the beach.
ⓒ How is your sister?
  → She is 17 years old.
ⓓ When is the movie?
  → It is at five.

9 다음을 괄호 안의 지시에 따라 바꾸시오.

1) Jack and Bill are my best friends. (부정문)
  → _____

2) You were angry at that time. (의문문)
  → _____

10 다음 문장을 영작하시오.
그는 배우였다. (actor)
  → _____

명사 , 대명사

Unit 02

1 Unit 셀 수 있는 명사

명사 (Nouns) ┬ 셀 수 있는 명사 (Countable) ┬ 단수 (Singular): **a friend, an apple**
            │   └ 복수 (Plural): **friends, apples**
            └ 셀 수 없는 명사 (Uncountable)

1 단수 명사

(1) a + 대부분의 명사

a dog, a school, a computer, a house, a cat, a book

(2) an + 발음이 모음으로 시작하는 명사

an <u>a</u>pple, an <u>e</u>gg, an <u>i</u>gloo, an <u>o</u>ven, an <u>u</u>mbrella

2 복수 명사

(1) 대부분 명사에는 -s

a dog → two dogs   an orange → many oranges

(2) [s, sh, ch, x, o]로 끝나면 -es

a dish → two di<u>sh</u>es   a church → many chur<u>ch</u>es

(3) [모음+y]로 끝나면 -s

a boy → three b<u>oy</u>s   a key → two k<u>ey</u>s

(4) [자음+y]는 y를 빼고 -ies

a candy → many cand<u>ies</u>   a city → some cit<u>ies</u>

(5) 불규칙하게 변화하는 명사들

a child → many children   a leaf → many leaves

▶ 1

명사는 사람, 사물, 장소 등의 이름을 나타낸다.

(1)
a pencil, a kitten

(2)
모음인 발음: [a, e, i, o, u, ʌ]
an elephant, an hour

▶ 2

(1)
pencils, kittens
(2)
tomato → tomatoes
예외) piano → pianos
        photo → photos
(3)
donkey → donkeys
toy → toys
(4)
baby → babies
(5)
deer → deer
tooth → teeth

Quick Test

Answers ▲ P. 4

1. <u>*a*</u> girl → <u>*girls*</u>
2. ___ house → _____
3. ___ book → _____
4. ___ orange → _____

5. ___ apple → _____
6. ___ cat → _____
7. ___ pencil → _____
8. ___ lily → _____

9. ___ strawberry → _____
10. ___ elephant → _____
11. ___ boy → _____
12. ___ fox → _____

20

E EXERCISE

A [   ] 안에서 알맞은 것을 고르시오.

1 [A, An] cow is an animal.

2 [A, An] banana is a fruit.

3 [A, An] fly is an insect.

4 [A, An] eagle is a bird.

5 [A, An] teddy bear is a doll.

6 [A, An] carrot is a vegetable.

7 [A, An] oak is a tree.

B [보기]에서 알맞은 단어를 골라 어법에 맞게 고쳐 문장을 완성하시오.

Word Bank	rose	ball	pineapple

1 _A rose_ is beautiful. → _____ are beautiful.

2 _____ is round. → _____ are round.

3 _____ is sweet. → _____ are sweet.

C 주어진 단어를 조건에 맞도록 고쳐 문장을 완성하시오.

1 ladybug

(단수) → _A ladybug_ is pretty.   (복수) → _Ladybugs_ are pretty.

2 orange

(단수) → _____ is delicious.   (복수) → _____ are delicious.

3 cat

(단수) → My pet is _____.   (복수) → My pets are _____.

4 fox

(단수) → _____ is a wild animal.   (복수) → _____ are wild animals.

Unit 02

2 셀 수 없는 명사

명사(Nouns) ┌ 셀 수 있는 명사(Countable)
└ 셀 수 없는 명사(Uncountable) ┌ a/an 쓸 수 없음: a friendship (X)
└ 복수형 쓸 수 없음: friendships (X)

1 셀 수 없는 명사

(1) 셀 수 없는 물질
Salt is salty.　(X) a salt
Air is light.　(X) an air

(2) 추상적인 개념
Love is wonderful.　(X) a love
People want peace.　(X) a peace

(3) 사람, 도시, 나라 등의 고유한 이름
Jay is my friend.　　Mrs. Wong is nice.
Seoul is a city.　　Korea is a country.

2 셀 수 없는 명사를 셀 때

(1) 단위 사용
a glass of water　　(X) a water
two glasses of water　(X) two waters

(2) 수나 양을 나타내는 말 사용
a little sugar　　　some tea
a lot of coffee　　lots of pie

1

(1)
water, juice, bread, coffee, money

(2)
beauty, happiness, health, life

- 셀 수 없는 명사의 다른 예
  soccer, news, homework

(3)
고유한 이름은 대문자로 시작한다.
Peter, Mr. Phil, Japanese, Europe

2

(1)
a cup of coffee, a carton of milk
a box (bar) of soap, a slice of pie

(2)
a little: 아주 약간
some: 조금, 어느 정도
a lot of (= lots of): 많은

Quick Test

Answers ▲ P. 4

| Word Bank | girl | house | Asia | air | strawberry | egg | airplane | London | envelope |

1. a ___girl___

a _____

a _____

2. an ___egg___

an _____

an _____

3. Ø ___London___

Ø _____

Ø _____

22

E EXERCISE

Answers P. 4

A [   ] 안에서 알맞은 것을 고르시오.

1 [A, An, ∅] Busan is a busy city.

2 [A, An, ∅] ant is a diligent insect.

3 [A, An, ∅] Carol is a nurse.

4 [A, An, ∅] owl is active at night.

5 [A, An, ∅] Asia is a big continent.

6 [A, An, ∅] Spain is a country in Europe.

7 [A, An, ∅] Korean is my mother tongue.

B [보기]에서 알맞은 단어를 골라 문장을 완성하시오.

Word Bank	baby	water	glass	Korea	some	Jason

1 My best friend is _____*Jason*_____ .

2 _____ is my country.

3 Here is a _____ of orange juice.

4 My sister is a _____ .

5 Would you like _____ tea?

6 _____ is important to us.

C 우리말과 같은 뜻이 되도록 주어진 단어를 이용하여 문장을 완성하시오.

1 축구는 흥미로운 스포츠이다. (soccer)

→ _____*Soccer*_____ is an exciting sport.

2 여기에 커피 한 잔이 있다. (cup, coffee)

→ Here is _____ .

3 프랑스는 아름다운 나라이다. (France)

→ _____ is a beautiful country.

4 이것은 한 통의 우유이다. (carton, milk)

→ This is _____ .

5 주스는 내가 가장 좋아하는 음료이다. (juice)

→ _____ is my favorite drink.

Unit 02

3 인칭/지시대명사

대명사(Pronouns) ┌ 인칭대명사(Personal): I, you, he, she, it, we, they
         └ 지시대명사(Demonstrative): this, that, these, those

1 인칭대명사

	단수	복수	예문
1인칭	I	We	I am a poet. Alex and I are poets. **We** are poets.
2인칭	You	You	**You** are a comedian. Paul and you are funny. **You** are funny.
3인칭	He She It	They	Richard is a doctor. **He** is an eye doctor. My sister is 17 years old. **She** is pretty. Busan is a city. **It** is in Korea. Alex and Paul are friends. **They** are tall.

1 대명사는 명사를 대신해서 쓰는 말이다. 단수형과 복수형에 주의해서 쓴다.

2 지시대명사

	단수	복수	예문
이것	This	These	**This** is a cat. It is an animal. **These** are cats. They are animals.
저것	That	Those	**That** is a rose. It is a flower. **Those** are roses. They are flowers.

2 this는 가까이 있는 사람/사물을, that은 멀리 있는 사람/사물을 지칭한다.

Quick Test

Answers P. 4

1. Tom   → *he*
2. a book   → _____
3. Mr. Smith   → _____
4. Mrs. Smith   → _____

5. Terry and I   → _____
6. an ant and a bear → _____
7. Sue and you   → _____
8. a country   → _____

EXERCISE

A [   ] 안에서 알맞은 것을 고르시오.

1 [This, These] is Tom. [He, She, It] is my friend.

2 [This, Those] is Mary. [We, You, She] is my mom.

3 [This, These] is an onion. [He, She, It] is a vegetable.

4 [That, Those] are my jeans. [We, You, They] are new.

5 [That, Those] is my car. [He, She, It] is red.

6 [That, Those] is Jim. [You, He, They] is my cousin.

7 [That, Those] are vegetables. [We, You, They] are delicious.

B 빈칸에 알맞은 말을 넣어 문장을 완성하시오.

1 My sister is 10 years old. _____*She*_____ is short.

2 You and John are firemen. _____ are brave.

3 Cleveland is a city. _____ is in Ohio.

4 Kevin is very strong. _____ is a police officer.

5 Sarah is very friendly. _____ is my best friend.

6 Jane and Helen are new students. _____ are from America.

C 우리말과 같은 뜻이 되도록 주어진 단어를 이용하여 문장을 완성하시오.

1 이것은 책이다. (a book)

→ _____*This*_____ is _____*a book*_____ .

2 그녀는 내 여동생이다. (my sister)

→ _____ is _____ .

3 이 사람은 새로 온 학생이다. (a new student)

→ _____ is _____ .

4 우리는 축구 선수들이다. (soccer players)

→ _____ are _____ .

5 그들은 멋진 청년들이다. (nice guys)

→ _____ are _____ .

📖 Grammar Drills
▲▲▲▲▲▲▲▲▲▲▲▲▲

A   [   ] 안에서 알맞은 것을 고르시오.

1 [Jack, A Jack] is a boy.

2 Two [bird, birds] are in the cage.

3 [A piece of bread, A bread] is on the plate.

4 A [potato, potatoes] is in the basket.

5 [A seal, Seals] are good swimmers.

6 [A vegetable, Vegetables] are good for one's health.

7 Two [cups of coffee, cup of coffees], please.

B   빈칸에 알맞은 것을 고르시오.

1 _____ are good for you.

  ⓐ Apples   ⓑ An apples   ⓒ A apple   ⓓ Apple

2 _____ is the capital city of South Korea.

  ⓐ Seoul   ⓑ A Seoul   ⓒ An Seoul   ⓓ Seouls

3 Three _____ are on the floor.

  ⓐ A box   ⓑ boxes   ⓒ boxs   ⓓ An box

4 _____ is a green parrot.

  ⓐ These   ⓑ Those   ⓒ They   ⓓ It

5 _____ are on the train.

  ⓐ A person   ⓑ A people   ⓒ People   ⓓ Persones

6 _____ is sweet.

  ⓐ Sugar   ⓑ A sugar   ⓒ An sugar   ⓓ Sugars

7 _____ is my breakfast.

  ⓐ Bowls of cereal   ⓑ A bowl of cereal   ⓒ Bowl of cereal   ⓓ An bowl of cereal

FURTHER STUDY

A Grammar in Speaking   주어진 단어를 이용하여 문장을 완성하시오.

1 **A** Two _____ are in the cage. (fox)

　　B No, only one fox is in the cage.

2 **A** I'm from Seoul, Korea.

　　B I'm from _____, U.K. (London)

3 **A** Whales are fish.

　　B No, they are _____. (mammal)

4 **A** Jack and Jill are _____. (soldier)

　　B Yes, they are brave.

5 **A** These girls are my _____. (daughter)

　　B Really? They are so cute!

6 **A** Mom, I'm very thirsty.

　　B Here is a _____ of water. (glass)

B Grammar in Writing   글을 읽고, 어법에 맞는 알맞은 말을 고르시오.

There are six (1) people / person in my family. My father is (2) an / a English teacher. My mother is (3) a / an cook. (4) A Sumi / Sumi is my sister. She is (5) a / an student. My brother is (6) a / an baseball player. (7) He / she is in L.A. My little sister is (8) a / an baby. (9) He / She is two months old. I am (10) a / an elementary school student. My name is Jude. (11) That / These are my family members!

1 다음 빈칸에 공통으로 들어갈 알맞은 것을 고르시오.

> • _____ apple is a fruit.
> • He is _____ artist.

ⓐ a
ⓑ an
ⓒ Ø
ⓓ this

[2-3] 다음 중 명사의 단수형과 복수형이 잘못 짝지어진 것을 고르시오.

2 ⓐ leaf - leafs   ⓑ school - schools
ⓒ boy - boys   ⓓ tomato - tomatoes

3 ⓐ box - boxes   ⓑ dish - dishes
ⓒ man - men   ⓓ child - childs

4 다음 중 셀 수 있는 명사를 고르시오.

ⓐ deer   ⓑ happiness
ⓒ Carl   ⓓ peace

5 다음 밑줄 친 부분의 쓰임이 잘못된 것을 고르시오.

ⓐ They are <u>my best friends</u>.
ⓑ New York is <u>a city</u>.
ⓒ An ant is <u>an insects</u>.
ⓓ <u>Two girls</u> are in my room.

6 다음 문장에서 밑줄 친 부분에 들어갈 수 <u>없는</u> 것을 고르시오.

> _____ is my bag. It is big.

ⓐ These   ⓑ This
ⓒ That   ⓓ It

7 다음 밑줄 친 부분의 쓰임이 바른 것을 고르시오.

ⓐ <u>Many water</u> is in the bottle.
ⓑ <u>A life</u> is wonderful.
ⓒ <u>Mark and Jason</u> are engineers.
ⓓ <u>It</u> are my books.

8 다음 대화의 빈칸에 들어갈 알맞은 것을 고르시오.

> **A** This is my car.
> **B** Wow, _____ is really nice.

ⓐ they   ⓑ it
ⓒ he   ⓓ these

9 다음 빈칸에 알맞은 인칭대명사를 쓰시오.

1) This is my brother. _____ is a student.
2) Ann and I are singers. _____ are famous.
3) My sister is in L.A. _____ is a pianist.

10 다음 주어진 단어를 이용하여 밑줄 친 부분을 영어로 옮기시오.

> A vase, a slice of pie, and <u>두 잔의 커피</u> are on the kitchen table. (cup, coffee)

 _____

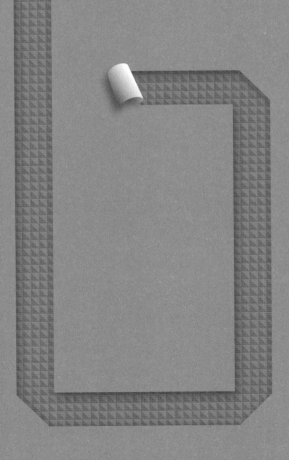

인칭대명사

Unit 03

인칭대명사의 주격과 목적격

	단수		복수	
	주격	목적격	주격	목적격
1인칭	I	me	We	us
2인칭	You	you	You	you
3인칭	He She It	him her it	They	them

1 주격 vs. 목적격

(1) 대명사의 주격과 목적격

I like them. They know me.

He loves her. She doesn't like him.

(2) 명사의 주격과 목적격 vs. 대명사의 주격과 목적격

Diana is a jazz singer. She is from Canada. (Diana = She)

I really like Diana. I really like her. (Diana = her)

My parents are nurses. They are busy. (My parents = They)

I love my parents. I love them. (my parents = them)

Jen and I are actors. We are famous. (Jen and I = We)

They know Jen and me. They know us. (Jen and me = us)

(3) 전치사의 목적어

Today is Jane's birthday. I bought a present for her.

They are good players. I played basketball with them.

1

(1)
주격 대명사와 목적격 대명사는 각각의
문장에서 주어와 목적어로 쓰인다.

(2)
명사는 격에 따라 형태가 변하지 않지만
대명사는 격에 따라 형태가 변한다.

(3)
전치사 뒤에는 목적격이 쓰인다.

Quick Test

Answers P. 5

1. Tom is gentle. → ___*He*___ is gentle.

2. You and Tom are nice. → _____ are nice.

3. Judy is a smart girl. → _____ is a smart girl.

4. Yon and I are famous. → _____ are famous.

5. My bag is new. → _____ is new.

6. I like Tom. → I like ___*him*___.

7. I like you and Tom. → I like _____.

8. Everybody likes Judy. → Everybody likes _____.

9. People like you and me. → People like _____.

10. I love my bag. → I love _____.

 **EXERCISE**

A [ ] 안에서 알맞은 것을 고르시오.

1 Jen likes [I, me] and Ken likes [she, her].

2 [It, This] was stormy and snowy yesterday.

3 Claire and I are in the Chess Club. [We, Us] play chess on Sundays.

4 Steve and Greg are students. I know [they, them].

5 Dan is busy. [He, Him] is in a meeting.

6 I like bananas. [They, Them] are my favorite fruit.

7 The chair is broken. [This, It] is very old.

B 빈칸에 알맞은 인칭 대명사를 넣어 문장을 완성하시오.

1 These are watermelons. I like _____*them*_____ very much.

2 This is my favorite book. I read _____ every day.

3 _____ is my teacher. I like her very much.

4 They are my nephews. I love _____.

5 _____ is my teacher. I respect him very much.

C 우리말과 같은 뜻이 되도록 주어진 단어를 이용하여 문장을 완성하시오.

1 나는 Sally를 알고 있습니다. 그녀는 작년에 우리 반이었습니다. (my classmate, last year, was)

→ I know Sally. _____*She was my classmate last year.*_____

2 그들은 좋은 차를 가지고 있습니다. 그들은 매일 그것을 운전합니다. (drive, every day)

→ They have a nice car. _____

3 원숭이들은 귀엽습니다. 나는 그들을 매우 좋아합니다. (like, very much)

→ Monkeys are cute. _____

4 그녀는 테니스를 좋아합니다. 그것은 그녀가 제일 좋아하는 운동입니다. (is, her, favorite sport)

→ She likes tennis. _____

Unit 03

인칭대명사의 소유격

	단수			복수		
	주격	소유격	소유대명사	주격	소유격	소유대명사
1인칭	I	my	mine	We	our	ours
2인칭	You	your	yours	You	your	yours
3인칭	He She It	his her its	his hers –	They	their	theirs

1 대명사의 소유격

I have a dog. **My** dog is cute.

He has a computer. **His** computer is new.

It has a wide screen. **Its** sound system is very good, too.

> 참고 **명사의 소유격**
>
> (1) 단수 명사+'s
>
> My brother's car is old.
>
> cf) The color of the car is unique.
>
> (2) 복수명사+'(s)
>
> These are my parents' computers.
>
> cf) There are several women's universities in Korea.

1

It의 소유격인 its와
It is의 축약형인 it's는
혼동되기 쉬우므로 주의한다.

(1) 대부분의 경우, '-'s를 붙인다.
cf) 사물의 소유격은 'of'를 이용하기도
한다.

(2) 복수 명사의 경우, 이미 해당 단어가
'-s'로 끝나므로, '(아포스트로피)만 붙인다.
cf) 복수 명사가 '-s'로 끝나지 않을 경우,
–'s를 붙인다.

2 소유대명사

This is <u>Jen's</u> cat.   → This is <u>her cat</u>.   → This is <u>hers</u>.

It is <u>my brother's</u> guitar   → It's <u>his guitar</u>.   → It's <u>his</u>.

<u>The cat's</u> ears are hairy.   → <u>Its</u> ears are hairy.

Quick Test

Answers   P. 5

1. I have a pencil.   →   This is ___*my*___ pencil.   →   This pencil is ___*mine*___.

2. You have a pen.   →   That is _____ pen.   →   That pen is _____.

3. He has a dog.   →   This is _____ dog.   →   The dog is _____.

4. She has a cat.   →   That is _____ cat.   →   The cat is _____.

5. It has pretty eyes.   →   _____ eyes are pretty.

6. They have a house.   →   This is _____ house.   →   This house is _____.

32

EXERCISE

A   [   ] 안에서 알맞은 것을 고르시오.

1   He drives a taxi. That's [he, him, his] job.

2   My answer is wrong. [You, Your, Yours] is right.

3   I have a dog. The dog sometimes bites [it's, its] tail.

4   These are [girls', girl's] shoes.

5   [Jenny's, Jenny] grandmother is 100 years old.

6   That is the [boys', boy's] washroom.

7   [We, Our, Ours] puppy is eight weeks old today.

B   괄호 안의 지시대로 빈칸에 알맞은 말을 넣어 문장을 완성하시오.

1   This is not my bag. _____*Mine*_____ is blue. (소유대명사)

2   I have three dolls. They can blink _____ eyes. (소유격)

3   He has a dragon kite. _____ kite is purple. (소유격)

4   Sarah has my phone number. But I don't have _____. (소유대명사)

5   This is my old camera. This one is _____. (소유대명사)

6   Kelly likes her new jacket. She loves _____ style. (소유격)

C   우리말과 같은 뜻이 되도록 주어진 단어를 이용하여 문장을 완성하시오.

1   그녀의 남자 친구는 잘생겼다. (boyfriend, is, handsome)

→ _____*Her boyfriend is handsome.*_____

2   이것이 그의 전화 번호니? (is, this, telephone number)

→ _____

3   Carl의 교실은 어디입니까? (where, is, Carl, classroom)

→ _____

4   내 가방은 가볍다. 네 것은 무겁다. (my bag, is, light, heavy)

→ _____

R REVIEW TEST

A   빈칸에 알맞은 것을 고르시오.

1 Bees eat honey. _____ like it a lot.

ⓐ They   ⓑ He   ⓒ That   ⓓ This

2 _____ girlfriend is at the door.

ⓐ You   ⓑ Your   ⓒ Yours   ⓓ You's

3 There is a dollar on the table. Is it _____?

ⓐ you   ⓑ your   ⓒ yours   ⓓ you's

4 Call _____ in the morning.

ⓐ mine   ⓑ me   ⓒ my   ⓓ I

5 I like Helen. I meet _____ every day.

ⓐ her   ⓑ he   ⓒ she   ⓓ hers

6 _____ five miles to my home.

ⓐ It   ⓑ Its'   ⓒ Its   ⓓ It's

7 The leg _____ the chair is loose.

ⓐ in   ⓑ at   ⓒ of   ⓓ it

B   빈칸에 알맞은 말을 넣어 문장을 완성하시오.

1 I see him every day. But I don't know _____ name.

2 This watch is $500. _____ is expensive.

3 Jack and I like music. _____ often go to concerts.

4 Her shirt is red. This blue one is not _____.

5 They are raising a dog. It's _____ dog.

6 My parents have lots of hats. These are _____ hats.

A **Grammar in Speaking** 빈칸에 알맞은 말을 넣어 대화를 완성하시오.

1 **A** Your phone number, please?

   B _____ number is 101-123-1234.

2 **A** Look at the cat! It's really cute!

   B Yeah, _____ eyes are pretty.

3 **A** Mike loves Sarah very much.

   B I know. He loves _____ very much.

4 **A** I brought my ball and bat.

   B I brought _____, too.

5 **A** These pancakes are so delicious.

   B Yeah, I just love _____.

B **Grammar in Writing** 글을 읽고, 빈칸에 알맞은 말을 넣어 문장을 완성하시오.

Hello, everyone. (1) _____ name is Shrek. Let me introduce my wife. (2) _____ name is Fiona. She is a princess. (3) _____ parents are a king and a queen. (4) _____ were not kind to me before, but now they are kind and good. They like (5) _____.

Fiona is not beautiful to other people. But, she is the most beautiful woman in the world to me. Fiona and I have three kids and (6) _____ live in the forest.

WRAP-UP TEST

SCORE:

1 다음 중 대명사의 격이 <u>다른</u> 하나를 고르시오.

ⓐ she   ⓑ I
ⓒ him   ⓓ they

2 다음 밑줄 부분을 대신하여 사용할 수 있는 것을 고르시오.

> Did <u>you and Jenny</u> play tennis?

ⓐ we   ⓑ they
ⓒ you   ⓓ she

3 다음 빈칸에 알맞은 말을 고르시오.

> I know Tom well.
> But he doesn't know _____.

ⓐ me   ⓑ I
ⓒ my   ⓓ mine

4 다음 밑줄 친 부분의 쓰임이 바르지 <u>않은</u> 것을 고르시오.

ⓐ Ann likes milk. She drinks <u>it</u> every day.
ⓑ I have two nieces. I love <u>they</u>.
ⓒ They are not <u>your</u> shoes.
ⓓ Cindy and I are friends. <u>We</u> live next door.

5 다음 밑줄 친 부분을 바르게 고친 것을 고르시오.

> I want to go to India with <u>she</u>.

ⓐ her   ⓑ them
ⓒ him   ⓓ you

6 다음 질문에 대한 답변으로 알맞지 <u>않은</u> 것을 고르시오.

> Is this your cell phone?

ⓐ No, it's hers.
ⓑ Yes, it's mine.
ⓒ No, it's his.
ⓓ No, it's Peter.

7 다음 문장에서 밑줄 친 부분을 바르게 고치시오.

I have a cat. It has beautiful eyes. <u>It's</u> claws are sharp.

→ _____

8 다음 글에서 밑줄 친 <u>It</u>를 나타내는 것을 고르시오.

> There is a big park near my house. Joe and I go there on weekends. There are always lots of people. A man walks a dog. A kid rides a bike. A woman lies on the grass and reads a book. **It** is a nice place for people.

ⓐ a dog   ⓑ a bike
ⓒ a book   ⓓ a park

9 다음 밑줄 친 두 단어를 한 단어로 바꿔 쓰시오.

> This is our ball. That is <u>their ball</u>.

→ _____

10 다음 밑줄 친 부분을 참고하여 빈칸에 알맞은 말을 쓰시오.

1) <u>My father</u> is a basketball player. _____ is tall.

2) Mike met <u>a woman</u>. _____ name is Jessica.

3) <u>We</u> just got off the train. We lost _____ bags.

4) A: Where do <u>your grandparents</u> live?
   B: _____ live in Springfield.

일반동사

일반동사의 현재형

Unit 04
1

동사 [be동사 – am / are / is
일반동사 [행동 표현 : run, walk, swim
상태 표현 : have, love, hate] 형태 변화 : I <u>run</u>. / He <u>runs</u>.

1 일반동사

(1) 행동 표현

I walk on the street.   I run in the park.

They push the door.   They pull the door.

(2) 상태 표현

They love animals.   They are animal-lovers.

They have a dog and two cats.

▶ **1**

(1) 행동을 나타내는 동사들
run, walk, swim, fly, move, push, pull, open, close, talk 등

*목적어: 일반동사 뒤에 위치, '~을'로 해석 ex) push the door

(2) 상태를 나타내는 동사들
think, like, love, hate, have, be 동사

2 일반동사의 형태 변화: 주어가 3인칭 단수인 경우

(1) 대부분의 일반 동사에는 -s

learn → learns   love → loves

(2) [-s, -ch, -sh, -x, -o]로 끝나면 -es

pass → passes   wash → washes

(3) [자음+y]로 끝나면 y를 i로 바꾸고 -es

try → tries   study → studies

(4) 불규칙 동사

have → has

▶ **2**

(2)
catch → catches
fix → fixes
do → does

(3) [모음+y]로 끝나면 -s
play → plays
buy → buys

Quick Test

Answers ▲ P. 7

1. talk → *talks*
2. do →
3. like →
4. pass →
5. watch →
6. go →
7. play →
8. make →

9. speak →
10. run →
11. sing →
12. dance →
13. catch →
14. fly →
15. cry →
16. buy →

38

E EXERCISE

A [   ] 안에서 알맞은 것을 고르시오.

1 She [like, likes] music.

2 Sue [help, helps] me with my homework every night.

3 I [has, have] a blue coat.

4 My sister [do, does] her chores every day.

5 We [write, writes] poems every week.

6 Students [visit, visits] the zoo in spring.

7 The temperature [rise, rises] in the morning.

B [보기]에서 알맞은 단어를 골라 어법에 맞게 고쳐 문장을 완성하시오.

Word Bank	cry	bark	smile

1 A baby _____*cries*_____ .   Babies _____ .

2 A dog _____ .   Dogs _____ .

3 A person _____ .   People _____ .

C 우리말과 같은 뜻이 되도록 주어진 단어를 이용하여 문장을 완성하시오.

1 그녀는 세수를 한다. (she, wash, her face)

→ _____ *She washes her face.* _____

2 그는 신발 끈을 묶는다. (he, tie, his shoes)

→ _____

3 꼬마들이 모래사장에서 논다. (kids, play, in the sand)

→ _____

4 그들은 많은 활동을 한다. (they, do, many activities)

→ _____

2 Unit

의문문과 부정문

	We love it.	He loves it.
부정문	→ We don't love it.	→ He doesn't love it.
의문문	→ Do we love it?	→ Does he love it?
대답	→ Yes, we do. / No, we don't.	→ Yes, he does. / No, he doesn't.

1 질문하고 답하기

(1) 1, 2인칭, 복수 주어: Do+주어+동사원형~?

You watch television. → A Do you watch television?
　　　　　　　　　　　 B Yes, I do.
　　　　　　　　　　　 B No, I do not (=don't).

They go to school. → A Do they go to school?
　　　　　　　　　　 B Yes, they do.
　　　　　　　　　　 B No, they do not (=don't).

(2) 3인칭 단수 주어: Does+주어+동사원형~?

He plays football. → A Does he play football?
　　　　　　　　　 B Yes, he does.
　　　　　　　　　 B No, he does not (=doesn't).

> 1
> 주어가 3인칭 단수일 때,
> does를 쓰고, 그 외의 경우엔 do를 쓴다.

2 부정문 만들기

(1) 1, 2인칭, 복수 주어: do not+동사원형

I know the song. → I don't know the song.
They read novels. → They don't read novels.

(2) 3인칭 단수 주어: does not+동사원형

Billy plays the piano. → Billy doesn't play the piano.
She likes horror movies. → She doesn't like horror movies.

> 2
> (1) don't+동사원형
>
> (2) doesn't+동사원형
> She don't know. (X)
> She don't knows. (X)
> She doesn't knows. (X)

Quick Test

Answers　P. 7

1. I know him. → _Do I know_ him? → _I don't know_ him.
2. You know her. → _____ her? → _____ her.
3. He knows me. → _____ me? → _____ me.
4. She knows them. → _____ them? → _____ them.
5. We know him. → _____ him? → _____ him.
6. They know you. → _____ you? → _____ you.

E EXERCISE

A [   ] 안에서 알맞은 것을 고르시오.

1 I [don't, doesn't] drink much water.

2 [Mary, They] doesn't read mystery books.

3 [Do, Does] we need glue?

4 Where does he [live, lives]?

5 She [do, does] her math homework in the morning.

6 He [don't, doesn't] know where the pharmacy is.

7 [Do, Does] they travel a lot?

B [보기]에서 알맞은 단어를 골라 문장을 완성하시오.

Word Bank	wear	have

1 _____Does_____ Kevin _____wear_____ glasses? _____, he _____.

2 _____ she _____ skirts? _____, she _____.

3 _____ they _____ a cat? _____, they _____.

C 우리말과 같은 뜻이 되도록 주어진 단어를 이용하여 문장을 완성하시오.

1 Mike는 김치를 좋아합니까? (Mike, like, kimchi)

→ _____*Does Mike like kimchi?*_____

2 그들은 일요일에는 학교에 가지 않습니다. (they, go to school, on Sundays)

→ _____

3 그 장난감 가게는 10시에 문을 엽니까? (the toy store, open, at 10)

→ _____

4 나의 고양이는 밤에는 울지 않습니다. (my cat, meow, at night)

→ _____

Unit 3

일반동사의 과거형

	현재형		과거형
규칙 변화	I like comic books.	→	I liked comic books.
불규칙 변화	I speak English.	→	I spoke English.

1 규칙변화

(1) 대부분의 동사에는 -ed

I listen to music. → I listened to music.

She watches TV. → She watched TV.

(2) [-e]로 끝나면 -d

He likes the book. → He liked the book.

I live in Busan now. → I lived in Busan last year.

(3) [자음+y]로 끝나면 y를 i로 고치고 -ed

They study English. → They studied English.

She cries a lot. → She cried a lot.

(4) [단모음+단자음]으로 끝나면 마지막 자음을 한 번 더 쓰고 -ed

I hug my mom every day. → I hugged her this morning.

Stop the car now! → He stopped the car.

2 불규칙변화

(1) 현재형과 과거형이 같은 동사

They cut the tree. → They cut the tree last night.

I always read the Bible. → I read the Bible last year.

(2) 현재형과 과거형이 다른 동사

They do their homework. → They did their homework.

I see him every day. → I saw him yesterday.

1

과거를 나타내는 표현
before : 이전에
yesterday : 어제
last month : 지난달에
last year : 지난해에
~ ago : ~전에
then (=at that time): 그때

(3)
[모음+y]로 끝나면 –ed
play → played

(4)
[자음+단모음+자음]으로 이루어진 단어의 경우이다.

2

(1) put - put / let - let / shut - shut

cf) 현재형 read [rid]
과거형 read [red] 발음이 다르다.

(2) swim - swam / come - came /
make - made / take - took /
eat - ate / bring - brought

Quick Test

Answers ▲ P. 7

1. have ___*had*___   **6.** come _____

2. do _____   **7.** make _____

3. run _____   **8.** go _____

4. cut _____   **9.** wash _____

5. help _____   **10.** fly _____

A [   ] 안에서 알맞은 것을 고르시오.

1 She [enjoy, enjoys, enjoyed] the show last year.

2 Elizabeth [do, did, does] the dishes last night.

3 Last year I [visit, visited, visits] Disneyland in California.

4 John [eat, eats, ate] breakfast every morning.

5 The baby [cry, cries, cried] a lot last night.

6 An hour ago, he [drive, drove, drives] her to the airport.

7 Linda [meet, meets, met] your sister at the concert last night.

B 주어진 단어를 이용하여 어법에 맞게 바꿔 문장을 완성하시오.

1 They _____saw_____ (see) an interesting magic show yesterday.

2 Linda _____ (fly) to Berlin last Sunday.

3 I _____ (take) a driving test 2 hours ago.

4 We _____ (go) hiking last Saturday.

5 My grandfather _____ (tell) me a scary story last night.

6 His friends _____ (give) him a present two weeks ago.

C 우리말과 같은 뜻이 되도록 주어진 단어를 이용하여 문장을 완성하시오.

1 그는 오늘 아침에 세수를 했다. (he, wash, his face, this morning)

   → _____ *He washed his face this morning.* _____

2 그녀는 나를 많이 도와주었다. (she, help, me, a lot)

   → _____

3 나는 작년에 공포 영화 한 편을 보았다. (I, see, a horror movie, last year)

   → _____

4 그들은 1950년에 돌아왔다. (they, come back, in 1950)

   → _____

4 Unit 의문문과 부정문

	We loved it.	He made it.
부정문	→ We didn't love it.	→ He didn't make it.
의문문	→ Did we love it?	→ Did he make it?
대답	→ Yes, we did. / No, we didn't.	→ Yes, he did. / No, he didn't.

1 질문하고 답하기

I helped my mom this morning.

→ **A** Did you help your mom this morning?
  B Yes, I did.
  B No, I didn't.

They went to the park last night.

→ **A** Did they go to the park last night?
  B Yes, they did.
  B No, they didn't.

> **1**
> Did + 주어 + 동사원형 ~?
> - Yes, 주어 did.
> - No, 주어 didn't.

2 부정문 만들기: did + not + 동사원형

Sam played the piano.	→	Sam didn't play the piano.
I helped my mom.	→	I didn't help my mom.
She wore glasses.	→	She didn't wear glasses.
They came home.	→	They didn't come home.

> **2**
> didn't + 동사원형
> She didn't know. (O)
> She didn't knew. (X)
> She didn't knows. (X)
>
> She doesn't know. (O)
> She doesn't knew. (X)
> She doesn't knows. (X)

Quick Test

Answers ▲ P. 7

1. I met a pretty girl. (의문문) → ___*Did*___ you ___*meet*___ a pretty girl?
2. He waited for her call. (부정문) → He ___*didn't*___ ___*wait*___ for her call.
3. She sent the postcard. (의문문) → _____ she _____ the postcard?
4. They got up late this morning. (부정문) → They _____ _____ late this morning.
5. They bought an expensive house. (의문문) → _____ they _____ an expensive house?
6. I broke the window. (부정문) → I _____ _____ the window.
7. Alice came to school yesterday. (의문문) → _____ Alice _____ to school yesterday?
8. We took a trip last summer. (부정문) → We _____ _____ a trip last summer.

44

E EXERCISE

A [   ] 안에서 알맞은 것을 고르시오.

1 [Did, Do, Was] Andersen write *The Ugly Duckling*?

2 I [didn't, don't, was not] have any plans last weekend.

3 Did the plane [arrive, arrived, arrives] on time?

4 Sally [don't, didn't, wasn't] meet Jim's parents.

5 They [doesn't, didn't, wasn't] think about the problem.

6 She [didn't has, didn't have] a fancy cell phone.

7 [Did, Do, Was] Ned talk to his teacher about his grade?

B 빈칸에 알맞은 말을 넣어 문장을 완성하시오.

Sandy's schedule (yesterday)						
13:00	study science	15:00	take a shower	16:00	go shopping with Jack	17:00	take a nap

1 **A** Did she study science yesterday?

  B Yes, she _____. She _____ science yesterday.

2 **A** Did she take a shower yesterday?

  B Yes, she _____. She _____ a shower yesterday.

3 **A** Did she go shopping with Jane?

  B No, she _____. She _____ shopping with Jack.

C 우리말과 같은 뜻이 되도록 주어진 단어를 이용하여 문장을 완성하시오. (필요 시, 동사 변형할 것)

1 Kelly는 점심으로 샌드위치를 먹지 않았다. (Kelly, have, a sandwich, for lunch)

  → *Kelly didn't have a sandwich for lunch.*

2 나는 어젯밤에 Mark를 만나지 않았다. (I, see, Mark, last night)

  → _____

3 너는 지난 일요일에 교회에 갔니? (you, go to church, last Sunday)

  → _____

4 Amy가 무릎을 다쳤니? (Amy, hurt, her knee)

  → _____

Unit 04

일반동사의 현재진행형

현재형		현재진행형
I study Japanese.	→	I am studying Japanese.
You study Chinese.	→	You are studying Chinese.
She studies French.	→	She is studying French.

1 현재 vs. 현재진행

(1) 현재: 반복되는 일, 습관, 일반적 사실
I always clean my room.
It usually snows in winter in Korea.
He climbs mountains every morning.

(2) 현재진행: 지금 현재 일어나고 있는 일
Mom! I'm cleaning my room now.
Look out the window! It's snowing!
He is climbing Bukhan Mountain now.

2 '동사-ing' 형태 만들기

(1) 동사원형에 -ing
read → reading   study → studying

(2) [단모음+단자음]으로 끝나면 마지막 자음을 한 번 더 쓰고 -ing
run → running   put → putting

(3) [-e]로 끝나면 e를 빼고 -ing
write → writing   live → living

(4) [-ie]로 끝나면 ie를 y로 바꾸고 -ing
lie → lying   die → dying

1

반복되는 습관을 나타낼 때 쓰는 표현
always: 항상
usually: 보통, 일상적으로
every ~: 매 ~마다

진행형과 함께 쓰이는 표현
(right) now: (바로) 지금

진행형으로 쓰지 않는 동사
: have, like, love, know, want

I have a book. (O)
I am having a book. (X)

She likes you. (O)
She is liking you. (X)

cf) I am having dinner.(O)
have가 '가지고 있다' 이외의 의미로
쓰일 때는 진행형이 가능하다.

Quick Test

Answers　P. 8

1. read → *reading*
2. have → _____
3. sit → _____
4. visit → _____
5. meet → _____

6. lie → _____
7. come → _____
8. pull → _____
9. plan → _____
10. make → _____

11. give → _____
12. lose → _____
13. swim → _____
14. study → _____
15. write → _____

EXERCISE

A   [   ] 안에서 알맞은 것을 고르시오.

1   We [have, are having] lots of rain in summer.

    They [have, are having] lunch right now.

2   Look at the boy! He [smiles, is smiling] at me.

    He is a kind person. He always [smiles, is smiling] at people.

3   He [sits, is sitting] on a chair now.

    He usually [sits, is sitting] beside her.

4   The mailman [delivers, is delivering] our mail every day.

    The milkman [delivers, is delivering] the milk now.

B   주어진 단어를 이용하여 어법에 맞게 바꿔 문장을 완성하시오.

1   My mom _____ (cook) our meals every day.

2   We _____ (lose) the game now.

3   This coffee shop usually _____ (open) at 10 a.m.

4   She _____ (take) a shower right now.

5   My team always _____ (win) the game.

6   He _____ (watch) a comedy show now.

C   우리말과 같은 뜻이 되도록 주어진 단어를 이용하여 문장을 완성하시오.

1   Tony는 미소를 짓고 있습니다. (Tony, smile)

    → _____ *Tony is smiling.* _____

2   그는 벤치에 앉아 있습니다. (he, sit, on the bench)

    → _____

3   그는 Sally에게 손을 흔들고 있습니다. (he, wave, to Sally)

    → _____

4   Sally는 그에게 다가가고 있습니다. (Sally, come, close to him)

    → _____

Unit 04

6 의문문과 부정문

	She is meeting Jack.	They are taking a vacation.
부정문	→ She isn't meeting Jack.	→ They are not taking a vacation.
의문문	→ Is she meeting Jack?	→ Are they taking a vacation?
대답	→ Yes, she is / No, she isn't.	→ Yes, they are. / No, they aren't

1 질문하고 답하기

I am bothering you. →

A Am I bothering you?
B Yes, you are.
B No, you are not.

You are talking to me. →

A Are you talking to me?
B Yes, I am.
B No, I am not.

She is having dinner. →

A Is she having dinner?
B Yes, she is.
B No, she is not.

> **1**
> Be동사+주어+동사-ing?
> -Yes, 주어+be동사
> -No, 주어+be동사+not

2 부정문 만들기: be+not+동사-ing

I am working now.
→ I'm not working now. I'm taking a break.

She is waiting for you.
→ She's not waiting for you. She's waiting for your present.

They are laughing at you.
→ They're not laughing at you. They're laughing at me.

Quick Test

Answers ▲ P. 8

1. My brother is following me. (부정문) → My brother ___is___ ___not___ ___following___ me.

2. It is snowing heavily. (의문문) → _____ it _____ heavily?

3. She is telling me the news. (부정문) → She _____ _____ _____ me the news.

4. They are catching fish. (의문문) → _____ they _____ fish?

5. I am calling my mom. (부정문) → I _____ _____ _____ my mom.

6. The doorbell is ringing. (의문문) → _____ the doorbell _____ ?

E **EXERCISE**

A [   ] 안에서 알맞은 것을 고르시오.

1 What [is, are, do] you doing now?

2 You [do not, are not, am not] listening to me.

3 [Is, Are, Do] you having a good time?

4 The boy [is not, do not, does not] teasing me.

5 [Is, Does, Do] he waiting for you?

6 I [am not, is not, do not] looking for shoes now.

7 What [is, are, do] his cousins doing here?

B [보기]에서 알맞은 단어를 골라 어법에 맞게 고쳐 문장을 완성하시오.

Word Bank	wash	ride	draw	bake

1   **A** ____Is____ the kid ___drawing___ a rabbit?

    B Yes, he _____.

2   **A** _____ he _____ a horse?

    B No, he _____ _____ a horse. He _____ _____
    a bicycle.

3   **A** _____ you _____ dishes?

    B No, I _____ _____. I _____ _____ cookies.

C 우리말과 같은 뜻이 되도록 주어진 단어를 이용하여 문장을 완성하시오.

1 그들은 대화를 하고 있지 않습니다. (they, have, a conversation)

   → _____*They are not having a conversation.*_____

2 그는 바닥에 누워 있습니까? (he, lie, on the floor)

   → _____

3 우리 언니는 TV를 보고 있지 않습니다. (my sister, watch, TV)

   → _____

4 너희 삼촌이 칠면조를 요리하고 계시니? (your uncle, cook, a turkey)

   → _____

A 빈칸에 알맞은 것을 고르시오.

1 Mike _____ an expensive car.

ⓐ drives   ⓑ is drive   ⓒ drive   ⓓ do drive

2 I _____ understand it.

ⓐ doesn't   ⓑ is not   ⓒ are not   ⓓ don't

3 He _____ his daughter a piggyback ride now.

ⓐ gave   ⓑ is giving   ⓒ giving   ⓓ do giving

4 _____ you feed your dog last night?

ⓐ Do   ⓑ Was   ⓒ Did   ⓓ Do was

5 _____ you moving the car now?

ⓐ Is   ⓑ Are   ⓒ Do   ⓓ Am

6 She usually _____ rice cakes for the holidays.

ⓐ makes   ⓑ make   ⓒ is making   ⓓ made

7 The student _____ the picture out of the newspaper at this time.

ⓐ cut   ⓑ cuts   ⓒ is cutting   ⓓ are cutting

8 The plane _____ to the airport twice a day.

ⓐ fly   ⓑ is flying   ⓒ does flying   ⓓ flies

B [ ] 안에서 알맞은 것을 고르시오.

1 She [hate, hates] gingerbread.

2 We [don't, are not] go to that Chinese restaurant.

3 [Are, Do] you listening to me?

4 Did you [have, had] chicken soup last night?

5 I [am not, do not] talking to you.

6 Did you [see, saw] the tornado on the news yesterday?

7 The mouse [hides, is hiding] in the hole now.

8 His house [has, is having] a brown roof.

9 I [take, took] the subway home last Friday.

F FURTHER STUDY

Integrated Drills

A **Grammar in Speaking** 빈칸에 알맞은 말을 넣어 대화를 완성하시오.

1 **A** What _____ you do last weekend?

   B I went to an amusement park and rode roller coasters.

2 **A** You look great today! Where did you buy that nice dress?

   B I _____ it at the mall.

3 **A** Where are you, Tom? Are you playing with your sister?

   B No! I _____ _____ _____ with her.

   She is sleeping now.

4 **A** What are you buying at the market?

   B I _____ _____ eggs and a melon.

5 **A** _____ you leaving now?

   B No, we are leaving in two hours.

B **Grammar in Writing** 괄호 안에 주어진 단어를 어법에 맞게 고쳐 글을 완성하시오.

Steven Spielberg is a famous movie director in America. He was born in 1946 in Ohio. One day, his father (1) _____ (give) him a camera. After that time, he (2) _____ (dream) of being a movie director. His first movie was *The Last Gun*. Spielberg (3) _____ (make) films like *E.T.*, *Jaws* and *Star Wars* in the 1970s and 1980s. He has won three Academy Awards. People (4) _____ (like) him and (5) _____ (enjoy) his movies.

1 다음 동사의 원형과 과거형의 연결이 바르지 <u>못한</u> 것을 고르시오.

ⓐ have - haved ⓑ go - went
ⓒ sit - sat ⓓ play - played

2 다음 빈칸에 들어갈 단어들이 순서대로 짝지어진 것을 고르시오.

• He usually _____ on the floor.
• He _____ English yesterday.

ⓐ sleeps - studyed
ⓑ is sleeping - studied
ⓒ slept - is studying
ⓓ sleeps - studied

3 다음 문장을 부정문으로 만든 것으로 알맞은 것을 고르시오.

Mike saw a comedy movie.

ⓐ Mike doesn't saw a comedy movie.
ⓑ Mike didn't see a comedy movie.
ⓒ Mike was not see a comedy movie.
ⓓ Mike saw not a comedy movie.

4 다음 밑줄 친 부분의 쓰임이 <u>잘못된</u> 것을 고르시오.

ⓐ John <u>goes</u> to church every Sunday.
ⓑ The baby <u>crys</u> a lot.
ⓒ She <u>lives</u> in Prague.
ⓓ He <u>has</u> a big mouth.

5 다음 질문의 대답으로 알맞은 것을 고르시오.

Does he know her name?

ⓐ Yes, he is.
ⓑ No, he don't.
ⓒ Yes, he does.
ⓓ No, he didn't.

6 다음 중 어법에 맞는 문장을 고르시오.

ⓐ She flyed to London last night.
ⓑ Do he walk to school?
ⓒ We are having a good time.
ⓓ Did they came to class?

7 다음 빈칸에 알맞지 <u>않은</u> 것을 고르시오.

He bought a nice car _____.

ⓐ yesterday ⓑ last year
ⓒ right now ⓓ two years ago

8 다음 문장을 괄호 안의 지시에 따라 바꾸시오.

1) She is singing a song. (부정문)

→ _____

2) They take piano lessons after school.
(의문문)

→ _____

9 다음 밑줄 친 동사를 알맞은 형태로 바꾸시오.

1) He <u>finish</u> his class at five.

→ _____

2) She <u>teach</u> English at school.

→ _____

3) Are they <u>set</u> the table now?

→ _____

10 다음 주어진 단어를 이용하여 밑줄 친 부분을 영어로 옮기시오.

A What are you doing now?
B <u>나는 지금 연을 만들고 있어.</u> (make, a kite)

→ _____

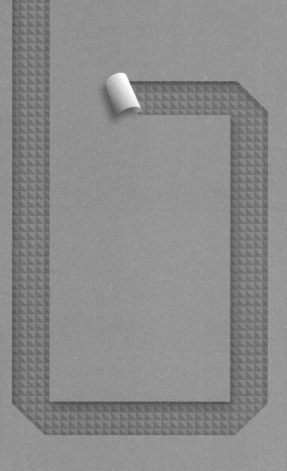

동사의 시제

Unit 05

현재/과거/미래

	현재	과거	미래
be동사	am / are / is	was / were	will / be going to
일반동사	원형 또는 3인칭 단수 –s	–ed 또는 불규칙 변화	

1 과거와 현재

(1) be동사

I **was** sick <u>yesterday</u>. I **am** better <u>now</u>.
She **was** short <u>last year</u>. She **is** tall <u>now</u>.
They **were** watching TV <u>before</u>. <u>Now</u> they **are** eating dinner.

(2) 일반동사

I **studied** English <u>before</u>. I **study** Chinese <u>now</u>.
She **lived** in London <u>then</u>. She **lives** in Paris <u>now</u>.
They **had** one cat <u>a year ago</u>. They **have** three cats <u>now</u>.

2 현재와 미래

(1) will+동사원형

I **am** 13 now. <u>Next year</u>, I **will be** 14.
It **is** windy and cloudy now. It **will rain** <u>tomorrow</u>.
They're studying hard. They **will have** an exam <u>next week</u>.

(2) be going to+동사원형

I'm home now. I'm **going to watch** a movie <u>soon</u>.
She doesn't have a car. She's **going to buy** one <u>later</u>.
We're studying lesson 1. We're **going to study** lesson 2 <u>tomorrow</u>.

▶ **1**
과거를 나타내는 표현들
yesterday : 어제
before : 지난번에
then : 그때
last~ : 지난 ~에
~ago : ~전에

▶ **2**
미래를 나타내는 표현들
soon: 곧
in the future: 미래에
tomorrow: 내일
next ~: 다음 ~에
~ later: ~후에

※ 현재나 현재 진행형으로 미래를 나타
내기도 한다.
The train <u>leaves</u> at 6.
The concert <u>starts</u> at 8.
He's <u>coming</u> at 8.
<u>I'm going</u> to the teacher.

Quick Test

Answers P. 9

원형	현재(3인칭 단수)	과거	미래
1. run	*runs*	*ran*	*will [be going to] run*
2. study			
3. travel			
4. go			
5. visit			

EXERCISE

A   [ ] 안에서 알맞은 것을 고르시오.

1   There [will be, is, was] a big tree by my house last year.

2   She [will see, sees, saw] *The Lord of the Rings* yesterday.

3   I usually [will walk, walk, walked] to school.

4   Dan [is going to stay, stay, stayed] in Rome next month.

5   The man [will change, change, changed] the light bulb soon.

6   His older brother now [will work, works, worked] in a bank.

7   The police officer [will be, is, was] near the bridge 30 minutes ago.

B   주어진 단어를 이용하여 어법에 맞게 바꿔 문장을 완성하시오.

1   The test was easy, and I _____*passed*_____ (pass) it yesterday.

2   I will _____ (call) you back in two weeks.

3   She _____ (be) at her aunt's house last weekend.

4   Yesterday, he _____ (cut) his fingers by accident.

5   They _____ (come) to the party on time tonight.

6   My father _____ (sell) his car last year.

C   주어진 조건을 이용하여 문장을 완성하시오.

1   We go hiking on Saturdays. (미래)

   → _____*We are going to [will] go hiking*_____ this Saturday.

2   He is really happy to receive her letter. (과거)

   → _____ to receive her letter.

3   I gave her nice flowers today. (미래)

   → _____ tomorrow night.

4   The man was in the office yesterday. (미래)

   → _____ tomorrow.

5   His friends will go to the movies soon. (과거)

   → _____ last Friday.

Unit 05

2 will/be going to

		They will help us.		He is going to come.
부정문	→	They won't help us.	→	He isn't going to come.
의문문	→	Will they help us?	→	Is he going to come?
대답	→	Yes, they will / No, they won't.	→	Yes, he is. / No, he isn't.

1 will

(1) 평서문: will ('ll)+동사원형

I will visit you soon.

They'll arrive next weekend.

(2) 부정문: will not (won't)+동사원형

I won't tell a lie. I will be honest with you.

They won't arrive this weekend. They'll come next week.

(3) 의문문과 응답

A Will it rain tomorrow?

B Yes, it will. / No, it won't.

2 be going to

(1) 긍정문: be going to+동사원형

I'm going to <u>listen</u> to her song all night long.

We're going to <u>eat</u> lunch at noon.

(2) 부정문: be+not+going to+동사원형

He's not going to <u>come</u> home before 9.

They are not going to <u>tell</u> you about that.

(3) 의문문과 응답

A Is she going to <u>go</u> to college?

B Yes, she is. She's going to study biology.

B No, she's not. She's going to get a job.

▶ 1

will의 의미 : ～할 것이다
- We will miss you. (단순한 미래)
- I will always love you. (의지)

▶ 2

be going to의 의미
- We're going to miss you.
  (단순한 미래)
- She's going to go to college.
  (예정)

Quick Test

Answers   P.10

1. They will go to Italy next year.

→ (의문문) _____*Will they go*_____ to Italy next year?

→ (부정문) _____ to Italy next year.

2. He's going to buy a new TV.

→ (의문문) _____ to buy a new TV?

→ (부정문) _____ buy a new TV.

56

EXERCISE

Answers P.10

A   [   ] 안에서 알맞은 것을 고르시오.

1 The show will [starts, start] soon.

2 They [not, won't] tell you the secret.

3 Sam [will not plant, will plant not] an apple tree in his yard.

4 [Will she, Is she] move to Boston?

5 [Will, Is] the police officer going to arrest the thief?

6 [Will he, Is he] make noodles for dinner tomorrow?

7 My parents [are not going to, are going not to] the zoo with us.

B   주어진 단어를 이용하여 문장을 완성하시오.

1 My father will sell his car. (be going to, not)

→ My father _____ *is not going to sell* _____ his car.

2 Will you give me a ride tonight? (be going to)

→ _____ me a ride tonight?

3 She stays at home on Sundays. (is going to)

→ She _____ at home this Sunday.

4 Your grandmother brought her dog. (will)

→ Your grandmother _____ her dog later.

5 I have a cup of green tea. (will)

→ I _____ a cup of green tea after dinner.

C   우리말과 같은 뜻이 되도록 주어진 단어를 배열하시오.

1 그는 내년에 고등학교를 졸업할 것이다. (graduate from / is going to / he / next year / high school)

→ _____ *He is going to graduate from high school next year.* _____

2 저와 함께 저녁을 드시겠어요? (have dinner / you / will / with me)

→ _____

3 우리는 이번 여름에 하와이에 갈 예정이다. (Hawaii / go to / are going to / we / this summer)

→ _____

4 나를 도와주지 않겠니? (you / help / won't / me)

→ _____

A   [   ] 안에서 알맞은 것을 고르시오.

1   They [were, will be] at the beach yesterday.

2   Sam [won't be, was] busy tomorrow.

3   I [will, will be] win the contest.

4   She [won't be, will be not] back for a few days.

5   Ben [ran, will run] in the marathon last year.

6   Kelly [were, will be] at the museum this afternoon.

7   I'll [grow, is growing] tomatoes this spring.

8   He's [will go, going to] the festival at 7 o'clock.

B   빈칸에 알맞은 것을 고르시오.

1   Will Jim _____ the test?

   ⓐ pass   ⓑ going to pass   ⓒ passing   ⓓ passes

2   I _____ to San Diego this Sunday.

   ⓐ goes   ⓑ am going to go   ⓒ don't went   ⓓ will going

3   She _____ school. She is sick.

   ⓐ will attend not   ⓑ not will attend   ⓒ will not attend   ⓓ won't attending

4   My class _____ at 9 o'clock.

   ⓐ begun   ⓑ begins   ⓒ be beginning   ⓓ will beginning

5   He _____ write the report.

   ⓐ will don't   ⓑ not going to   ⓒ isn't going   ⓓ won't

6   We _____ a birthday party next Sunday.

   ⓐ will have   ⓑ is going to   ⓒ had   ⓓ won't be have

7   Did you _____ my letter?

   ⓐ will read   ⓑ read not   ⓒ be reading   ⓓ read

FURTHER STUDY

A

Grammar in Speaking 주어진 단어를 이용하여 대화를 완성하시오.

1 **A** Will you do me a favor?

   B Sure, I _____. What is it?

2 **A** Your room is very messy.

   B I know. I _____ it this weekend. (clean)

3 **A** What are you doing next Monday evening?

   B I _____ a paper. (write)

4 **A** Are the children going to play in the park this afternoon?

   B No. They _____ their grandparents at 2 p.m. (visit)

5 **A** Was the weather warm at the beach this morning?

   B Yes, it was. However, it _____ warm tomorrow. (be)

B

Grammar in Writing 주어진 단어를 어법에 맞게 고쳐 편지를 완성하시오.

Dear Anne,

I (1) _____ (be) on the train to London now. It (2) _____ (leave) Paris an hour ago. I (3) _____ (stay) in Paris for two weeks.

I (4) _____ (go) to many beautiful places in Paris, and I

(5) _____ (forget) them. I (6) _____ (take) many pictures, too. I (7) _____ (stay) in London for one week.

Unfortunately, my stay (8) _____ (be) too short in London.

My plane (9) _____ (leave) on the 15th. I (10) _____ (show) you my wonderful pictures in a few weeks!

Love,

sarah

WRAP-UP TEST

SCORE:

1 다음 빈칸에 들어갈 말이 바르게 짝지어진 것을 고르시오.

> • It _____ windy yesterday.
> • It _____ warm today.
> • It _____ cold tomorrow.

ⓐ will be - is - was
ⓑ were - is - is going to be
ⓒ is - was - be will
ⓓ was - is - will be

2 다음 동사의 원형과 과거형의 연결이 바르지 <u>못한</u> 것을 고르시오.

ⓐ study – studied   ⓑ say – said
ⓒ hold – holded   ⓓ get – got

3 다음 빈칸에 will이 들어갈 수 <u>없는</u> 문장을 고르시오.

ⓐ I _____ not invite him to the party.
ⓑ _____ you attend the meeting?
ⓒ Simon _____ wearing a cap now.
ⓓ She _____ visit her aunt this Friday.

4 다음 밑줄 친 부분의 쓰임이 <u>잘못된</u> 것을 고르시오.

ⓐ <u>Will you have</u> dinner with her?
ⓑ He <u>is not going to</u> buy the car.
ⓒ She <u>will does</u> her homework.
ⓓ <u>Are you going to</u> work until 9?

5 다음 어법상 옳지 <u>않은</u> 문장을 고르시오.

ⓐ We are going to paint our house this weekend.
ⓑ Jack makes a huge mistake on the test yesterday.
ⓒ She enjoys playing the piano.
ⓓ There was a big sculpture in the park.

6 다음 밑줄 친 곳을 바르게 고치시오.

He will not <u>shares</u> his room with his brother.

→ _____

7 다음 빈칸에 알맞은 것을 고르시오.

> He _____ fourteen next year.

ⓐ is   ⓑ was
ⓒ will be   ⓓ is going to

8 다음 두 문장이 같은 뜻이 되도록 빈칸에 알맞은 말을 쓰시오.

She will write a letter to her grandmother.
= She _____ a letter to her grandmother.

[9-10] 다음 글을 읽고 물음에 답하시오.

> A What are you going to do (A)_____?
> B (B)나는 도서관에 갈 거야. (go to the library)

9 (A)에 알맞지 <u>않은</u> 것을 고르시오.

ⓐ after school   ⓑ last Friday
ⓒ this weekend   ⓓ tomorrow

10 주어진 표현을 이용하여 (B)를 영어로 옮기시오.

→ _____

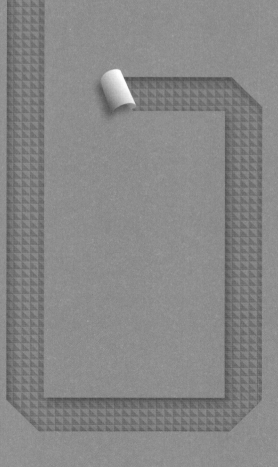

조동사

Unit 06

1 능력을 나타내는 조동사

현재	I can <u>finish</u> it by myself.
과거	I could <u>finish</u> it thanks to your help.
미래	I will be able to <u>finish</u> it if you help me.

1 can: 현재나 가까운 미래의 능력

(1) 평서문: can+동사원형

I can <u>do</u> it. We can <u>do</u> it!

He can <u>cook</u> very well.

(2) 부정문: cannot (can't)+동사원형

I can't <u>go</u> to the movies tonight.

She cannot <u>swim</u> at all.

(3) 의문문: can(not)+주어+동사원형

A Can you <u>speak</u> English?

B Yes, I can, but not very well.

A Can't you <u>say</u> the alphabet?

B No, I can't. What is that?

2 could, be able to: 과거/미래의 능력

(1) 과거

She could <u>win</u> the game.

= She was able to <u>win</u> the game.

(2) 미래

She will be able to <u>win</u> the game. (O)

She will can win the game. (X)

1

can : ~할 수 있다

can+동사원형
He can go. (O)
He can goes. (X)

2

can = be able to

Quick Test ___

Answers ▲ P.11

1. She can speak five languages.

(의문)	*Can she speak*	five languages?
(부정)	_____	five languages.
(미래)	_____	five languages.
(과거)	_____	five languages.
=	_____	five languages.

2. They can eat fish.

(의문)	_____	fish?
(부정)	_____	fish
(미래)	_____	fish.
(과거)	_____	fish.
=	_____	fish.

62

E EXERCISE

A   [   ] 안에서 알맞은 것을 고르시오.

1 She [able to, can] count in English.

2 Steve could [answer, answers] the question.

3 Can you [rides, ride] a bike?

4 You can [park, parked] your car here.

5 [Was, Could] he able to find you?

6 She [wasn't, cannot] return the book.

7 My uncle [will can, can] paint the fence today.

B   주어진 단어를 이용하여 문장을 완성하시오.

1 I _____*could solve*_____ (solve) the problem with his help before.

2 James _____ (be able to) have lunch with us tomorrow.

3 He _____ (find, not) the books for you.

4 Was Deborah _____ (book) the plane tickets?

5 He _____ (send, not) the file last night.

6 Brian _____ (be able to, not, call) Tina now.

7 I _____ (be able to, finish) the work tomorrow.

C   우리말과 같은 뜻이 되도록 주어진 단어를 배열하시오.

1 이전에 그녀는 노래를 잘 부를 수 있었다. (sing / before / well / was able to / she)

   → _____*She was able to sing well before.*_____

2 어젯밤 Mary는 강아지를 찾을 수 없었다. (find / last night / her dog / Mary / could not)

   → _____

3 나는 지금 달을 볼 수가 없다. (see / the moon / right now / can't / I)

   → _____

4 우리는 곧 만날 수 있을 것이다. (be able to / soon / meet / we / will)

   → _____

Unit 06

허가를 나타내는 조동사

A Could I get your number?
B Yes, you can.

A Will you give me your number?
B Yes, I will.

1 'I'를 주어로: can, could, may

(1) 부탁하기

Can I use your cell phone? (허물없는 표현)
Could I use your cell phone? (정중한 표현)
May I use your cell phone? (매우 예의 바른 표현)

(2) please 넣기: 좀 더 정중한 표현

May I get your autograph, please?
May I please take a picture with you?

(3) 대답하기

A Can I go home now?
B Of course, you can.

A May I sit here?
B I'm sorry. You may not.

2 'You'를 주어로: can, will, could, would

(1) 부탁하기

Can you pass me the salt, please? (허물없는 표현)
Will you pass me the salt, please? (허물없는 표현, 약간 명령조)
Could you pass me the salt, please? (정중한 표현)
Would you pass me the salt, please? (매우 예의 바른 표현)

(2) 대답하기

A Could you do me a favor?
B Sure, I could [can / will].

A Would you go with me?
B Sorry, I cannot.

(2) 부탁할 때 대답하는 표현

Yes	No
Of course.	I'm sorry.
Certainly.	I'm afraid not.
Sure.	Surely not.
Okay.	
My pleasure.	
I'd be happy to.	

Quick Test

Answers ▲ P.11

1. Can I go to bed now? •
2. May I use your car? •
3. Will you lend me some money? •
4. Would you put this in my car? •
5. May I please borrow your garden tools? •

• (a) Sorry, you can't. It's in the repair shop.
• (b) Of course, you can go to bed now.
• (c) Sure, I will. Give me the car key.
• (d) I'm sorry, I can't. I don't have any money now.
• (e) Sure, but I can't find the tools anywhere.

64

E EXERCISE

A [   ] 안에서 알맞은 것을 고르시오.

1 Will you [opens, open] the door for me?

2 [May, Would] I have your phone number?

3 [Can, Would] I have a cup of coffee?

4 Can you [turn, to turn] off the radio?

5 [Can, May] she make a dessert for the party?

6 [May, Would] I listen to your new song?

7 Can you [fly, flies] a kite?

B [보기]에서 알맞은 단어를 골라 조동사 **can**과 함께 문장을 완성하시오.

Word Bank	wait	borrow	have	call	help	go

1 I don't have my math book. ___*Can*___ I ___*borrow*___ yours?

2 I'm very late. _____ you _____ a taxi for me?

3 This bag is very heavy. _____ you _____ me with it?

4 She is at the meeting. _____ you _____ for a moment?

5 I'm so thirsty. _____ I _____ something to drink?

6 You look so tired. You _____ _____ home early today.

C 주어진 조건에 맞도록 문장을 완성하시오.

1 You can order some food. (의문문으로)

  → _____*Can you order some food?*_____

2 You can go out and play. (부정문으로)

  → _____

3 Say your name again. (좀 더 공손하게)

  → _____

4 Can you get me some lemonade? (매우 예의 바르게)

  → _____

5 Would you show me your ID? (허물없는 표현으로)

  → _____

Unit 06

3 의무를 나타내는 조동사

This cake is tasty. You should try it.

You must not make any noise in the library.

You don't have to keep silent in the cafeteria.

1 should: 조언, 금지, 의무

You should <u>eat</u> healthy food.

You shouldn't <u>eat</u> too much fast food.

Should I <u>stop</u> eating hamburgers?

2 must (=have to): 의무

(1) 현재

I have to <u>come</u> to class earlier.

= I must <u>come</u> to class earlier.

(2) 과거

I had to <u>come</u> to class earlier.

*must는 과거형이 없다.

(3) 미래

I will have to <u>come</u> to class earlier.

*will must (X)

(4) 의문문

Do I have to <u>come</u> to class earlier?

*Do I must~? (X)

(5) 부정문

I must not <u>be</u> late for class. (금지)

I don't have to <u>come</u> to class earlier. (불필요)

(5)
must가 '강한 추측(~임에 틀림없다)'의 의미를 나타내기도 한다.
You must be tired.

Quick Test

Answers ▲ P.11

Word Bank	의무	조언	불필요	추측

1. You should close the windows. _조언_

2. She's eating very fast. She must be hungry. _____

3. We don't have to do that. _____

4. All students must bring their own textbooks. _____

66

E EXERCISE

A [　] 안에서 알맞은 것을 고르시오.

1 Children should [go, to go] to bed early.

2 You must [not bring, bring not] your pet into the building.

3 I will [have to, must] wear a school uniform.

4 Will you have [return, to return] that book?

5 You [not may, may not] eat or drink during the performance.

6 [Do you must, Do you have to] finish your homework right now?

7 He shouldn't [watch, watches] too much TV.

B 주어진 조건에 맞도록 문장을 완성하시오.

1 I must study hard to prepare for the exam. (미래시제로)

→ _____*I will have to study hard*_____ to prepare for the exam.

2 She must open the black box. (부정문으로)

→ _____ the black box.

3 I should take some medicine. (의문문으로)

→ _____ some medicine?

4 They must get on the train at 7 a.m. (과거시제로)

→ _____ the train at 7 a.m.

C 우리말과 같은 뜻이 되도록 주어진 단어를 배열하시오.

1 여기서 수영하면 안 됩니다. (not / here / must / swim / you)

→ _____*You must not swim here.*_____

2 당신은 은행 계좌를 개설해야 합니다. (open / you / a bank account / must)

→ _____

3 당신은 집에 일찍 가야 합니다. (home / go / you / early / should)

→ _____

4 어젯밤 그녀는 언니를 돌봐야 했다. (take care of / she / her sister / had to / last night)

→ _____

5 그는 아픈 것임에 틀림없다. (sick / he / be / must)

→ _____

REVIEW TEST

A [　　] 안에서 알맞은 것을 고르시오.

1 We will have dinner at 7. So you [will, must] come home before 7.

2 I [could, can] catch the last bus yesterday.

3 [Can, Will] you be able to fix my computer?

4 [Do, Must] they have to make a plan?

5 May I [shook, shake] your hand, please?

6 Doris [will have to, will must] change her clothes before the party.

7 Steve [cannot, not can] read English newspapers.

8 Erica [can, was able to] pick me up last night.

B 빈칸에 알맞은 것을 고르시오.

1 The school does not allow long hair. You _____ keep your hair short.
   ⓐ could　　　　　ⓑ may　　　　　ⓒ must　　　　　ⓓ would

2 He lost his wallet. So he _____ walk all the way home yesterday.
   ⓐ musted　　　　ⓑ had to　　　　ⓒ should　　　　ⓓ must

3 My sister _____ the violin with me tomorrow.
   ⓐ can plays　　　ⓑ played　　　　ⓒ is play　　　　ⓓ won't play

4 _____ me a snack?
   ⓐ Could buy you　ⓑ Could you buy　ⓒ Buy you can　　ⓓ May you buy

5 Charlie _____ find a job soon.
   ⓐ will be able to　ⓑ was be able to　ⓒ cannot　　　　ⓓ couldn't

6 _____ see a doctor?
   ⓐ Can I have to　ⓑ Could I have to　ⓒ Could I must　　ⓓ Do I have to

7 I can _____ another copy.
   ⓐ be make　　　ⓑ makes　　　　ⓒ make　　　　　ⓓ make not

FURTHER STUDY

A Grammar in Speaking 빈칸에 알맞은 조동사를 넣어 문장을 완성하시오.

1 　　2 　　3 　　4

5 　　6 　　7 　　8

1 **A** Can I smoke here?

　B No, you _____ smoke here.

2 **A** How fast can I drive here?

　B You _____ drive under 30 miles an hour.

3 **A** Can I turn right here?

　B No, you can't. You _____ turn left.

4 **A** Can I drive a car here?

　B No, but you _____ ride your bike here.

5 **A** Can I drive fast here?

　B No, you _____ drive slowly. Kids are playing around here.

6 **A** I can't find the way out!

　B Follow the exit sign. You _____ find the way out.

7 **A** Watch out! There is a sign.

　B Oh, yeah. People _____ be careful because of the big dog.

8 **A** I brought my lunch with me.

　B Oh, look at the sign. You _____ eat or drink here.

WRAP-UP TEST

1 다음 빈칸에 공통으로 들어갈 단어를 고르시오.

> • They _____ play the violin well.
> • _____ I try this on?

ⓐ do
ⓑ can
ⓒ must
ⓓ would

2 다음 빈칸에 들어갈 수 <u>없는</u> 것을 고르시오.

> _____ you open the window?

ⓐ Can
ⓑ Could
ⓒ Would
ⓓ Should

3 다음 밑줄 친 부분을 바르게 고치시오.

> You will <u>must</u> show your ID to the security guard.

→ _____

4 다음 중 어법상 옳지 <u>않은</u> 문장을 고르시오.

ⓐ You should take an umbrella.
ⓑ We must not use our cell phones during the movie.
ⓒ He will can finish reading this book in two hours.
ⓓ Do I have to get there before ten?

5 다음 can의 쓰임이 <u>다른</u> 하나를 고르시오.

ⓐ Can you jump high?
ⓑ Can he find his car?
ⓒ Can they win the game?
ⓓ Can you help me with this?

6 다음 대화를 읽고 대답으로 알맞은 것을 고르시오.

> A May I go out and play?
> B _____

ⓐ Yes, you may.
ⓑ No, I should.
ⓒ No, you don't.
ⓓ Yes, I would.

7 다음 밑줄 친 부분의 쓰임 다른 하나를 고르시오.

ⓐ You <u>must</u> wear a hat under the strong sun.
ⓑ You <u>must</u> be careful on city streets.
ⓒ You <u>must</u> be very tired after your long flight.
ⓓ You <u>must</u> do your homework before dinner.

8 다음 두 문장이 같은 뜻이 되도록 빈칸에 알맞은 말을 쓰시오.

He can ride a horse.
= He _____ _____ _____ ride a horse.

9 다음 우리말과 같은 뜻이 되도록 빈칸에 알맞은 말을 쓰시오.

나는 어제 동생을 돌봐야만 했어.
= I _____ _____ take care of my sister yesterday.

10 다음 빈칸에 알맞은 단어를 쓰시오.

> Last night, I went to bed at one o'clock. I got up late and was late for school. I will _____ _____ come to class earlier tomorrow.

형용사

Unit 07

형용사의 의미와 쓰임

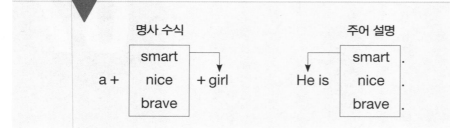

1 명사 수식

(1) 명사 앞에 위치

Sue is a small girl.

These are good pictures.

Sue is a big girl.

Those are bad pictures.

(2) 명사 뒤에 위치하는 경우

something cold   (X) cold something

nothing special   (X) special nothing

2 주어 설명

(1) be동사 뒤에서 주어의 상태를 설명한다.

Paris is romantic. (Paris → romantic)

Venice is beautiful. (Venice → beautiful)

(2) 명사와 함께 주어의 상태를 설명한다.

Venice is beautiful.

Venice is a city.

→ Venice is a beautiful city. (Venice → a beautiful city)

1

(1) 형용사는 관사 뒤, 명사 앞에 온다.
She's smart a girl. (X)
She's a smart girl. (O)
형용사가 단독으로 쓰일 때 관사를 붙이지 않는다.

(2) ~thing, ~body, ~one으로 끝나는 명사는 대부분 뒤에서 수식한다.

2

주어를 보충 설명하는 말을 보어라고 부른다. 명사도 보어로 쓰인다.
I am a boy.
He is a doctor.
Venice is a city.
Roses are flowers.

Quick Test

Answers ▲ P.13

Word Bank	short	hot	dirty	full	young [new]	difficult	weak	small

1. big   ↔   *small*

2. clean   ↔

3. cold   ↔

4. easy   ↔

5. strong   ↔

6. hungry   ↔

7. long   ↔

8. old   ↔

E EXERCISE

A [   ] 안에서 알맞은 것을 고르시오.

1 A dog is [a cute, cute].　　　　　A dog is [a cute, cute] animal.

2 An elephant is [a big, big].　　　An elephant is [a big, big] animal.

3 Ants are [small, a small].　　　　Ants are [small, a small] insects.

4 Baseball and soccer are [fun, a fun].　　Baseball and soccer are [fun, a fun] sports.

5 She is [a happy, happy].　　　　She is [happy, a happy] girl.

6 This is [exciting, an exciting].　　This is [an exciting, exciting] movie.

7 I am [honest, a honest].　　　　I am [an honest, honest] person.

B [보기]에서 알맞은 단어를 골라 문장을 완성하시오.

Word Bank	happy	big	small	short	sad	long

1 I'm _____happy_____. I'm not _____.

2 Polar bears are _____. They are not _____.

3 Her hair is _____. It is not _____.

C 주어진 두 문장을 한 문장으로 바꿔 쓰시오.

1 She is a girl. She is pretty.

→ _____ She is a pretty girl.

2 He is a doctor. He is kind.

→ _____

3 It is a book. It's old.

→ _____

4 Pigs are animals. They are fat.

→ _____

Unit 07

2 여러 가지 형용사

지시형용사	부정 수량형용사
This is a cabin.	I have **a lot of** time.
→ This is a **small** cabin.	I have **some** time.
→ This cabin **is small**.	I have **a little** time.

1 지시형용사

(1) 뒤따라오는 명사를 지칭

This <u>movie</u> is exciting. That <u>movie</u> is scary.
These <u>movies</u> are exciting. Those <u>movies</u> are scary.

(2) 단, 복수 구분 필요

These <u>books</u> are difficult. (X) This books are difficult.
That <u>pen</u> is expensive. (X) Those pen is expensive.

(3) 지시 형용사 vs. 지시 대명사

That <u>ring</u> is expensive. <u>That</u> is an expensive ring.
These <u>cookies</u> are yummy. <u>These</u> are yummy cookies.

2 부정 수량형용사: 정해지지 않은 수나 양 표시

셀 수 있는 명사	공통 적용	셀 수 없는 명사
many	a lot of [lots of]	much
a few [a couple of]	some [any]	a little
few		little

A Are there **any** <u>girls</u> in your class?
B There are **some** (=a few) <u>girls</u> in our class.
B There are not **any** <u>girls</u> in our class.

▶ 1

(2)
This/That+단수명사+is
These/Those+복수명사+are

(3)
┌ 지시형용사 : 이~, 저~
└ 지시대명사 : 이 사람(들), 이것(들)
          저 사람(들), 저것(들)

▶ 2
many / much / a lot of: '많은'
a few / a little: '조금 있는'
few / little: '거의 없는'
some: '약간의'
주로 긍정문에 쓴다.
any: some과 같은 의미이다.
      주로 의문문/부정문에 쓴다.

There is/are~ : '~가 있다'
이때, there를 '거기'라고 해석하지 않는다.

Quick Test

옳은 표현에는 O, 틀린 표현에는 X를 표시하시오.

Answers ▲ P.13

1. that movie   O
2. bad kids   _____
3. a few water   _____
4. some people   _____

5. these balloon   _____
6. a good books   _____
7. many money   _____
8. much girls   _____

EXERCISE

Answers P.13

A [   ] 안에서 알맞은 것을 고르시오.

1 [This, These] watch is nice.

2 [That, Those] boys are good at sports.

3 [This, These] peaches are delicious.

4 This [panda, pandas] is cute.

5 These [candies, candy] are sweet.

6 That [sweater, sweaters] is warm.

7 Those [orange, oranges] are sour.

B [보기]에서 알맞은 단어를 골라 문장을 완성하시오.

Word Bank	many	a little	a few

1 Are there any birds in the cage?

There are _____*a few*_____ birds in the cage.

2 Is there any water in the bottle?

There is _____ water in the bottle.

3 Are there many books in the bookcase?

There are _____ books in the bookcase.

C 우리말과 같은 뜻이 되도록 주어진 단어를 배열하시오.

1 책장에 많은 책이 있습니다. (lots of / there are / in the bookcase / books)

→ _____*There are lots of books in the bookcase.*_____

2 연못에 물이 조금 있습니다. (a little / there is / water / in the pond)

→ _____

3 이것들은 재미난 이야기입니다. (are / interesting / these / stories)

→ _____

4 저 곰 인형은 귀엽습니다. (that / teddy bear / is / cute)

→ _____

A [ ] 안에서 알맞은 것을 고르시오.

1 She is [a lovely, lovely].

2 They are [clever girls, girls clever].

3 Those are [a yellow, yellow] butterflies.

4 It was [red something, something red].

5 [These, This] cookies are delicious.

6 They are [real diamonds, diamonds real].

7 There is not [any, some] jam in the jar.

8 Seattle is a [city rainy, rainy city].

B 빈칸에 알맞은 것을 고르시오.

1 New York is _____ .

   ⓐ a city big   ⓑ a big city   ⓒ big a city   ⓓ city a big

2 Is she _____ ?

   ⓐ a pretty   ⓑ pretty   ⓒ pretty girl   ⓓ girl

3 Would you like _____ cold to drink?

   ⓐ any   ⓑ it   ⓒ something   ⓓ what

4 He is _____ boy.

   ⓐ honest a   ⓑ a honest   ⓒ honest   ⓓ an honest

5 Is there _____ salt in the bottle?

   ⓐ any   ⓑ many   ⓒ few   ⓓ a few

6 _____ sneakers are dirty.

   ⓐ This   ⓑ That   ⓒ It   ⓓ Those

7 There is _____ milk in the glass.

   ⓐ a few   ⓑ many   ⓒ a little   ⓓ two

A

Grammar in Speaking 주어진 단어를 이용하여 대화를 완성하시오.

1 A Was it sunny yesterday?

B No, it _____ _____ _____ . (not sunny)

2 A Who is your mother in this picture?

B Her hair _____ _____ (long), and she _____ _____ . (beautiful)

3 A Is your room clean?

B No, it _____ _____ . (dirty)

4 A Is this a long video game?

B No, this _____ _____ _____ _____ . (short game)

This _____ _____ _____ . (not long)

5 A Was it cold this morning?

B No, It _____ _____ . (warm)

6 A Is that an expensive shirt?

B No, this _____ _____ . (cheap)

This _____ _____ _____ . (not expensive)

B

Grammar in Writing 다음 광고를 보고, 빈칸에 알맞은 말을 넣어 문장을 완성하시오.

For Rent - Apartment	**- Furnished living room**
	with a large TV, a cozy couch, a blue carpet
	- One bathroom
	very clean
- One bedroom	**- Others**
with a new bed, a large closet	quiet neighbors
- kitchen	**Call for more information: 555-3258**
with a gray table, 2 brown chairs	

Here is a perfect apartment for you. There is one bedroom with a bed and a closet. The bed is (1) _____ , and the closet is (2) _____ . The kitchen table is gray and the chairs are (3) _____ . The living room is all furnished. There is a (4) _____ TV and a cozy couch in the living room. There is a carpet, too. It is a (5) _____ carpet. The bathroom is (6) _____ _____ . Moreover, the neighbors are (7) _____ . If you need more information, please call 555-3258.

1 다음 빈칸에 들어갈 말이 바르게 짝지어진 것을 고르시오.

> • _____ are nice watches.
> • _____ watch is nice.

ⓐ Those – These ⓑ That – This
ⓒ This – Those   ⓓ These – That

2 다음 빈칸에 알맞지 <u>않은</u> 것을 고르시오.

> She is _____.

ⓐ a girl   ⓑ pretty
ⓒ a tall woman ⓓ a happy

3 다음 밑줄 친 부분과 바꾸어 쓸 수 있는 것을 고르시오.

> There is <u>much</u> money in his wallet.

ⓐ many   ⓑ lots of
ⓒ a few   ⓓ few

4 다음 괄호 안의 단어의 순서가 바르게 나열된 것을 고르시오.

> He is (boy, a, handsome).

ⓐ He is handsome a boy.
ⓑ He is a boy handsome.
ⓒ He is a handsome boy.
ⓓ He is handsome boy a.

5 다음 밑줄 친 부분의 쓰임이 잘못된 것을 고르시오.

ⓐ Paris is <u>a romantic city</u>.
ⓑ This diamond is <u>real</u>.
ⓒ She is <u>kind a nurse</u>.
ⓓ <u>Those spiders</u> are fast.

6 다음 밑줄 친 부분을 바르게 고치시오.

> There isn't <u>some</u> cake in the oven.

→ _____

7 다음 주어진 우리말과 같은 뜻이 되도록 빈칸에 알맞은 말을 고르시오.

> 우리는 새로운 것이 필요해.
> → We need _____.

ⓐ a something new
ⓑ something new
ⓒ a new something
ⓓ new something

8 다음 주어진 문장을 지시형용사를 이용한 문장으로 바르게 고친 것을 고르시오.

> These are nice postcards.

ⓐ These postcards are nice.
ⓑ These postcards are nices.
ⓒ This postcards is a nice.
ⓓ These postcard are nice.

9 다음 주어진 우리말과 같은 뜻이 되도록 빈칸에 알맞은 단어를 쓰시오.

> **A** How many apples are there in the apple tree?
> **B** 사과나무에 사과가 거의 없어.

→ There are _____ _____ in the apple tree.

10 다음 두 문장을 한 문장으로 만드시오.

1) An elephant is an animal. An elephant is big.
   → An elephant is _____ _____ _____.

2) Jason is a man. Jason is honest.
   → Jason is _____ _____ _____.

부사

Unit 08

Unit 1 부사의 의미와 쓰임

English is really fun.

I study English hard.

I am working quite hard.

Luckily, I passed the test!

1 부사의 역할

(1) 형용사 수식

English is fun. → English is really fun.

We are good friends. → We are very good friends.

(2) 동사 수식

I study English. → I study English hard.

They are speaking. → They are speaking loudly.

(3) 다른 부사 수식

I am working hard. → I am working quite hard.

You run fast! → You run very fast!

(4) 문장 전체 수식

I passed the test! → Luckily, I passed the test!

He left me. → Sadly, he left me.

2 부사의 의미

(1) 시간 / 장소(방향)

I get up early.

He gets up late.

I am standing up.

He is sitting down.

(2) 방법(태도) / 정도

I sing quietly.

He sings loudly.

She is quite pretty.

He is very handsome.

2

시간
now, then, soon, today

장소(방향)
here, there, near, up, down

방법
happily, slowly, loudly, fast, hard

정도
very, so, pretty(꽤), really, quite, too

Quick Test

Answers ▲ P.14

Word Bank	up	late	slowly	far	badly	hard

1. early ⟷ _____late_____

2. fast ⟷ _____

3. down ⟷ _____

4. well ⟷ _____

5. close ⟷ _____

6. easily ⟷ _____

80

E EXERCISE

A [   ] 안에서 알맞은 것을 고르시오.

1 Mr. Choi plays golf [good, well].

2 The movie *Transformer* is [very, many] exciting.

3 I was at the beach [then, hard].

4 She is [pretty, fast] good at dancing.

5 The weather is [too, many] cold.

6 I'm [so, a lot of] glad to meet you.

7 There is an old museum [near, soon] the park.

B [보기]에서 알맞은 단어를 골라 문장을 완성하시오.

Word Bank	well	carefully	early	easily	quietly	happily

1 I went to sleep _____*early*_____ last night, but I got up late today.

2 My mom is a chef, so she cooks _____.

3 Please speak _____. The baby is asleep.

4 She's strong. She opened the jar _____.

5 Please listen to me _____.

6 They got married and lived _____ ever after.

C 우리말과 같은 뜻이 되도록 주어진 단어를 이용하여 문장을 완성하시오.

1 그 책은 꽤 재미있다. (the book, is, interesting)

→ _____*The book is quite interesting.*_____

2 슬프게도, 그들은 경기에 졌다. (they, lost, the game)

→ _____

3 그녀는 굉장히 시끄럽게 말한다. (she, talks, very)

→ _____

4 그는 영어를 잘한다. (he, speaks, English)

→ _____

Unit 08

2 부사의 형태

He is a <u>bad</u> guy.　　→　　He treats people **badly**.

It is <u>heavy</u> rain.　　→　　It rains **heavily**.

1 형용사+ly

(1) -ly

He is a <u>nice</u> dancer.　→　He dances **nicely**.

It is a <u>sad</u> story.　　→　**Sadly**, it is true.

(2) [-y]로 끝나면 y를 i로 바꾸고 -ly

They live a <u>happy</u> life. →　They live **happily**.

That is an <u>easy</u> job.　→　I make money **easily**.

(3) [-le]로 끝나면 le를 빼고 -ly

The system is <u>simple</u>. →　We **simply** operate it.

His voice is <u>gentle</u>.　→　He speaks **gently**.

(3) [-e]로 끝나면 e를 빼고 -ly.
true → truly
gentle → gently

2 주의해야 할 형태

(1) 명사+ly = 형용사

They are <u>friendly</u>.　　The <u>weekly</u> news is on TV.

(2) 부사+ly = 다른 의미를 가진 부사

I study English <u>hard</u>.　I <u>hardly</u> study English.

(3) 형용사와 같은 형태를 가지는 경우

I don't like <u>fast</u> food.　I run <u>fast</u>.

I like <u>hard</u> mattresses.　Work <u>hard</u> and play <u>hard</u>.

I don't have <u>enough</u> money.　I worked <u>enough</u> today.

2

(1) 부사와 혼동하지 않도록 주의한다.
- friendly 친절한
- weekly 주간의, 매주의

(2) 기존의 부사와 다른 의미를 갖는다.
- hard 열심히, 힘든
　hardly 거의 ~하지 않는
- late 늦은, 늦게
　lately 최근에
- near 가까운, 가까이에
　nearly 거의

Quick Test

Answers　P.14

1.	simple	→	*simply*	7.	*gentle*	→	gently
2.	clean	→		8.		→	carefully
3.	good	→		9.		→	quickly
4.	happy	→		10.		→	smartly
5.	large	→		11.		→	poorly
6.	easy	→		12.		→	strongly

82

EXERCISE

A   [   ] 안에서 알맞은 것을 고르시오.

1   They are really [friend, friendly].

2   She is a [kind, kindly] person.

3   The task is [actually, actual] easy.

4   They smiled at each other [happy, happily].

5   [Sudden, Suddenly], it started to rain.

6   He speaks very [clear, clearly].

7   Cindy talked to her mom [cheerful, cheerfully].

B   [보기]에서 알맞은 단어를 골라 문장을 완성하시오.

Word Bank	poorly	really	gently	loudly	brightly	usually

1   They were _____*really*_____ surprised at the noise.

2   They played the music _____.

3   The sun shines _____.

4   He touched the butterfly _____.

5   The student is _____ prepared for the test.

6   The bank is _____ open until 6.

C   우리말과 같은 뜻이 되도록 주어진 단어를 배열하시오.

1   그는 빠르게 뛰었다. (ran / fast / he)

    → _____*He ran fast.*_____

2   열차는 일찍 떠났다. (early / the train / left)

    → _____

3   다행히도, 그 새는 새장을 탈출했다. (escaped / the cage / the bird / luckily)

    → _____

4   그는 파티에 늦게 왔다. (came / late / he / to the party)

    → _____

Unit 08

3 빈도부사

He **always** wears a blue jacket.
He **usually** wears a white shirt under it.
He **often** wears a yellow tie with the shirt.
He **sometimes** wears a gray coat with that outfit.
He **never** wears sunglasses.

1 빈도부사의 위치: be 동사 뒤, 일반동사 앞

Jason <u>is</u> **always** late for school.
Jason **usually** <u>comes</u> to school after 9 o'clock.
The teacher <u>is</u> **often** upset with him.
Jason **sometimes** <u>promises</u> not to be late again.
The teacher **never** <u>trusts</u> him.

2 질문하고 답하기

(1) 빈도부사를 이용해서 물어보기

A Is Jason **always** late for school?
B Yes, he is.
B No, he isn't **always** late for school.
  (= he **sometimes** comes to school on time.)

(2) 의문사를 이용해서 물어보기

A How often is Jason late for school?
B Jason is **always** late for school.

A How many times a week is Jason late for school?
B Jason is late for school **five times** a week.

1

빈도부사	빈도	의미
always	100%	언제나, 항상
usually	around 80~90%	대개, 보통
often	around 50~60%	종종
sometimes	around 30%	가끔
never	0%	절대 ~않다

(2)
how often 얼마나 자주?
how many times 몇 번?

Quick Test

Answers ▲ P.15

1. It rains in Seattle. (often)
→ It _____*often rains*_____ in Seattle.

2. I am afraid of ghosts. (never)
→ I _____ of ghosts.

3. Jenny calls her grandfather. (sometimes)
→ Jenny _____ her grandfather.

4. Your sisters are lazy. (always)
→ Your sisters _____ lazy.

5. I order soup for lunch. (usually)
→ I _____ soup for lunch.

6. He walks to school. (never)
→ He _____ to school.

E EXERCISE

Answers ▾ P.15

A　[　] 안에서 알맞은 것을 고르시오.

1 Tina [often goes, goes often] hiking.

2 I will [never tell, tell never] a lie to you.

3 [What, How] many times does she meet him in a week?

4 They [usually have, have usually] lunch in the cafeteria.

5 Ed [often makes, makes usually] pizza for us.

6 I walk my dog [five time, five times] a week.

7 How [often, usually] do you go shopping?

B　주어진 표를 참고하여 문장을 완성하시오.

	Sun	Mon	Tue	Wed	Thu	Fri	Sat
Anne	○		○		○	○	
Mike	○	○	○	○	○	○	○
Lisa		○			○		
Chris	○	○		○	○	○	
Paul							

(○ = busy day)

1 Anne is _____*often*_____ busy.

2 Mike is _____ busy.

3 Lisa is _____ busy.

4 Chris is _____ busy.

5 Paul is _____ busy.

C　우리말과 같은 뜻이 되도록 주어진 단어를 배열하시오.

1 그는 얼마나 자주 연을 날립니까? (does / fly / how often / he / a kite)

　→ _____*How often does he fly a kite?*_____

2 그들은 가끔 남은 음식을 집으로 가져옵니다. (leftovers / sometimes / bring / they / home)

　→ _____

3 그 반은 항상 좋은 점수를 받습니다. (always / good grades / the class / gets)

　→ _____

4 Susan은 직장에 절대 늦지 않습니다. (is / late / never / Susan / for work)

　→ _____

5 Brad는 요즘 자주 일찍 일어납니다. (often / gets up / Brad / these days / early)

　→ _____

REVIEW TEST

▲▲▲▲▲▲▲▲▲▲▲▲

A [   ] 안에서 알맞은 것을 고르시오.

1 They came to the party [late, lately]. There was no food left.

2 Is [he often, often he] ill?

3 The math test was [many, very] difficult.

4 How [often, many] does she make mistakes?

5 He opened his birthday present [quickly, quick].

6 The boy ran [very, many] fast.

7 She [studies usually, usually studies] hard.

8 The crowd is yelling [loud, loudly].

B 빈칸에 알맞은 것을 고르시오.

1 I had a fight with Billy. I will _____ talk to him again.

ⓐ every day   ⓑ no   ⓒ usually   ⓓ never

2 My father drives his car _____.

ⓐ fastly   ⓑ fast   ⓒ easy   ⓓ tough

3 _____, I lost my little dog.

ⓐ Unfortunate   ⓑ Unhappy   ⓒ Bad   ⓓ Sadly

4 He spoke _____ to the injured child.

ⓐ quiet   ⓑ luckily   ⓒ kindly   ⓓ helpful

5 We _____ hike in the forest on weekends.

ⓐ sometimes   ⓑ no   ⓒ much   ⓓ fast

6 How _____ do they travel?

ⓐ usually   ⓑ sometimes   ⓒ often   ⓓ never

FURTHER STUDY

🔆 Integrated Drills

▲▲▲▲▲▲▲▲▲▲▲▲

A   **Grammar in Speaking**   빈칸에 알맞은 것을 골라 대화를 완성하시오.

Word Bank	fast	always	many	never	really

1 **A** How _____ times a week do you eat ice cream?

   B Around three times a week, maybe.

2 **A** I had an accident. I drove too _____.

   B You are such a careless driver.

3 **A** I never go to the beach in the summer. How about you?

   B I _____ go there in the summer.

4 **A** He's really smart. He speaks English well, too.

   B He's _____ fortunate.

5 **A** Do you go swimming every day?

   B No, I _____ go swimming. I can't swim.

B   **Grammar in Writing**   빈칸에 알맞은 것을 골라 글을 완성하시오.

Word Bank	soon	hopefully	luckily	really	hard	always	late

I have many bad habits. I get up (1) _____ every morning. So, I (2) _____ skip breakfast. I sometimes borrow money from other children and don't pay it back. I don't study (3) _____. I usually sleep in class. I (4) _____ need to change. (5) _____, I have good parents. I also have good teachers and friends. I'm now asking them for some help. (6) _____, they will offer good advice. I promise to change my bad habits (7) _____.

1 다음 중 성격이 <u>다른</u> 하나를 고르시오.

ⓐ beautiful   ⓑ heavily
ⓒ kindly   ⓓ soon

2 다음 빈칸에 알맞지 <u>않은</u> 것을 고르시오.

> It is _____ nice to meet you.

ⓐ so   ⓑ really
ⓒ very   ⓓ many

3 다음 빈칸에 알맞은 말을 순서대로 나열한 것을 고르시오.

> • He is a _____ cook.
> • He cooks _____.

ⓐ good - goodly   ⓑ bad - badly
ⓒ well - good   ⓓ badly - bad

4 다음 문장에서 sometimes가 들어갈 곳을 고르시오.

He ⓐ sends ⓑ me ⓒ a postcard ⓓ.

5 다음 중 어법상 옳지 <u>않은</u> 문장을 고르시오.

ⓐ She studies economics hard.
ⓑ The train left early.
ⓒ He drove a car fastly.
ⓓ Please listen carefully.

6 다음 밑줄 친 부분의 쓰임이 <u>잘못된</u> 것을 고르시오.

ⓐ She <u>often</u> smiles at me.
ⓑ There are <u>always</u> many people there.
ⓒ Paul <u>usually</u> cleans his room on Sunday.
ⓓ He <u>never</u> is lonely.

7 다음 형용사와 부사가 <u>잘못</u> 짝지어진 것을 고르시오.

ⓐ real - really
ⓑ week - weekly
ⓒ gentle - gently
ⓓ easy - easily

8 다음 밑줄 친 부분을 바르게 고치시오.

1) Stars twinkle <u>bright</u> in the sky.
   → _____

2) She is a <u>happily</u> woman.
   → _____

3) He got up <u>lately</u> this morning.
   → _____

9 다음 대화의 빈칸에 알맞은 말을 쓰시오.

> **A** _____ _____ do you eat out?
>
> **B** I usually eat out once a week.

10 다음 두 문장을 한 문장으로 만들 때 빈칸에 알맞은 말을 쓰시오.

> He passed the test. he was lucky.
> → _____, he passed the test.

비교

Unit 09

비교/최상급의 의미와 형태

규칙 변화		원급	비교급[-er, more]	최상급 [-est, most]
규칙 변화	1음절	tall	taller	tallest
	2음절 이상	important	more important	most important
불규칙 변화		good / well	better	best

1 비교급과 최상급

(1) 원급: '～한'

He is young.   He runs fast.

(2) 비교급: 비교급+than '…보다 더 ～한'

He is younger than I.   He runs faster than I.

(3) 최상급: the＋최상급 '가장 ～한'

He is the youngest child.   He runs fastest.

2 비교급, 최상급을 만드는 방법

(1) 규칙변화 1: 형용사/부사+-(e)r/-(e)st

❶ smart – smarter – smartest

❷ large – larger – largest

❸ heavy – heavier – heaviest

❹ fat – fatter – fattest

(2) 규칙변화 2: more/most＋형용사/부사

interesting – more interesting – most interesting

(3) 불규칙 변화

good / well – better – best

bad / badly – worse – worst

many / much – more – most

▶ **1**
형용사와 부사 모두 비교급과 최상급을 만들 수 있다.
- 비교급: 두 가지 대상을 비교할 때
  (비교급+than+비교 대상)
- 최상급: 여러 가지 대상 가운데
  「가장 ～ 한 것」을 나타낼 때
  (the+최상급)
* 부사의 최상급에는 원칙적으로
  the를 붙이지 않는다.

▶ **2**
(1)
규칙변화 1: 1음절 단어
❶ 대부분 -er/-est
❷ [-e]로 끝나면 -s/-st
❸ [자음+y]로 끝나면
  y를 i로 고치고 -er/-est
❹ [단모음+단자음]으로 끝나면 마지막
  자음을 덧붙이고 -er/-est

(2)
규칙변화 2: 대부분 2음절 이상의
단어 (y로 끝나는 형용사 제외)

(3)
He cooks well.
He cooks better than his wife.
He is the best cook in his family.

Quick Test

Answers ▲ P.16

1. big – *bigger* – *biggest*
2. hot – _____ – _____
3. beautiful – _____ – _____
4. happy – _____ – _____
5. many – _____ – _____

6. good – _____ – _____
7. fast – _____ – _____
8. easy – _____ – _____
9. badly – _____ – _____
10. wise – _____ – _____

EXERCISE

A [   ] 안에서 알맞은 것을 고르시오.

1 She is [pretty, prettier] than her sister.

2 Today is the [hotter, hottest] day of this summer.

3 Her cat is [biger, bigger] than mine.

4 I like fantasy novels [better, best] than mystery novels.

5 This exam was [worse, worst] than the last one.

6 My gift was [more, much] costly than his.

7 He is the [older, oldest] of the three boys.

B 주어진 단어를 이용하여 어법에 맞게 고쳐 문장을 완성하시오.

1 My bag is _____ (light) than yours.

2 The weather is _____ (bad) than yesterday.

3 This building is _____ (tall) in our city.

4 I drink milk _____ (much) than water.

5 Mrs. Smith is _____ (kind) teacher in my school.

6 This movie is _____ (interesting) than *Finding Nemo*.

7 She is _____ (beautiful) girl in the world.

C 우리말과 같은 뜻이 되도록 주어진 단어를 이용하여 문장을 완성하시오.

1 개들은 고양이들보다 더 친근하다. (dogs, are, friendly, than, cats)
→ _____ *Dogs are friendlier than cats.* _____

2 내 방은 우리 집에서 가장 작다. (my room, is, small, in my house)
→ _____

3 빨간 구두가 검정 구두보다 비싸다. (red shoes, are, expensive, than, black shoes)
→ _____

4 당신은 어제보다 좋아 보이는군요. (you, look, good, than, yesterday)
→ _____

Unit 09

Unit 2 비교 표현

동등 비교	Your brother is not as tall as you.
비교급의 강조	You are much taller than your brother.
최상급 표현	Your father is one of the tallest men in your family.

1 as+원급+as: '…만큼 ～한'

Rachel is as tall as Paul.
(= Rachel is 5 feet tall. Paul is also 5 feet tall.)
Justine is not as tall as Rachel.
(= Rachel is taller than Justine.)

> **1**
> 동등 비교 구문
> not as ～ as는 비교급 구문으로 바꿀 수 있다.

2 much, far, a lot, still, even+비교급: '…보다 훨씬 더 ～한'

You are much smarter than she is.
She speaks English a lot better than you.

> **2**
> 비교급의 강조
> (x) very smarter

3 one of the 최상급: '가장 ～한 것 중 하나'

Seoul is one of the busiest cities in Asia.
Matt is one of the most handsome guys in the world!

> **3**
> 'one of the 최상급' 뒤에는 항상 '복수 명사'가 온다.

4 최상급을 나타내는 다른 표현들

Jen is the smartest girl in my class.
= Jen is smarter than any other girl in my class. (비교급 이용)
= No other girl in my class is as smart as Jen. (원급 이용)

> **4**
> 비교급이나 원급을 이용해 최상급의 의미를 나타낼 수 있다.

Quick Test

Answers ▲ P.16

1. He is as old as she is. *그는 그녀만큼 나이가 많다.*

2. Kelly doesn't like movies as much as John.

3. His score was much better than he expected.

4. My grandma is sweeter than any other person.

5. He is one of the strongest guys in my class.

E EXERCISE

A   [   ] 안에서 알맞은 것을 고르시오.

1 The Rhine is one of the [more, most] famous rivers in the world.

2 He is [even, more] younger than I thought.

3 She is as [clever, cleverer] as you are.

4 I am [very, much] taller than my brother is.

5 Sally is [not as, as not] sad as David.

6 The sun is [far, more] bigger than the Earth.

7 This repair shop is [cleaner, cleanest] than any other repair shop in the area.

B   주어진 단어를 이용하여 어법에 맞게 고쳐 문장을 완성하시오.

1 A The movie was terrible.
   B Right, it was _____ (bad) than I thought.

2 A She can speak English _____ (well) than any other student in our class.
   B I know. She's the best.

3 A Yesterday was colder than today.
   B That's true. Today is _____ (cold) yesterday.

4 A His boat goes 70km/h. Mine also goes 70km/h.
   B Then, his boat is _____ (fast) your boat.

C   우리말과 같은 뜻이 되도록 주어진 단어를 이용하여 문장을 완성하시오.

1 아빠는 엄마만큼 화가 나셨다. (my father, is, as, angry, my mother)
   →   _My father is as angry as my mother._

2 "I"는 영어에서 가장 짧은 단어 중의 하나이다. ("I", is, one of, short, words, in English)
   → _____

3 KTX는 한국의 다른 어떤 기차들보다 빨리 달린다. (the KTX, runs, fast, than, any other train, in Korea)
   → _____

4 넌 네 어머니보다 훨씬 크게 웃는구나. (you, laugh, much, loud, than, your mother)
   → _____

A   [   ] 안에서 알맞은 것을 고르시오.

1 Tom is [brave, braver, bravest] than Johnny.

2 I am [much, more] healthier than before.

3 She can play tennis as [well, better, best] as Alex Agassi.

4 What is the [most important, importantest] thing in your life?

5 Jane is one of the cutest [girls, girl] in my class.

6 Cape Town is one of the [more, most] beautiful cities in the world.

7 This bag is [heavy, heavier, heaviest] than mine.

8 The play was [very, a lot] better than I expected.

B   빈칸에 알맞은 것을 고르시오.

1 Gary is _____ than Jim.
   ⓐ more strong   ⓑ stronger   ⓒ strong   ⓓ strongest

2 A cat is _____ clever as a fox.
   ⓐ as   ⓑ than   ⓒ so   ⓓ of

3 The oranges look _____ fresher than the apples.
   ⓐ very   ⓑ many   ⓒ a lot of   ⓓ much

4 His voice is _____ in my class.
   ⓐ louder   ⓑ the loudest   ⓒ the louder   ⓓ most loud

5 Athens is one of _____ in the world.
   ⓐ the older city   ⓑ the oldest cities   ⓒ the oldest city   ⓓ the old city

6 You are _____ kinder than I thought.
   ⓐ many   ⓑ very   ⓒ much   ⓓ most

7 Warren is the _____ man in our company.
   ⓐ more honest   ⓑ honestest   ⓒ honester   ⓓ most honest

A `Grammar in Speaking` 주어진 단어를 이용하여 어법에 맞게 고쳐 대화를 완성하시오.

1 **A** Did you arrive early?

   B No, I only got here five minutes _____ than you. (early)

2 **A** I don't read as much as my sister does.

   B She reads a lot _____ than you. (much)

3 **A** Did you see the new student in your class? Is she pretty?

   B Of course, she is _____ girl in the school. (pretty)

4 **A** Is Hawaii a popular island?

   B Yes, it is one of _____ islands in the world. (popular)

5 **A** New York City is _____ any other city in the U.S.A. (big)

   B Right. It's the biggest city in the country.

B `Grammar in Reading` 빈칸에 알맞은 말을 골라 어법에 맞게 고쳐 글을 완성하시오.

Word Bank	fast	strong	large

Teacher:

All right, guys. Here's the first question. Listen and think about it. Which can move faster, heat or cold? The answer is heat. Heat moves (1) _____ than cold. Why? Because you can catch a cold! Do you get it? Then, here goes the next one. What is the strongest creature in the world? It is the snail! It carries its house on its back. A snail is (2) _____ than me! Interesting, isn't it? The last one is: What is the largest ant in the world? The elephant! An elephant is a lot (3) _____ than an ant. Of course, they are not the same creatures, but it is a good joke anyway! Right?

1 다음 중 원급-비교급-최상급이 연결이 잘못된 것을 고르시오.

ⓐ nice - nicer - nicest
ⓑ busy - busier - busiest
ⓒ hot - hotter - hottest
ⓓ well - weller - wellest

2 다음 빈칸에 공통으로 들어갈 알맞은 말을 고르시오.

> • This scarf is _____ expensive than that scarf.
> • She is _____ famous than he.

ⓐ more   ⓑ better
ⓒ most   ⓓ best

3 다음 밑줄 친 부분의 쓰임이 바른 것을 고르시오.

ⓐ I have manyer books than he has.
ⓑ Math is the difficultest subject to study.
ⓒ She is the oldest child in the family.
ⓓ The movie was most exciting than I expected.

4 다음 빈칸에 들어갈 수 없는 것을 고르시오.

> She is _____ prettier than I thought.

ⓐ much   ⓑ very
ⓒ even   ⓓ a lot

5 다음 두 문장을 한 문장으로 만든 것으로 알맞은 것을 고르시오.

> The oranges are fresh.
> The apples are fresh, too.

ⓐ The oranges are as fresh as the apples.
ⓑ The oranges are fresher than the apples.
ⓒ The apples are more fresh than the oranges.
ⓓ The apples are the freshest fruit in the grocery store.

6 다음 중 문장의 의미가 나머지와 다른 것을 고르시오.

ⓐ James is the tallest boy in my class.
ⓑ No other boy in my class is as tall as James.
ⓒ James is taller than any other boy in my class.
ⓓ James is taller than my classmate.

7 다음 주어진 우리말을 영어로 바르게 옮긴 것을 고르시오.

> 그녀는 우리 학교에서 가장 똑똑한 학생 중 한 명이다.

ⓐ She is a smart student in my school.
ⓑ She is smarter than the student.
ⓒ She is one of the smartest students in my school.
ⓓ She is the smartest student in my school.

8 다음 두 문장의 뜻이 같도록 빈칸에 알맞은 말을 쓰시오.

> The plane is faster than the train.
> = The train is _____ as the plane.

[9-10] 다음 글을 읽고 물음에 답하시오.

> **A** The movie was terrible.
> **B** Really? Was it ⓐbad than you thought?
> **A** No, ⓑ그것은 가장 지루한 영화였어. (boring)
> **B** I should not see it.

9 ⓐ를 바르게 고치시오.

→ _____

10 ⓑ를 영작하시오.

→ _____

10

여러 가지
동사

목적어를 가지는 동사

Unit 10
1

자동사 (목적어를 갖지 않는다)	I sleep late in the morning.
타동사 (목적어를 한 개 갖는다)	I like him very much.
수여동사 (목적어를 두 개 갖는다)	I gave her flowers.

1 목적어를 갖지 않는 동사: 자동사

주어	동사	기타 어구
I	jog	in the morning.
The class	starts	at 11:00 in the morning.
The bus	arrives	at 9 o'clock.

1
의미: '주어가 ∼하다'

2 목적어를 한 개 갖는 동사: 타동사

주어	동사	목적어	기타 어구
She	likes	him	very much.
I	sold	my guitar.	
They	play	baseball	after school.

2
의미: 주어가 …를 ∼하다
같은 동사가 경우에 따라 자동사로 쓰이기도 하고, 타동사로 쓰이기도 한다.
예) We play baseball.
We play in the garden.

3 목적어를 두 개 갖는 동사: 수여동사

주어	동사	간접목적어	직접목적어
He	sent	her	a package.
Grandma	told	him	the story.
They	showed	her	some pictures.

3
의미: 주어가 …에게 …를 ∼하다
간접목적어(= 간목): 사람
직접목적어(= 직목): 사물

*수여동사의 의미
give 주다, send 보내다, 보내 주다
buy 사 주다, tell 말해 주다
show 보여 주다, teach 가르쳐 주다
pass 건네주다, make 만들어 주다

*주+동+간목+직목
주+동+직목+(to/for/of)+간목

to: teach, send, bring, give, show
for: buy, make, cook, sing, get
of: ask, demand

※ 목적어를 한 개 가지는 문장으로 바꿔 말하기 (to나 for를 이용한다.)
She gave me a present.
→ She gave a present to me.
My father bought us a bicycle.
→ My father bought a bicycle for us.

Quick Test 각 문장의 목적어에 밑줄을 긋고, 목적어가 없으면 X를 하시오.   Answers P.17

1. I told him the truth.

2. I don't drink coffee.

3. I run around the park every day.

4. He sent me nice flowers.

5. Thomas sent me a Christmas card.

6. I caught a big fish from the river.

7. The weather is windy and cool in fall.

8. Please do your homework now.

E EXERCISE

A 밑줄 친 동사의 목적어가 있으면 목적어를, 없으면 **X**를 쓰시오.

1 She <u>passed</u> him the ball.   *him, the ball*

2 I <u>looked</u> into the rabbit hole with him.   _____

3 The visitor <u>asked</u> the woman for directions. _____

4 The student <u>wrote</u> a letter to his aunt.   _____

5 They <u>saw</u> the boat in the water.   _____

6 The plane <u>is flying</u> high in the air.   _____

7 My sister <u>told</u> them the news.   _____

B 빈칸에 알맞은 말을 넣어 문장을 완성하시오.

1 My mom bought me a doll.

→ My mom bought a doll _____.

2 I sent my relatives a Christmas card.

→ I sent a Christmas card _____.

3 Are you going to show the picture to me?

→ Are you going to show me _____?

4 We give chocolates to our friends on Valentine's Day.

→ We give our friends _____ on Valentine's Day.

C 우리말과 같은 뜻이 되도록 주어진 단어를 배열하시오.

1 그녀는 나에게 그의 사진을 보여 주었다. (me / she / his pictures / showed)

→ _____ *She showed me his pictures.* _____

2 Mary는 우리에게 공연 표를 사 주었다. (tickets / us / bought / Mary / for the concert)

→ _____

3 우리 삼촌은 태권도 도장을 열었다. (my uncle / a Taekwondo gym / opened)

→ _____

4 그 목수가 우리 개의 집을 만들어 주었다. (built / for my dog / the carpenter / a doghouse)

→ _____

5 그 코치는 승리를 장담했다. (a victory / guaranteed / the coach)

→ _____

Unit 10

2 보어를 가지는 동사

보어를 갖는 be동사	You **are** <u>pretty</u>.
보어를 갖는 감각동사	You **look** <u>pretty</u> today.
목적보어를 갖는 동사	The music **makes** you <u>happy</u>.

1 보어를 갖는 동사

(1) be동사

주어	동사	보어	기타 어구
I	**am**	hungry.	
He	**is**	a nice guy.	
They	**are**	kind	to me.

(2) 감각동사

주어	동사	보어	기타 어구
You	**look**	nice	today.
It	**smells**	bad.	
That	**sounds**	good!	
The jam	**tastes**	sweet.	
I	**feel**	sick.	

2 목적어와 목적격 보어를 갖는 동사

주어	동사	목적어	목적격 보어
You	**make**	me	happy.
People	**call**	me	Chris.
My father	**made**	me	clean the room.
We	**chose**	him	the leader.
They	**elected**	Sonya	president.

1
보어는 주어를 설명한다.
(1) 의미: (주어는) ~하다, (주어는) ~이다
be동사 외에도 become(~가 되다)도
보어를 갖는다.

(2)
look (=seem) : (주어가) ~하게 보이다
smell: (주어가) ~하게 냄새나다
sound: (주어가) ~하게 들리다
taste: (주어가) ~하게 맛나다
feel: (주어가) ~하게 느껴지다

2
목적격 보어는 목적어를 설명한다.
의미: (주어가) …를 ~하게 (~가 되게)
하다
want, name, lend, wish

Quick Test 보어에 밑줄을 그으시오.

Answers ▲ P.18

1. She became <u>the president</u> of the club.
2. My parents are never angry with us.
3. Lamb's wool feels soft.
4. She looks beautiful in a red dress.
5. I want the package ready soon.
6. My son painted the fence white.
7. The movie was exciting.
8. I feel sorry to hear that.
9. We became roommates this year.
10. Are you mad at me?
11. I will name my son John.
12. That smells so good.

EXERCISE

A [   ] 안에서 알맞은 것을 고르시오.

1 The pie smells [good, well].

2 Do you want [to stay him, him to stay] here?

3 The pumpkin pie tastes [sweet, sweetly].

4 I named [my dog Tom, Tom my dog].

5 This chicken soup seems very [oil, oily].

6 He sometimes makes [her sad, sad her].

7 Tom became [famous, famously] right after his first movie.

B 주어진 단어를 배열하여 문장을 완성하시오.

1 It _____sounds_____ _____wonderful_____ to me. (wonderful, sounds)

2 The news _____ _____ _____. (me, surprised, made)

3 We _____ _____ _____. (wish, a merry Christmas, you)

4 We _____ _____. (very tired, feel)

5 I _____ _____ _____ for the test. (them, ready, want)

6 The soup _____ _____ to us. (spicy, tastes)

C 우리말과 같은 뜻이 되도록 주어진 단어를 배열하시오.

1 그녀는 웹디자이너가 되었다. (became / a web designer / she)

→ _____ *She became a web designer.* _____

2 사람들은 그를 천재라 부른다. (call / a genius / him / people)

→ _____

3 그 아이디어는 흥미로울 것 같다. (interesting / sounds / the idea)

→ _____

4 그 영화는 나를 미소 짓게 만들었다. (made / smile / the movie / me)

→ _____

REVIEW TEST

A [   ] 안에서 알맞은 것을 고르시오.

1 Philip always [makes, gives] me angry.

2 My son [lied to me, lied me] yesterday.

3 My grandfather told [me stories, stories me] about his childhood.

4 The man looked [busy, busily] at the moment.

5 The audience was [quiet, quietly] during the performance.

6 He showed [me a picture, a picture me] of himself.

7 He [lent me, me lent] some money.

B 빈칸에 알맞지 <u>않은</u> 것을 고르시오.

1 She sent _____.
   ⓐ me a postcard   ⓑ him a letter   ⓒ a letter them   ⓓ a package to him

2 Mary and Tom arrived _____.
   ⓐ at the party   ⓑ early   ⓒ late   ⓓ the airport

3 They looked _____.
   ⓐ friendly   ⓑ greatly   ⓒ sick   ⓓ healthy

4 His friend feels _____.
   ⓐ cold   ⓑ grateful   ⓒ warmly   ⓓ sad

5 She taught _____ in the library.
   ⓐ me English   ⓑ English to me   ⓒ me kind   ⓓ me

6 I told _____.
   ⓐ her about it   ⓑ him to go   ⓒ the morning   ⓓ the police my name

7 Please call _____.
   ⓐ me a taxi   ⓑ in the evening   ⓒ again   ⓓ frequent

A   Grammar in Speaking   빈칸에 알맞은 말을 골라 어법에 맞게 고쳐 대화를 완성하시오.

Word Bank	open	look	give	good	rise

1 **A** Wow, you _____ beautiful in that dress. Are you going to a party?

   B Yes, my friend is holding a birthday party for me.

2 **A** Where did you get those nice sneakers?

   B My mom _____ them to me as a Christmas gift.

3 **A** The sun _____ in the east and sets in the west.

   B How about the moon?

4 **A** He is a very _____ friend.

   B Yes, he is. He often helps me with my homework.

5 **A** Please keep the window _____. It's hot inside.

   B Sorry, but it's too cold outside.

B   Grammar in Writing   글을 읽고, 주어진 단어를 문맥에 맞게 배열하시오.

Last night, I dreamed that I could fly like a bird. (1) in the sky / flew / I . I was hungry and I ate clouds. (2) tasted / they / sweet like cotton candy. My face was dirty. (3) some rain / me / gave / the clouds and I washed my face. I felt sleepy and (4) on / the clouds / I / lay . They were very soft. The clouds, the moon and the stars were my friends. (5) an angel / me / they / called . Suddenly, the sun came out. My wings disappeared, and I fell to the ground. I woke up then.

(1) _____

(2) _____

(3) _____

(4) _____

(5) _____

1 다음 빈칸에 공통으로 들어갈 알맞은 것을 고르시오.

   • I _____ a mistake.
   • She _____ her son a pilot.

   ⓐ called   ⓑ made
   ⓒ became   ⓓ showed

2 다음 빈칸에 알맞은 것을 고르시오.

   Alex sent _____ two letters.

   ⓐ he   ⓑ mine
   ⓒ them   ⓓ yours

3 다음 빈칸에 들어갈 수 <u>없는</u> 것을 고르시오.

   She looks _____.

   ⓐ lovely   ⓑ friendly
   ⓒ greatly   ⓓ pretty

4 다음 밑줄 친 부분의 쓰임이 잘못된 것을 고르시오.

   ⓐ Mike became <u>famous</u>.
   ⓑ He told <u>me an interesting story</u>.
   ⓒ I forgot <u>her phone number</u>.
   ⓓ You always make me <u>happily</u>.

5 다음 중 어법상 옳지 <u>않은</u> 문장을 고르시오.

   ⓐ He arrived the airport on time.
   ⓑ They won the soccer game.
   ⓒ Jim is a hard worker.
   ⓓ Please pass me the book.

6 다음 빈칸에 알맞은 말을 고르시오.

   My father bought me a bike.
   → My father bought a bike _____ me.

   ⓐ of   ⓑ for
   ⓒ to   ⓓ from

7 다음을 주어진 우리말에 맞게 알맞게 배열하시오.

   내 친구들은 나를 Jimmy라 부른다.
   (call, Jimmy, me, my friends)

   → _____

8 다음 문장을 to와 of를 사용하여 바꾸시오.

   1) She gave him a pen.
      → _____

   2) My teacher asked me a question.
      → _____

[9-10] 다음 글을 읽고 물음에 답하시오.

   Barbara is my favorite teacher. (A) <u>She teaches
   English us</u>. She studied math at college, but
   she ___(B)___ an English teacher. She always
   smiles at us.

9 밑줄 친 (A) 문장을 바르게 고치시오.

   → _____

10 빈칸 (B)에 알맞은 말을 고르시오.

   ⓐ made   ⓑ became
   ⓒ was   ⓓ wanted

UNIT
11

여러 가지
문장

1   명령문
2   감탄문
3   부가/선택의문문

Unit 11

1 명령문

Eat healthy food! → You should eat healthy food.

Don't eat too much fast food. → You shouldn't eat too much fast food.

Let's eat lots of vegetables. → We should eat lots of vegetables.

1 명령문: [동사원형 ~]

(1) 'be'나 일반동사로 시작한다.

Be confident.   Be nice!

Leave me alone.   Go back to your seat.

Fasten your seat belt.   Please answer the question.

(2) 명령문, and … : '~ 해라, 그러면 …'

명령문, or … : '~ 해라, 그렇지 않으면 …'

Give me the password, and I will let you in.

Give me the password, or I will not let you in.

2 부정 명령문 [Don't+동사원형]

Don't be shy.   Don't be a fool.

Don't waste your time.   Don't give up your dream.

Please don't leave your seat.

Do not use your cell phone in the classroom.

3 권유 명령문 [Let's (not)+동사원형]

Let's dance!   Let's take a break.

Let's not make any noise.   Let's not skip meals.

1

(1) be동사의 원형은 'be'이다.

(2) 명령문의 앞, 뒤에 please를 넣으면 '~해 주십시오'와 같이 공손한 의미를 갖는다.

2 부정 명령문도 please를 붙여서 공손하게 만든다.

*강조할 때는 축약형을 쓰지 않는다.

3 권유 명령문의 부정 표현은 '~하지 말자'의 의미로 쓰인다.

Quick Test

Answers ▲ P.19

1. You open the door. → _____Open_____ the door.

2. You are happy. → _____ happy.

3. You don't worry. → _____ worry.

4. You are not lonely. → _____ be lonely.

5. You are a good boy. → _____ a good boy.

E EXERCISE

A [   ] 안에서 알맞은 것을 고르시오.

1 [Are, Be] careful!

2 [Watch, Watches] out for that car.

3 [Don't, Not] be afraid of failure.

4 Hurry up, [and, or] you will miss the bus.

5 Take this pill, [and, or] you will feel better.

6 Let's [don't, not] play outside.

7 [Are, Be] nice to your little brother.

B [보기]에서 빈칸에 알맞은 것을 골라 문장을 완성하시오.

Word Bank	have	be	take	give	watch

1 _____*Give*_____ the newspaper to your father.

2 Don't _____ TV too much.

3 Let's _____ pizza for dinner.

4 _____ an umbrella, or you will get wet.

5 _____ kind to them.

C 우리말과 같은 뜻이 되도록 주어진 단어를 이용하여 문장을 완성하시오.

1 6시에 만나자. (meet, at six)

→ _____*Let's meet at six.*_____

2 열심히 공부해, 그러면 시험에 합격할 거야. (study, hard, you, will, pass the test)

→ _____

3 이 강에서는 수영을 하지 마. (swim, in this river)

→ _____

4 오늘 밤에는 외출하지 말자. (go out, tonight)

→ _____

5 어떤 소리도 내지 마. (make any noise)

→ _____

Unit 11

2 감탄문

She is a very cute baby.

→ **What** a cute baby (she is)!

→ **How** cute (the baby is)!

---

1 What 감탄문: [What+(a / an)+형용사+명사+(주어+동사)]

(1) 단수 명사

You have a very nice sister.

→ What <u>a</u> <u>nice</u> <u>sister</u> (you have)!

It is a very small world.

→ What <u>a</u> <u>small</u> <u>world</u> (it is)!

(2) 복수 명사 / 셀 수 없는 명사

You have great ideas.

→ What <u>great</u> <u>ideas</u> (you have)!

It is very cold water.

→ What <u>cold</u> <u>water</u> (it is)!

2 How 감탄문: [How+형용사+(주어+동사)]

I am very foolish.

→ How <u>foolish</u> (I am)!

You swim very fast.

→ How <u>fast</u> (you swim)!

She is very pretty.

→ How <u>pretty</u> (she is)!

1

(1)
단수 명사일 때는 관사를 꼭 넣어야
한다.
(주어+동사)는 생략이 가능하다.

(2)
(주어+동사)는 생략이 가능하다.

2
(주어+동사)는 생략이 가능하다.

Quick Test

Answers ▲ P.19

1. _____What_____ a handsome boy he is!

2. _____ a cute dog it is!

3. _____ smart the girl is!

4. _____ a nice car it is!

5. _____ beautiful the beach is!

6. _____ a beautiful day!

7. _____ delicious the cookie is!

8. _____ pretty Mary is!

9. _____ heavy the box is!

10. _____ an expensive scarf it is!

E EXERCISE

Answers P.19

A   [   ] 안에서 알맞은 것을 고르시오.

1 [What, How] a nice car you have!

2 [What, How] big it is!

3 What [wonderful, a wonderful world] it is!

4 How [honest, an honest man] you are!

5 What beautiful [eyes, eye] you have!

6 What a [funny, funnily] story it is!

7 How [joyful, joyfully] they are!

B   [보기]에서 빈칸에 알맞은 것을 골라 문장을 완성하시오.

Word Bank	nice	cute	old

1 **A** This lamp is the same age as my great-grandmother.

   B What an _____ lamp it is!

2 **A** Look at the penguins.

   B What _____ animals they are!

3 **A** My daughter always helps me.

   B What a _____ girl!

C   주어진 문장을 감탄문으로 바꿔 완성하시오.

1 They are very huge animals.

   → What _____ *huge animals (they are)* _____ !

2 It is very bad news.

   → What _____ !

3 It is a very old church.

   → What _____ !

4 He is a very strong man.

   → What _____ !

Unit 11

3 부가/선택의문문

It's your fault, isn't it?   You made a mistake, didn't you?

It's not your fault, is it?   You didn't make a mistake, did you?

1 부가의문문

(1) 긍정문 뒤에는 부정문

be동사   It is beautiful today, isn't it?

일반동사   He liked her, didn't he?

조동사   They can help you, can't they?

(2) 부정문 뒤에는 긍정문

be동사   They are not helping you, are they?

일반동사   He doesn't like her anymore, does he?

조동사   It cannot be better, can it?

(3) 답변

A She liked me, didn't she?

B Yes, she did. / No, she didn't.

2 선택의문문

(1) 의문사가 없는 경우

Is this yours or his?

Do you drink coffee with sugar or without sugar?

(2) 의문사가 있는 경우

Who is taller, Rachel or Justine?

What is your favorite subject, English or art?

Which do you like better, coffee or tea?

1

부가의문문 만들기
- 주어는 대명사로 바꾸어야 한다.
- 동사의 종류를 맞추어야 한다.
- 시제(현재, 과거, 미래)를 맞추어야 한다.

(2)
He will not come, will he?
He will come, won't he?

(3)
답변은 질문에 상관없이 긍정은 Yes,
부정은 No로 대답한다.

2

의문사

Who: 누구?
What: 무엇?
Where: 어디?
When: 언제?
Why: 왜?
How: 어떻게?
Which: 어느 것?

Quick Test

Answers ▲ P.20

1. This is Tom's bike, _isn't it_ ?

2. They are in your class, _____ ?

3. She will come to the party, _____ ?

4. Tony doesn't drink milk, _____ ?

5. The weather was nice, _____ ?

6. Your father is a dentist, _____ ?

7. He likes dancing, _____ ?

8. The ant has six legs, _____ ?

9. You drink coffee, _____ ?

10. It's cold today, _____ ?

110

E EXERCISE

A [   ] 안에서 알맞은 것을 고르시오.

1 This is a new movie, [isn't it, is it]?

2 Andy wasn't at the farewell party, [was Andy, was he]?

3 You ordered a salmon sandwich, [didn't you, did you]?

4 You [don't understand, understand] him, do you?

5 [How, What] do you want to do, go fishing or hiking?

6 Damon [can, can't] ride a snowboard, can he?

7 [Who, which] do you like more, Britney or Christina?

B [보기]에서 빈칸에 알맞은 것을 골라 문장을 완성하시오.

Word Bank	who	is	when	did	which

1 _____Who_____ is more popular, Harry or Ron?

2 _____ flies faster, a bee or a butterfly?

3 _____ is better for you, Monday or Friday?

4 _____ you go there by bus or by train?

5 _____ he your father or brother?

C 우리말과 같은 뜻이 되도록 주어진 단어를 배열하시오.

1 너는 녹차를 좋아하지, 그렇지 않니? (green tea / you / don't you / like)

   → _____ _You like green tea, don't you?_ _____

2 그들은 작년에 아프리카에 있었어, 그렇지 않니? (in Africa / they / were / weren't they / last year)

   → _____

3 그 컴퓨터는 작동하지 않을 거야, 그렇지? (the computer / will it / work / won't)

   → _____

4 그들은 Mary를 볼 수 있었어, 그렇지 않니? (they / could / couldn't they / see / Mary)

   → _____

A [   ] 안에서 알맞은 것을 고르시오.

1 [Don't, Not] be so upset.

2 Let's [go, goes] shopping after school.

3 Follow me, [or, and] you will be lost.

4 [What, How] a nice dress you have!

5 [What, How] delicious it is!

6 Patrick is going to apologize to her, [isn't he, doesn't he]?

7 You didn't copy this, [don't you, did you]?

8 [Who, Which] do you prefer, milk or juice?

B 빈칸에 알맞은 것을 고르시오.

1 You can wait for a moment, _____ you?

    ⓐ don't   ⓑ do   ⓒ can't   ⓓ can

2 Let's _____ about his score.

    ⓐ don't   ⓑ not talk   ⓒ not to talk   ⓓ not talking

3 What a _____ mouth he has!

    ⓐ bigger   ⓑ bigly   ⓒ biggest   ⓓ big

4 _____ is harder, a diamond or an emerald?

    ⓐ Where   ⓑ Which   ⓒ How   ⓓ Who

5 _____ open your test booklets!

    ⓐ Not do   ⓑ Do not   ⓒ Doesn't   ⓓ Did not

6 _____ silly he looks!

    ⓐ How   ⓑ Which   ⓒ When   ⓓ What

7 _____ answer the telephone.

    ⓐ Be   ⓑ Not do   ⓒ Let   ⓓ Please

A **Grammar in Speaking 1** 빈칸에 알맞은 말을 넣어 대화를 완성하시오.

1 A I'm talking on the phone. Please _____ quiet.

B Sorry, I will be quiet.

2 A She broke her promise again. This is the fifth time.

B You won't forgive her, _____?

3 A Mom, I'm starving. I could eat a horse.

B _____ hungry you are! Wait and I will get you something to eat.

4 A What do you want to do on our vacation, son?

B _____ go camping, Dad.

5 A How do you play this game?

B Name the song, _____ you win a prize.

6 A Do you want a large dog _____ a small dog?

B I want a small dog because I live in an apartment.

B **Grammar in Speaking 2** 다음 대화를 읽고, 어법에 알맞은 것을 고르시오.

A Summer vacation is coming. Where do you want to go this year?

B I want to go somewhere in Asia. How about Bali?

A Hmm, I want to go to Egypt. (1) [Let's, Let] go to Egypt.

B You went there two years ago, (2) [did, didn't] you?

A Yes, but I want to see the pyramids again. (3) [Let's not, Let don't] go to Bali.

B OK. Please (4) [call, calls] the travel agency and book our tickets for the flight.

A Thank you.

B By the way, which is (5) [hotter, hottest], Egypt or Bali?

A Egypt, I think.

1 다음 빈칸에 알맞은 말을 고르시오.

> Let's _____ a walk.

ⓐ taking   ⓑ take
ⓒ takes   ⓓ to take

2 다음 빈칸에 들어갈 말이 나머지 하나와 다른 것을 고르시오.

ⓐ _____ a small world it is!
ⓑ _____ big eyes you have!
ⓒ _____ beautiful she is!
ⓓ _____ a happy girl you are!

3 다음 빈칸에 들어갈 말이 바르게 짝지어진 것을 고르시오.

> • Get up now, _____ you will be late.
> • Work hard, _____ you will succeed.

ⓐ or, and   ⓑ and, but
ⓒ and, or   ⓓ but, or

4 다음 빈칸에 알맞은 것을 고르시오.

> _____ careful!

ⓐ Do   ⓑ Be
ⓒ Does   ⓓ Being

5 다음 중 어법에 맞는 문장을 고르시오.

ⓐ Barbara will stay with us, won't she?
ⓑ Jane is not a teacher, is Jane?
ⓒ Mr. Smith couldn't meet her, did he?
ⓓ He didn't understand it, can he?

6 다음 문장에서 쓰임이 잘못된 곳을 찾아 바르게 고치시오.

It is raining outside. Let's not going fishing.

→ _____

7 다음 중 어법상 옳지 않은 문장을 고르시오.

ⓐ Don't be so angry.
ⓑ Please help me.
ⓒ Doesn't waste your money.
ⓓ Stay away from the dog!

8 다음 주어진 문장을 보기와 같이 바꾸시오.

> 〈보기〉 You should do your homework.
> → Do your homework.

1) You should not open the door.
  → _____

2) You should be proud of yourself.
  → _____

9 다음 문장을 감탄문으로 고치시오.

1) You have a very nice dream.
  → What _____

2) The mountain is very high.
  → How _____

10 다음 빈칸에 알맞은 말을 쓰시오.

Which do you like better, roses _____ lilies?

to부정사

Unit 12
1 명사적 쓰임

동사	We <u>run</u> along the riverside.	
to부정사	We <u>love</u> to run along the riverside.	명사의 기능
동명사	We <u>love</u> running along the riverside.	

1 to부정사가 명사처럼 쓰이는 경우

(1) **목적어 역할**

I like **to ride** roller coasters.

I love **to read** *Harry Potter*.

(2) **보어 역할**

The most fun thing is **to ride** roller coasters.

My favorite activity is **to read** *Harry Potter*.

(3) **주어 역할**

To ride roller coasters is fun.

To read *Harry Potter* is exciting.

> ※ 동명사(동사-ing)가 명사처럼 쓰이는 경우
>
> (1) **목적어 역할**
>
> I like **riding** roller coasters.
>
> I love **reading** *Harry Potter*.
>
> (2) **보어 역할**
>
> The most fun thing is **riding** roller coasters.
>
> My favorite activity is **reading** *Harry Potter*.
>
> (3) **주어 역할**
>
> **Riding** roller coasters is fun.
>
> **Reading** *Harry Potter* is exciting.

1

to부정사만 목적어로 취하는 동사:
decide, need, want, hope, plan, wish
(O) I want <u>to go</u> home.
(×) I want going home.

*동명사만 목적어로 취하는 동사:
enjoy, mind, finish, give up, quit, stop
(O) I enjoy <u>swimming</u>.
(×) I enjoy to swim.

*to부정사와 동명사 모두 목적어로 취하는 동사: love, like, begin, start
(O) I love <u>singing</u>.
(O) I love <u>to sing</u>.

Quick Test 밑줄 친 부분이 문장에서 어떤 역할을 하는지 쓰시오. Answers ▲ P.21

1. I love <u>to see</u> movies. 목적어

2. <u>To swim</u> is good for health. _____

3. My hobby is <u>listening</u> to classical music. _____

4. <u>Learning</u> English is fun. _____

5. I enjoy <u>skiing</u> in winter. _____

6. My dream is <u>to be</u> an astronaut. _____

E EXERCISE

A   [   ] 안에서 알맞은 것을 고르시오.

1   He hopes [seeing, to see] you there.

2   She enjoys [to knit, knitting] sweaters.

3   He gave up [to smoke, smoking] cigarettes.

4   My dream is [to flies, to fly] over a rainbow.

5   She wants [to be, being] an actress.

6   Do you mind [to open, opening] the window?

7   I finished [having, to have] lunch.

B   주어진 문장과 같은 뜻이 되도록 빈칸에 알맞은 말을 넣어 문장을 완성하시오.

1   He likes to drive his son to school.

    → He likes _____ *driving* _____ his son to school.

2   Collecting coins is her hobby.

    → _____ coins is her hobby.

3   Jessica doesn't like to eat carrot cakes.

    → Jessica doesn't like _____ carrot cakes.

4   I love listening to Latin music.

    → I love _____ to Latin music.

C   우리말과 같은 뜻이 되도록 주어진 단어를 배열하시오.

1   그녀는 케이크 굽는 것을 좋아한다. (baking / she / cakes / enjoys)

    → _____ *She enjoys baking cakes.* _____

2   나의 목표는 아홉 시까지 일을 마치는 것이다. (is / my goal / finishing / by 9 / the work)

    → _____

3   책을 쓰는 것이 내 직업이다. (books / my job / is / write / to)

    → _____

4   그는 병원에 갈 필요가 있다. (a doctor / to / see / needs / he)

    → _____

5   그의 취미는 희귀한 식물을 기르는 것이다. (is / unusual plants / his / hobby / growing)

    → _____

Unit 12

2

형용사적/부사적 쓰임

형용사적 쓰임	부사적 쓰임
I have a book to read.	I'm sorry to hear that.
I have an interesting book.	I am very sorry.

1 to부정사가 형용사처럼 쓰이는 경우

(1) 명사/대명사 수식: '~할, ~하는'

I have two people to invite.

There is no water to drink in the refrigerator.

I need some money to buy new shoes.

I need something to drink!

(2) It's time to~: '~할 시간이다'

It's time to get up and go out!

It's time to go to bed.

2 to부정사가 부사처럼 쓰이는 경우

(1) '~하기 위해'

I'm going to the amusement park to ride roller coasters.

I'm going to the market to buy some milk.

cf) in order to

He came here in order to say hello.

= He came here to say hello.

(2) '~하다니, ~하게 되어서'

I'm glad to meet you.

He is foolish to believe it.

1

(1)
이때 to부정사는 명사 뒤에서 명사를 수식한다.

2

(1)
이때 to부정사는 동사, 형용사, 부사를 수식한다.

cf) to+동사원형
= in order to+동사원형

Quick Test to부정사의 의미에 유의하며 다음 문장을 해석하시오.

Answers P.21

1. He bought some water to drink. — *그는 마실 물을 좀 샀습니다.*

2. She swims to become healthy.

3. It's time to study English.

4. I'm happy to meet you.

5. Do you have something to tell me?

6. I went shopping to buy a gift.

118

EXERCISE

A [   ] 안에서 알맞은 것을 고르시오.

1 I have something [to do, doing].

2 She needed some books [reading, to read].

3 He was surprised [to hear, hear] the news.

4 They were happy [to see, to seeing] their aunt.

5 I have lots of homework [do, to do].

6 Michelle skips dinner [in order to, in order for] lose weight.

7 It's [time to, time for] say good-bye.

B [보기]에서 빈칸에 알맞은 말을 골라 문장을 완성하시오. (to부정사를 활용할 것)

Word Bank	play	pour	work	pick up	go	hear

1 There is no juice _____*to pour*_____ into the glass.

2 I'm sad _____ the bad news.

3 He came to this city _____ for them.

4 You need two computers _____ the game.

5 It's time _____ to the concert.

6 She came to the school _____ her son.

C 우리말과 같은 뜻이 되도록 주어진 단어를 배열하시오.

1 Miami는 방문하기 좋은 곳이다. (Miami / visit / a good place / to / is)

   → _____*Miami is a good place to visit.*_____

2 나는 그녀와 점심을 먹으려고 그녀에게 전화했다. (her / have lunch / I / to / with her / called)

   → _____

3 일어날 시간이다. (to / wake up / time / It's)

   → _____

4 John은 오늘 오후에 마쳐야 할 과제가 있다. (a report / this afternoon / John / to / finish / has)

   → _____

A [   ] 안에서 알맞은 것을 고르시오.

1 We wanted [to help, helping] poor people.

2 [Watching, To watching] movies is one of my hobbies.

3 Here is your bill [to pays, to pay].

4 English grammar is fun [to study, studying].

5 I enjoy [hiking, to hike] in the forest.

6 It's time [to go, going] home.

7 He left the office [in order for, in order to] meet a client.

8 [To pass, Pass] the test is very difficult.

B 빈칸에 알맞은 것을 고르시오.

1 Baseball is fun _____.

ⓐ to playing　　　ⓑ playing　　　ⓒ to play　　　ⓓ play

2 My father quit _____.

ⓐ smoke　　　ⓑ smoking　　　ⓒ to smoke　　　ⓓ to smoking

3 _____ up early is hard for me.

ⓐ Getting　　　ⓑ To gets　　　ⓒ To getting　　　ⓓ Get

4 She was shocked _____ the ghost.

ⓐ seeing　　　ⓑ to seeing　　　ⓒ to sees　　　ⓓ to see

5 _____ the map is easy for me.

ⓐ Read　　　ⓑ To reads　　　ⓒ Reading　　　ⓓ To reading

6 The fireman ran into the house _____ the woman.

ⓐ saves　　　ⓑ to save　　　ⓒ to saving　　　ⓓ for save

7 It's time _____ her for the mistake.

ⓐ to forgiving　　　ⓑ forgive　　　ⓒ forgiving　　　ⓓ to forgive

F FURTHER STUDY

A Grammar in Speaking 빈칸에 알맞은 것을 골라 어법에 맞게 고쳐 대화를 완성하시오.

> **Word Bank**   see   close   pack   drink   interview

1 A Long time, no see! How are you?

  B Hi, Jack. It's nice _____ you again.

2 A Mom, I'm thirsty. I need something _____ .

  B There is cold water in the refrigerator.

3 A I am very cold. Do you mind my _____ the window?

  B Of course not, go ahead.

4 A Why is she coming?

  B She's an interviewer. She is coming in order _____ people.

5 A Steve, it's time _____ for our family vacation.

  B OK, Mom. Where is my bag?

B Grammar in Writing 글을 읽고, 어법에 알맞은 것을 고르시오.

Yesterday, I went to Sea World. There were many creatures (1) to see / seeing and many activities (2) to do / doing . First, I went to the seal tank. Seals are fun animals (3) to watch / watching ! My favorite activity was feeding the whale. The whale jumped and splashed in the water. Water went into the crowd! I took many pictures (4) to show / showing my family. Finally, it was time (5) to go / going home. I didn't want (6) to leave / leaving . I had a great time at Sea World!

1 다음 빈칸에 알맞은 말을 고르시오.

To _____ the test is my goal.

ⓐ passing ⓑ passes
ⓒ passed ⓓ pass

2 다음 밑줄 친 부분과 바꾸어 쓸 수 있는 것을 고르시오.

She studied hard to get a good score.

ⓐ in order for ⓑ in order to
ⓒ so as for ⓓ so that

3 다음 밑줄 친 부분의 쓰임이 잘못된 곳을 찾아 바르게 고치시오.

ⓐ Riding a bike is fun.
ⓑ I have two assignments to do.
ⓒ She quit smoking cigarettes.
ⓓ My hobby is to taking pictures.

4 다음 빈칸에 들어갈 수 없는 것을 고르시오.

I _____ reading the newspaper.

ⓐ finished ⓑ enjoyed
ⓒ need ⓓ like

5 다음 대화의 밑줄 친 부분을 바르게 고친 것을 고르시오.

A Do you mind open the door?
B Of course not.

ⓐ to opening ⓑ to open
ⓒ opening ⓓ opened

6 다음 밑줄 친 부분과 쓰임이 같은 것을 고르시오.

This store is a nice place to buy fresh fruits.

ⓐ To go shopping is my favorite activity.
ⓑ I need time to change my clothes.
ⓒ He was glad to see her again.
ⓓ We love to learn English.

7 다음 문장에서 쓰임이 잘못된 곳을 찾아 바르게 고치시오.

They really enjoyed to see the magic show last night.

→ _____

8 다음 주어진 우리말에 맞게 배열하시오.

내 직업은 학생들에게 수학을 가르치는 것이다.
(math, my job, teach, to, students, is)

→ _____

[9-10] 다음 글을 읽고 물음에 답하시오.

A (A) 넌 뭐가 되고 싶니?
B My dream is ___(B)___ (be) an astronaut.
A Astronaut! Wow...
B Yes, I really want to travel to Mars.

9 (A)를 우리말로 옮긴 것으로 가장 알맞은 것을 고르시오.

ⓐ What do you want being?
ⓑ What do you want to be?
ⓒ What do you want to being?
ⓓ What do you want for be?

10 주어진 단어를 이용하여 (B)에 알맞은 말을 쓰시오.

→ _____

장소 전치사,
There is / are

Unit 13

1 장소 전치사 1

A <u>Where</u> are the books?

B The books are in the bookstore.

A <u>Where</u> is the bookstore?

B The bookstore is next to the post office.

1 기본 전치사

A basket is on the table.

A bottle of wine is in the basket.

Candies are in front of the wine.

A box of chocolate is behind the candies.

Two wine glasses are by the basket.

A present box is under the table.

2 기타 전치사

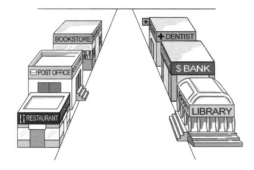

The bookstore is next to (= beside) the post office.

The post office is across from the bank.

The bank is between the library and the dental clinic.

The library is in front of the restaurant.

1

전치사는 명사와 더불어 장소에 대한 정보를 제공한다.

전치사 뒤에 오는 명사에는 정관사 'the' 를 쓰는 것이 일반적이다.

on: ～위에

in: ～안에

in front of: ～앞에

behind: ～뒤에

by: ～옆에

under: ～아래에

2

next to(=beside): ～옆에

across from: ～반대편에, 맞은편에

between A and B: A와 B 사이에

in front of: ～앞에

EXERCISE

A 주어진 그림에 맞도록 전치사를 이용하여 문장을 완성하시오.

1 A mirror is _____*on*_____ the wall.

2 A cat is _____ the desk.

3 A plant is _____ the desk.

4 A dog is _____ the bed.

5 A pillow is _____ the bed.

6 A chair is _____ the desk.

7 A dog is _____ the chair _____ the bed.

B 주어진 그림에 맞도록 전치사를 이용하여 문장을 완성하시오.

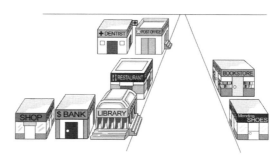

1 The library is _____*by [beside / next to]*_____ the bank.

2 The restaurant is _____ the library.

3 The bookstore is _____ the restaurant.

4 The shoe store is _____ the library.

5 The post office is _____ the dental clinic.

Unit 13

2 장소 전치사 2

at school	on the floor	in the theater
at home	on the wall	in France
at the meeting	on the train	in class

1 at

(1) 장소를 하나의 지점으로 생각할 때

Brian is at the door.　　　　Tom is at the bus stop.

(2) 행사가 벌어지는 장소, 특정한 목적이 있는 곳

Mike is at the party.　　　　Paul is at the airport.

2 on

(1) 접촉하는 표면 위

Mike is on the street.　　　　Paul is on the roof.

(2) 기차, 비행기, 버스를 타고 있는 상태

Sarah is on the bus.　　　　Brian is on the flight.

3 in

(1) 도시 이름, 나라 이름 앞, 특정 장소의 안쪽

Mike is in the library.　　　　Paul is in the States.

(2) 어떤 상태에 있을 때

Sarah is in class.　　　　Brian is in the army.

1

at은 대체로 좁은 장소 앞에 사용한다.
at은 그 장소의 실제 규모보다는 말하는
사람의 관점이 중요하다.

2

(2)
승용차를 타고 있을 때는 in the car이다.

(2)
in class 수업 중
in the army 복역 중(군대)

Quick Test

Answers ▲ P.23

1. Mike is _on_ the bus.

2. His friend, Jake, is _____ the taxi.

3. Jamie is _____ the party.

4. Brian is still _____ his way.

5. Paula is _____ Vancouver.

6. She is a student _____ a college _____ Vancouver.

E EXERCISE

A [　] 안에서 알맞은 것을 고르시오.

1 The singer is [on, in] the stage.

2 My brother is [on, in] London.

3 The boy is [on, in] the living room.

4 The sweater is [in, at] the drawer.

5 She is [on, at] the office.

6 The train is [on, at] the station.

7 Sunglasses are [on, in] the fourth floor.

B [보기]에서 빈칸에 알맞은 말을 골라 문장을 완성하시오.

Word Bank	at the bus stop	in the garden	on the school bus

1 Kids are _____.

2 Butterflies are _____.

3 A woman is _____.

C 우리말과 같은 뜻이 되도록 주어진 단어를 이용하여 문장을 완성하시오.

1 James는 파티장에 있습니다. (James, is, the party)

→ _____ *James is at the party.* _____

2 Tom은 프랑스에 있습니다. (Tom, is, France)

→ _____

3 내 고양이가 지붕 위에 있습니다. (my cat, is, the roof)

→ _____

4 Dan은 비행기를 타고 있습니다. (Dan, is, the plane)

→ _____

Unit 13

3 There is/are

There is a bird in the nest. → Is there a bird in the nest?
There are lots of birds on the tree. → Are there lots of birds on the tree?

1 There is, There are

(1) There is+단수, There are+복수
There is an apple on the table.
There are beautiful houses on the hill.

(2) 수에 주의한다.
There are cookies in the basket.
There is cookies in the basket. (X)

2 부정문: not

There is a post office next to the store.
→ There is not [isn't] a post office next to the store.

There are students in the classroom.
→ There are not [aren't] any students in the classroom.

3 질문하고 답하기

There is an apple on the table.
→ A Is there an apple on the table?
  B Yes, there is.
  B No, there isn't.

There are apples on the table.
→ A Are there apples on the table?
  B Yes, there are.
  B No, there aren't.

1
이때, there을 '거기'라고 해석하지 않으며, 뒤에 따라오는 명사가 단수인지 복수인지에 따라 be동사의 종류가 결정된다.

2
there+be동사+not

3
be동사+there~?
- Yes, there+be동사
- No, there+be동사+not

Quick Test

Answers P.23

1. There is a picture on the wall.
   A: _____Is there_____ a picture on the wall?
   B: Yes, _____.
   B: No, _____.

2. There are soccer balls on the floor.
   A: _____ soccer balls on the floor?
   B: Yes, _____.
   B: No, _____.

E EXERCISE

A [   ] 안에서 알맞은 것을 고르시오.

1 There [is, are] a car in the garage.

2 There [are not, not are] 10 bananas in the basket.

3 [Was there, There was] a man in the room last night?

4 [There, It] are dishes on the table.

5 There [is, are] a woman on the phone.

6 [Is there, There is] pepper in my soup?

7 [There are, Are there] flowers in the garden.

B 빈칸에 알맞은 말을 넣어 문장을 완성하시오.

1 A Is there a pen in the pencil case?

   B Yes, _____. _____ a pen in the pencil case.

2 A _____ many mirrors on the wall?

   B _____, there aren't. _____ only one mirror on the wall.

3 A _____ gift boxes on the table?

   B _____, _____. _____ gift boxes on the table.

C 우리말과 같은 뜻이 되도록 주어진 단어를 배열하시오.

1 집 앞에 차가 한 대 있습니다. (a car / in front of / there is / the house)

   → _____*There is a car in front of the house.*_____

2 바구니 안에 고양이 다섯 마리가 있습니다. (five kittens / in the basket / there are)

   → _____

3 우체국 옆에 은행이 있습니까? (the post office / there / a bank / is / next to)

   → _____

4 서랍 안에 숟가락이 하나 있습니까? (there / a spoon / in the drawer / is)

   → _____

REVIEW TEST

📖 Grammar Drills

▲▲▲▲▲▲▲▲▲▲▲▲

A [　] 안에서 알맞은 것을 고르시오.

1 Steve is [on, at, in] Michigan.

2 John and Mike were [on, at, in] the flight to London.

3 [There, They] is a big dog in front of my house.

4 [Where, Who] is the post office?

5 The department store is [in, on, across from] the bakery.

6 [These is, There are] seven students in the classroom.

7 [Where was, Where were] the twin boys last night?

8 [There are not, There isn't] an Italian restaurant in the city.

B 빈칸에 알맞은 것을 고르시오.

1 They are _____ the meeting now.

ⓐ at   ⓑ on   ⓒ behind   ⓓ across from

2 There _____ a big cinema here 10 years ago.

ⓐ were   ⓑ is   ⓒ are   ⓓ was

3 _____ are my socks?

ⓐ Who   ⓑ Why   ⓒ Where   ⓓ When

4 There _____ a road next to the building.

ⓐ aren't   ⓑ is not   ⓒ are   ⓓ were

5 _____ is the TV guide?

ⓐ Where   ⓑ There   ⓒ Who   ⓓ That

6 _____ is a trail beside the river.

ⓐ What   ⓑ Who   ⓒ They   ⓓ There

7 Is Ben _____ a field trip?

ⓐ at   ⓑ on   ⓒ in   ⓓ beside

A

Grammar in Speaking 빈칸에 알맞은 말을 넣어 대화를 완성하시오.

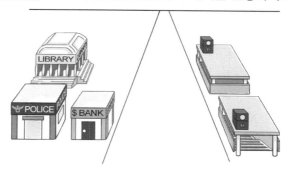

1 **A** Excuse me. Where _____ the subway station?

 B The subway station is _____ the bank.

2 **A** I'm sorry, but _____ is the bank?

 B The bank is _____ the police station.

3 **A** Oh, is the library in front of the police station?

 B No, the library is _____ the police station.

 A Thank you very much.

B

Grammar in Writing 빈칸에 알맞은 말을 넣어 문장을 완성하시오.

This is my room. I have a bed, a desk, some books, and a big window with curtains in my room. There is a clock (1) _____ the wall. There is a chair (2) _____ the desk. There are some books (3) _____ the desk. Look at the window! It is (4) _____ the door. I love my room.

1 다음 빈칸에 공통으로 들어갈 단어를 고르시오.

> • A nice picture was _____ the wall.
> • Kids are _____ the school bus.

ⓐ in   ⓑ on
ⓒ at   ⓓ under

2 다음 밑줄 친 부분과 의미가 같은 것을 고르시오.

> There is a big tree <u>next to</u> the castle.

ⓐ across from   ⓑ in front of
ⓒ between   ⓓ beside

3 다음 빈칸에 들어갈 수 없는 것을 고르시오.

> Toy soldiers are _____ the box.

ⓐ between   ⓑ behind
ⓒ in   ⓓ on

4 다음 중 어법상 옳지 않은 문장을 고르시오.

ⓐ Your backpack is under the table.
ⓑ Are there a kangaroo in the zoo?
ⓒ There is not a library on 5th Street.
ⓓ The bank is beside the bookstore.

5 다음 우리말과 같은 뜻이 되도록 빈칸에 알맞은 말을 고르시오.

> 기차역은 우체국 맞은편에 있습니까?
> → Is there a train station _____ the post office?

ⓐ across from   ⓑ beside
ⓒ next to   ⓓ in front of

6 다음 중 in이 들어갈 수 <u>없는</u> 것을 고르시오.

ⓐ My sisters are _____ Seoul.
ⓑ Jay is _____ class.
ⓒ They were _____ the car.
ⓓ Birds are _____ the roof.

7 다음 빈칸에 알맞은 전치사를 쓰시오. (in, at, on)

1) Brian is _____ home.
2) There are many people _____ the drugstore.
3) Jamie is _____ the theater.

8 다음 우리말과 같은 뜻이 되도록 빈칸에 알맞은 말을 쓰시오.

> 교실에는 학생들이 있습니다.

→ _____ _____ students in the classroom.

[9-10] 다음 대화를 읽고 물음에 답하시오.

> A Excuse me, ___(A)___ is the library?
> B (B) <u>in front of, it, is, the gallery</u>.

9 (A)에 알맞은 의문사를 쓰시오.

→ _____

10 (B) 안의 단어들을 배열하여 문장을 완성하시오.

→ _____

전치사

Unit 14

1

시간 전치사 1

A <u>When</u> is your wedding?

B It's <u>at</u> <u>12 o'clock</u>.

B It's <u>on</u> <u>Saturday</u>.

B It's <u>in</u> <u>March</u>.

1 at

(1) 한 시점

Let's meet **at** 3 o'clock.

I always eat lunch **at** noon.

(2) 한 시점으로 간주되는 기간

Some people work **at** night.

We give New Year's cards **at** this time of the year.

2 on

(1) 특정한 날, 요일, 날짜

Please come and visit me **on** my birthday.

The jazz festival starts **on** Friday.

(2) 특정한 날의 일부분

I have an English conversation class **on** Friday morning.

We have a party **on** Christmas Eve.

3 in

(1) 월, 계절, 한 해

The jazz festival is **in** September.

We always go snowboarding **in** winter.

(2) 하루의 일부분

My mom always has a cup of black tea **in** the afternoon.

I don't have any classes **in** the morning.

▶ 1
(1)
at 7:30
at lunch time
at that time

(2)
at this time tomorrow
at the end of the year

▶ 2
(1)
on Sundays
on February 23rd

(2)
on the 17th of August
on a rainy day

▶ 3
(1)
in 1993

(2)
in the evening
cf) at night

Quick Test

Answers ▲ P.24

1. She often goes skiing ____*in*____ winter. (겨울에)

2. He got a nice present _____ his birthday. (그의 생일에)

3. She got her first job _____ 2014. (2014년에)

4. The party starts _____ 9 o'clock. (아홉 시에)

A   [   ] 안에서 알맞은 것을 고르시오.

1   We have a barbecue party [at, on, in] Independence Day.

2   My grandmother was born [at, on, in] 1940.

3   Where did you go [at, on, in] lunchtime?

4   Do you feel blue [at, on, in] a rainy day?

5   He has a meeting [at, on, in] 7 o'clock.

6   The class begins [at, on, in] September.

7   Grace's package arrived [at, on, in] Monday.

B   빈칸에 알맞은 전치사를 넣어 문장을 완성하시오. (at, on, in)

1   **A** When do you usually go to bed?

   B I always go to bed _____ midnight.

2   **A** Does she go to church _____ Sundays?

   B Yes, she does.

3   **A** I don't remember the date of the concert.

   B It's _____ March 19th.

4   **A** When is the festival?

   B It's _____ May.

5   **A** Do you take a shower _____ the morning?

   B Yes, I do.

C   우리말과 같은 뜻이 되도록 주어진 단어와 전치사를 이용하여 문장을 완성하시오.

1   영화는 자정에 끝났습니다. (the movie, was, over, midnight)

  → _____ *The movie was over at midnight.* _____

2   그는 2014년에 졸업했습니다. (he, graduated, 2014)

  → _____

3   Fred는 아침에 약속이 있습니다. (Fred, has, an appointment, the morning)

  → _____

4   나는 내일 이 시간에 그를 만날 것입니다. (I, will meet, him, this time tomorrow)

  → _____

Unit 14

2 시간 전치사 2

A <u>When</u> do you work out?　**B** I work out **before** breakfast.

　　　　　　　　　　　　　　　B I work out **after** dinner.

　　　　　　　　　　　　　　　B I work out **around** 11 in the morning.

　　　　　　　　　　　　　　　B I work out **from** 7 **to** 9.

　　　　　　　　　　　　　　　B I work out **during** lunchtime.

---

1 before, after

(1) before: ～전에

I ate my lunch before 12 o'clock.

Before dinner, I finished my homework.

(2) after: ～후에

We went to the movies after school.

He arrived after two months.

2 around (= about): ～즈음에

It's around 4 o'clock.

I saw him around 7:30.

3 from~ to…: ～부터 …까지

She has classes from 2 to 7.

I was in Paris from September to November.

4 for, during

(1) for: ～동안 (for+기간)

I stayed in Paris for three months.

I went to Busan for a day.

(2) during: ～동안 (during+때를 나타내는 명사)

He was at his uncle's during the summer vacation.

They did their best during the exam.

1

(2)

in : ～후에, (시간이) 지나서

I'll come back in two days.

4

while+주어+동사 : ～동안

He watched TV while I studied.

136

EXERCISE

A [   ] 안에서 알맞은 것을 고르시오.

1 Do your homework [before, during] dinner.

2 I take piano lessons [from, at] 5 to 6.

3 Please turn off your mobile phone [from, during] the meeting.

4 I will call you [around, during] 3 o'clock.

5 He visited his grandmother [from, on] Friday to Sunday.

6 Brush your teeth [before, during] going to bed.

7 Steve stayed in Korea [for, during] 3 months.

B 빈칸에 알맞은 전치사를 넣어 문장을 완성하시오. (at, on, from~to)

<Jean's time schedule>

	Mon	Tue	Wed
9:00	Math	English	Korean
10:00	History	Korean	Math
11:00	Music	Physics	Art

<Terry's time schedule>

	Mon	Tue	Wed
9:00	English	Math	Korean
10:00	History	English	Physics
11:00	Art	Music	Math

1 Jean has history class _____ 10:00 _____ Mondays.

2 Jean has art class _____ 11:00 a.m. _____ Wednesdays.

3 Terry doesn't have English class _____ Wednesday mornings.

4 Terry has math class _____ 9:00 _____ 10:00 _____
   Tuesday mornings.

C 우리말과 같은 뜻이 되도록 주어진 단어와 전치사를 이용하여 문장을 완성하시오.

1 나는 시험 전에 굉장히 긴장했다. (I, was, so nervous, the test)

   → _____ *I was so nervous before the test.* _____

2 그들은 해변에 5시간 동안 누워 있었다. (they, lay, on the beach, five hours)

   → _____

3 너는 봄 방학 동안 무엇을 했니? (what, did, you, do, spring break)

   → _____

4 사무실은 월요일부터 수요일까지 휴무입니다. (the office, is closed, Monday, Wednesday)

   → _____

Unit 14

3 기타 전치사

A Thank you for coming.

B You were great. You won the contest without any help.

A It is very kind of you to say so.

1 about, for, by, of

Mary told me about the accident.

Let's talk about the movie.

I bought a Christmas gift for my wife.

He opened the door for me.

Did you come here by bus?

I'd like to pay by credit card.

Let's meet on top of the mountain.

It's very sweet of you to say that.

1

about: ~에 관한

for: ~를 위한, ~에 대해
I'm sorry for the mistake.

by: ~를 타고 (교통수단)
    ~에 의해(통신, 지불 수단)
pay by credit card
: 신용 카드로 지불하다

of: ~의
형용사 of 사람: 사람이 ~하다
It's kind of you to help me.

2 with, without

Are you coming with us?

I like the girl with red hair. Her name is Anne.

I can't live without you.

He usually drinks coffee without cream and sugar.

2

with: ~를 가지고, ~와 함께
without: ~없이

3 between, among

The building is between Maple and Main Streets.

I like the color between purple and violet.

She is very popular among boys in my school.

He is the fastest one among them.

3

between A and B
: ~ (둘) 사이에

among: ~ (셋 이상) 사이에
: ~ 중에서

Quick Test

Answers ▲ P.24

1. Would you like to dance _____*with*_____ me? (나와 함께)

2. Thank you _____ the gift. (선물에 대해)

3. I went there _____ plane. (비행기를 타고)

4. Do you know the story _____ Hansel and Gretel? (헨젤과 그레텔의)

5. Who is the tallest _____ the three guys? (남자 세 명 중에서)

E **EXERCISE**

A   [   ] 안에서 알맞은 것을 고르시오.

1 I made a nice dog house [with, by, about] my father.

2 She took a picture [to, for, among] me.

3 There are many cars [between, among, in] 4th and 5th Streets.

4 She goes to school [by, on, in] subway.

5 I can't eat soup [on, by, without] a spoon.

6 She lives [with, in, about] a roommate.

7 She stood [about, among, of] the trees.

B   주어진 뜻과 일치하도록 [보기]에서 빈칸에 알맞은 말을 골라 문장을 완성하시오.

Word Bank	about	for	by	of	among	with

1 She always talks _____*about*_____ her new boyfriend. (그녀의 새 남자 친구에 대하여)

2 I found a book about robots _____ the books on the bookcase. (책 사이에)

3 Jenny always goes to school _____ bicycle. (자전거로)

4 I play a game _____ his computer. (그의 컴퓨터를 가지고)

5 He made a bookcase _____ my uncle. (우리 삼촌을 위해)

6 Berlin is the capital _____ Germany. (독일의)

C   우리말과 같은 뜻이 되도록 주어진 단어와 전치사를 이용하여 문장을 완성하시오.

1 신용 카드로 지불하겠습니다. (I, am going to pay, credit card)
   → _____*I am going to pay by credit card.*_____

2 이 그림은 Craig을 위한 것입니다. (this picture, is, Craig)
   → _____

3 나는 바다표범에 대한 신문 기사를 읽었다. (I, read, an article, seals)
   → _____

4 그 비행기는 내 짐을 빠뜨린 채 도착했다. (the plane, arrived, my luggage)
   → _____

A   [　] 안에서 알맞은 것을 고르시오.

1 She went shopping [with, by] a friend.

2 Did you go to Rome [by, on] plane?

3 We don't usually work [on, at] holidays.

4 I went to the gym [between, at] 9 and 11.

5 Give me a wake-up call [at, on] 6 o'clock.

6 [During, Before] the accident, he drank a lot of alcohol.

7 The bus runs [from, to] 5 a.m. to midnight.

8 She is the best [among, about] the students in school.

B   빈칸에 알맞은 것을 고르시오.

1 She sang the same song _____ an hour.

   ⓐ during   ⓑ for   ⓒ in   ⓓ at

2 We had a chat _____ 4 to 9.

   ⓐ from   ⓑ by   ⓒ for   ⓓ of

3 The speaker talked _____ her new novel.

   ⓐ before   ⓑ to   ⓒ in   ⓓ about

4 The bank closes _____ national holidays.

   ⓐ at   ⓑ in   ⓒ on   ⓓ from

5 My friends played _____ the puppy.

   ⓐ for   ⓑ after   ⓒ during   ⓓ with

6 He is going to meet them _____ noon.

   ⓐ at   ⓑ in   ⓒ on   ⓓ to

7 He painted many pictures _____ the summer vacation.

   ⓐ from   ⓑ at   ⓒ for   ⓓ during

F FURTHER STUDY

A **Grammar in Speaking** 빈칸에 알맞은 말을 넣어 대화를 완성하시오.

1 **A** Did you go to the theater by yourself?

　B I went there _____ my friends.

2 **A** What did you do _____ Thanksgiving Day?

　B We had a big family dinner.

3 **A** How long were you in Europe?

　B I was there _____ June to August.

4 **A** I usually park my car _____ the underground parking lot.

　B I park my car there, too.

5 **A** Please choose a nice hat _____ me.

　B This might look good on you.

B **Grammar in Writing** 표를 보고 빈칸에 알맞은 말을 넣어 글을 완성하시오.

<Tom's Timetable>

	Mon.	Tue.	Wed.	Thu.	Fri.
09:00~10:00	English	Korean	Society	Math	English
10:00~11:00	Math	History	Science	Korean	Art
11:00~12:00	Science	English	Math	English	History
12:00~13:00	Lunch Break				
13:00~14:00	Art	Music	Music	P.E.	Science
14:00~15:00	P. E.	Math	English	P.E.	Music

My classes always start (1) _____ 9 a.m. We have our lunch break at noon.

We have our lunch (2) _____ one hour. (3) _____ Mondays, we have

an art class (4) _____ lunch. On Tuesdays, we have a history class at 10. We

study (5) _____ the Civil War in history class. On Thursdays, we have P.E.

(6) _____ 1 to 3 p.m. We are learning how to swim this month. Among the

many subjects, my favorite is English. Luckily, I have an English class every day.

WRAP-UP TEST

SCORE:

1 다음 빈칸에 한 번도 쓰이지 않는 것을 고르시오.

> • The show starts _____ 7.
> • I went to Egypt _____ Sue.
> • She made a cake _____ her mother.

ⓐ at   ⓑ on
ⓒ with   ⓓ for

2 다음 밑줄 친 부분을 바르게 고친 것을 고르시오.

> He read the book <u>during</u> five hours.

ⓐ at   ⓑ on
ⓒ for   ⓓ around

3 다음 빈칸에 공통으로 들어갈 알맞은 것을 고르시오.

> • I read a newspaper _____ the morning.
> • She was born _____ 1992.
> • It snows a lot _____ winter.

ⓐ in   ⓑ on
ⓒ at   ⓓ of

4 다음 중 어법상 옳지 <u>않은</u> 문장을 고르시오.

ⓐ He called you around 10 p.m.
ⓑ I slept from 10 a.m. to 8 p.m. yesterday.
ⓒ She is writing a story about magic.
ⓓ Did you go there of bus?

5 다음 밑줄 친 부분의 쓰임이 <u>잘못된</u> 것을 고르시오.

ⓐ She practices the piano <u>after</u> school.
ⓑ They stayed in Japan <u>during</u> vacation.
ⓒ Did you see the man <u>for</u> gray hair?
ⓓ I use the computer <u>without</u> a mouse.

6 다음 빈칸에 on이 쓰일 수 없는 것을 고르시오.

ⓐ We don't go to school _____ Sundays.
ⓑ They have a party _____ Friday night.
ⓒ She got a nice dress _____ her birthday.
ⓓ I have a meeting _____ this time tomorrow.

7 다음 문장에서 잘못된 곳을 찾아 바르게 고치시오.

> I bought a red cap between many colors.

→ _____

8 다음 우리말과 같은 뜻이 되도록 빈칸에 알맞은 말을 쓰시오.

> 9시 전에는 집에 들어오너라.

→ Please come home _____ 9.

[9-10] 다음 대화를 읽고 물음에 답하시오.

> **A** Did you hear the news (A) <u>그녀에 대한</u>?
> **B** No. What is it?
> **A** She got a D on her math test.
> **B** Really? That's too bad.
> **A** Anyway, (B) <u>between, and, you, me, a secret, it's</u> (그것은 너와 나만 아는 비밀이야).

9 (A)를 영작하시오.

→ _____

10 우리말과 일치하도록 밑줄 친 (B)를 배열하시오.

→ _____

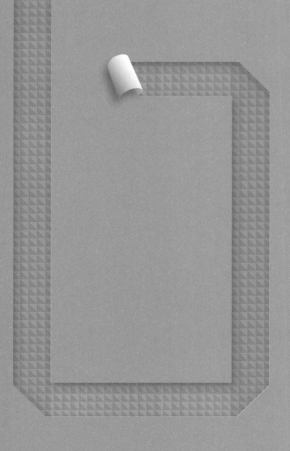

접속사

Unit 15

Unit 1 and/but/or/so

A and B	A와 B	I want a pizza and a hamburger.
A but B	A이지만 B는 아니다	I want a pizza but a hamburger.
A or B	A 또는 B	I want a pizza or a hamburger.
A, so B	A이다, 그래서 B이다.	I want a pizza, so I ask my mom to buy it.

1 and: '~과, 그리고'

I ordered a hamburger and a Coke.

I ordered a hamburger, a Coke and French fries.

I went to the Burger Queen and ate a burger.

1
비슷하거나 대등한 내용을 연결한다.
- 단어와 단어를 연결한다.
- 세 단어를 연결할 때: A, B and C
- 구 또는 절끼리 연결한다.

2 but: '하지만, ~는 아니다'

I ordered a burger and a Coke but not French fries.

I ordered a burger and a Coke, but didn't order French fries.

2
반대되는 내용을 연결한다.
- 단어, 구 또는 절끼리 연결한다.
- comma(,)를 쓰기도 한다.

3 or: '~ 혹은 …, ~ 또는 …, 그렇지 않으면'

Here or to go?

Would you like French fries or a green salad?

3
둘 중 하나를 선택할 때 쓰인다.
- 단어, 구 또는 절끼리 연결한다.

4 so: '그래서, 따라서~'

I didn't get French fries, so I saved money.

I ordered a green salad instead of French fries, so my meal became much healthier.

4
원인과 결과를 나타낸다.
- 단어, 구 또는 절끼리 연결한다.
- 원인[이유], so 결과[결론]

Quick Test

Answers ▲ P.26

1. I can speak Korean _____and_____ English. (한국어와 영어)

2. She is beautiful _____ unkind. (아름답지만 불친절한)

3. Are you a magician _____ a musician? (마술사 또는 음악가)

4. He was very tired _____ he went to bed early. (피곤해서 일찍 잤다)

5. We had dinner _____ saw a movie. (저녁을 먹고 영화를 봤다)

6. He didn't study hard, _____ he passed the test. (공부를 열심히 하지 않았지만 시험에 통과했다)

144

EXERCISE

A [   ] 안에서 알맞은 것을 고르시오.

1 He is young [so, but, or] wise.

2 Do you want to leave now [or, so, but] later?

3 Martin was sick [but, so, or] he didn't go to school.

4 I brought a pencil, a notebook [and, or, so] an eraser.

5 Would you prefer green peppers [or, so, but] white onions on your pizza?

6 Andrew was tired [and, so, or] he went to bed early last night.

7 Cindy practiced hard [but, so, or] she passed her driving test.

B [보기]에서 빈칸에 알맞은 말을 골라 문장을 완성하시오.

Word Bank	or	and	but	so

1 I went swimming yesterday, _____ my sister didn't.

2 Karen _____ Lindsey visited a museum on Saturday.

3 I came home late _____ my mother was worried.

4 Let's buy some ice cream _____ a cake for dessert tonight.

C 주어진 단어를 이용하여 한 문장으로 완성하시오.

1 Would you like hot coffee? Would you like iced coffee? (or)

→ _____ *Would you like hot coffee or iced coffee?* _____

2 There was nothing to eat. We ordered a pizza. (so)

→ _____

3 I met him before. I couldn't remember his name. (but)

→ _____

4 Mary can play the violin. Mary can play the cello. (and)

→ _____

5 Henry looks weak. Henry is very strong. (but)

→ _____

Unit 15
2 기타 접속사

I saw Jessica. I went into the shop <u>at that time</u>.
→ I saw Jessica **when** I went into the shop.

1 when, before, after

(1) when : '~할 때'

He was doing the dishes **when** I came home.
I will call you back **when** I get home.

(2) before : '~하기 전에'

The concert is at 8 o'clock. Let's meet **before** 8.
Before you go home, please turn off the computer.

(3) after : '~한 후에'

I get very tired **after** jogging.
The war ended **after** many people died.

2 because (= since): '~하기 때문에'

I didn't say hello to her **because** I didn't see her.
Since I didn't see her, I didn't say hello to her.

3 if: '만약 ~라면'

Do you mind **if** I sit here?
If you have any questions, please let me know.

1
(1)
시간을 나타내는 when절에서는 현재시제가 미래를 나타낸다.

2
결과[결론]+because+원인[이유]
since+원인[이유], 결과[결론]
because와 since는 위치를 바꿀 수 있다.

3
if 뒤에서는 현재시제가 미래를 나타낸다.

Quick Test

Answers ▲ P.26

1. _____*When*_____ I went out, it was snowing. (밖에 나왔을 때)

2. It started snowing _____ I went out. (밖으로 나온 후)

3. _____ I went out, it snowed heavily. (외출하기 전에)

4. _____ it snowed heavily, I didn't go out. (눈이 엄청 내렸기 때문에)

5. _____ it snows heavily, I won't go out. (눈이 엄청 내린다면)

146

E EXERCISE

A   [   ] 안에서 알맞은 것을 고르시오.

1 [If, After] the weather is nice this weekend, we will go swimming.

2 [Since, After] it was hot, I opened the window.

3 [When, Since] I entered her room, she was sleeping.

4 We should brush our teeth [before, after] we go to bed.

5 [If, After] Tina finished her homework, she went to the movies.

6 I feel very tired [because, if] I didn't get enough sleep last night.

7 [Before, If] you go to the supermarket, please get some grapes.

B   [보기]에서 알맞은 말을 골라 문장을 완성하시오.

Word Bank	since	when	after	before

1 _____ the traffic light turns red, you should stop the car.

2 _____ he has no money, he can't go on a trip.

3 She couldn't meet him because she arrived _____ he left.

4 Please finish your homework _____ dinner.

C   주어진 단어를 이용하여 한 문장으로 완성하시오.

1 I got up late. I was late for school. (because)

   → _____ *I was late for school because I got up late. [Because I got up late, I was late for school.]*

2 You do your best. You can get a good result. (if)

   → _____

3 Jenny finishes school. She takes ballet lessons. (after)

   → _____

4 Ken drove too fast. We had an accident. (since)

   → _____

5 He comes home. I will tell him. (when)

   → _____

A   [   ] 안에서 알맞은 것을 고르시오.

1   I dropped the glass [and, or, but] broke it.

2   [If, But, When] my grandmother stayed with us, she told us interesting stories.

3   [Before, After, If] you don't want to go out, you may stay home.

4   [Since, After, So] she lost her wallet, she couldn't buy the ticket.

5   I went to the mall [so, or, but] didn't buy anything.

6   Do you want a present [so, or, but] some money for your birthday?

7   I sometimes run a mile [when, after, if] I finish the class.

8   I met my aunt [and, or, so] uncle at the park yesterday.

B   빈칸에 알맞은 것을 고르시오.

1   He got up early, _____ he was late for work.

ⓐ and   ⓑ so   ⓒ but   ⓓ when

2   I went on a diet _____ I put on some weight.

ⓐ so   ⓑ but   ⓒ if   ⓓ when

3   _____ he saw a shooting star, he decided to be an astronaut.

ⓐ After   ⓑ Since   ⓒ Before   ⓓ Or

4   Would you like some lemonade _____ some tea?

ⓐ but   ⓑ or   ⓒ when   ⓓ so

5   They didn't have tickets, _____ they watched the game on TV.

ⓐ and   ⓑ but   ⓒ so   ⓓ or

6   Do you mind _____ I sit in this chair?

ⓐ since   ⓑ if   ⓒ after   ⓓ before

7   She wore a green dress, a white hat _____ an orange scarf.

ⓐ or   ⓑ so   ⓒ but   ⓓ and

A Grammar in Speaking 빈칸에 알맞은 말을 넣어 대화를 완성하시오.

1 A We are going to play basketball. Are you in _____ out?

   B I'm out because it's too hot to play.

2 A Did you turn off all the lights?

   B Of course. _____ I went out, I turned off all of them.

3 A When did you see him?

   B _____ I was parking my car, he was running down the street.

4 A I like our math class best.

   B My favorites are science _____ English.

5 A Don't you think Kelly is nice?

   B I don't think so. I spoke to her, _____ she didn't answer me.

B Grammar in Writing 빈칸에 알맞은 접속사를 넣어 글을 완성하시오.

Jim Carrey is a famous comedian (1) _____ actor. He looks funny and happy, (2) _____ his life was not very happy. When he was young, he had to work in a factory (3) _____ his family was poor. After he decided to be a famous comedian, he went to America. At that time, he was poor, (4) _____ he lived in a small car. Since he didn't have money, he had to eat one hamburger a day. Finally, he became famous (5) _____ he acted in *Dumb and Dumber* in 1995.

WRAP-UP TEST

SCORE:

1 다음 빈칸에 알맞은 것을 고르시오.

> She was beautiful _____ unkind.

ⓐ or   ⓑ and
ⓒ but   ⓓ so

2 다음 밑줄 친 부분을 바르게 고친 것으로 알맞은 것을 고르시오.

> He didn't study hard, <u>but</u> he failed the test.

ⓐ since   ⓑ so
ⓒ after   ⓓ when

3 다음 빈칸에 공통으로 들어갈 알맞은 것을 고르시오.

> • Hurry up, _____ you will catch the train.
> • Mike _____ I joined the folk music club.

ⓐ and   ⓑ or
ⓒ but   ⓓ if

4 다음 밑줄 친 부분의 쓰임이 잘못된 것을 고르시오.

ⓐ <u>Because</u> I was sick, I went to the hospital.
ⓑ <u>After</u> we had dinner, we went to the concert.
ⓒ Do you want to go out <u>or</u> stay home?
ⓓ <u>Before</u> I had no money, I couldn't buy the bag.

5 다음 밑줄 친 When의 쓰임이 다른 것을 고르시오.

ⓐ <u>When</u> did you come home?
ⓑ <u>When</u> you get up, can you give me a call?
ⓒ <u>When</u> do you go to sleep?
ⓓ <u>When</u> will we meet again?

6 다음 빈칸에 알맞은 것을 고르시오.

> If you are busy now, I _____ you back later.

ⓐ call   ⓑ will call
ⓒ to call   ⓓ called

7 다음 두 문장의 뜻이 같아지도록 빈칸에 알맞은 말을 쓰시오.

They missed the bus, so they took a taxi.
= _____ they missed the bus, they took a taxi.

8 다음 두 문장을 한 문장으로 연결하시오.

We went to a museum. The museum was closed.
→ We went to a museum, _____ it was closed.

[9-10] 다음 글을 읽고 물음에 답하시오.

> A   What were you doing ___(A)___ you heard the scream?
> B   (B) 잠을 잘 수가 없었기 때문에, I was reading a magazine.

9 (A)에 알맞은 접속사를 고르시오.

ⓐ if   ⓑ because
ⓒ when   ⓓ Since

10 (B)를 영작하시오.

→ _____

150

Concise and Core Grammar Points!

The Grammar

Nexus Contents Development Team

Starter

Answers

NEXUS Edu

The Grammar

Nexus Contents Development Team

Starter

Answers

NEXUS Edu

Answers ▸▸

Unit 01

1 be동사의 현재형

1	is, s	2	am, m
3	is, s	4	am, m
5	are, re	6	are, re
7	is, s	8	is, s

EXERCISE ▼ P.9

A   1   are   2   are   3   am   4   is
    5   are   6   isn't   7   is

B   1   is, He's   2   is, She's
    3   is not, He isn't [He's not]

C   1   Linda is a ballet dancer.
    2   He's not [He isn't] a new student.
    3   They aren't [They're not] her neighbors.
    4   She is [She's] a movie star.

2 be동사의 과거형

1	was, wasn't	2	were, weren't
3	were, weren't	4	was, wasn't

EXERCISE ▼ P.11

A   1   were   2   was not
    3   were   4   wasn't
    5   was   6   weren't
    7   wasn't

B   1   is, wasn't   2   is, wasn't
    3   am, wasn't   4   are, weren't
    5   is, wasn't   6   are, weren't

C   1   She was not [wasn't] a writer.
    2   They were lawyers.
    3   It was a mistake.
    4   I am not [I'm not] a photographer.
    5   He was not [wasn't] happy.

3 be동사의 일반 의문문

1	Is he	2	Are we
3	Is this	4	Are Jim and Harry
5	Was she	6	Are they
7	Is that		

EXERCISE ▼ P.13

A   1   Is, is   2   Is, isn't
    3   Are, are   4   Are, are
    5   Are, am not   6   Is, is
    7   Are, aren't

B   1   Is, is, He is
    2   Is, she isn't, She is
    3   Are, No, they aren't, They are

C   1   They are doctors.
        Are they doctors?
        Yes, they are.
        No, they aren't [are not].

    2   I am a police officer.
        Are you a police officer?
        Yes, I am.
        No, I am not [I'm not].

4 be동사의 의문사 의문문

1	Who	2	Where
3	How	4	When
5	What		

EXERCISE ▼ P.15

A   1   What, is   2   Who, is
    3   What day, is   4   Where, are
    5   When, is   6   How, is
    7   How old, are

B   1   What are   2   What time is
    3   Who is   4   Where are

C 1 Who are they?
They are my parents.

2 How tall are you?
I am 1.5 meters tall.

3 What is that?
It is my hat.

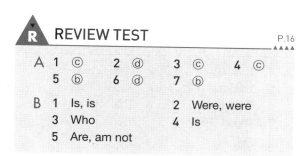

REVIEW TEST

P.16

A 1 ⓒ   2 ⓓ   3 ⓒ   4 ⓒ
5 ⓑ   6 ⓓ   7 ⓑ

B 1 Is, is   2 Were, were
3 Who   4 Is
5 Are, am not

A 1 그녀는 학교 연극의 감독이다.
2 Cathy가 미국에서 온 네 사촌이니?
3 작년에 그녀는 요리사가 아니었다.
4 이긴 사람이 누구니?
5 그들이 그의 남동생들이야?
6 당신의 직업은 무엇입니까?
7 저는 의사가 아닙니다. 간호사입니다.

B 1 A Sarah는 지금 집에 있습니까?
B 아니오, 없습니다. 그녀는 학교에 있습니다.
2 A Nate와 Fred는 어제 일을 했습니까?
B 네, 그렇습니다.
3 A Mr. Ford는 누구니?
B 그분은 새로 온 선생님이셔.
4 A Karen이 그의 누나니?
B 아니, 그녀는 그의 사촌이야.
5 A 당신은 컴퓨터 기술자입니까?
B 아니오, 그렇지 않습니다.

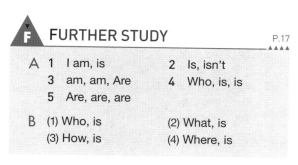

FURTHER STUDY

P.17

A 1 I am, is   2 Is, isn't
3 am, am, Are   4 Who, is, is
5 Are, are, are

B (1) Who, is   (2) What, is
(3) How, is   (4) Where, is

A 1 A 안녕. 나는 Jenny야.
B 안녕, 만나서 반가워. 내 이름은 Brian이야.
2 A 그는 우리 선생님이니?
B 아니, 그렇지 않아.
3 A 안녕. 나는 Ed라고 해. 네가 Gail이니?
B 네, 그렇습니다. 새로 오신 선생님이신가요?

4 A 그녀는 누구입니까?
B 그녀는 Grace입니다. 그녀는 미국에서 왔습니다.
5 A 이것들은 당신의 펜입니까?
B 네, 그렇습니다.
A 그것들은 색이 매우 다양하네요. 제가 그것들을 써도 될까요?

B (1) 그녀는 누구입니까?
→ 그녀의 이름은 J. K. Rowling입니다.
(2) 그녀의 직업은 무엇입니까?
→ 그녀는 작가입니다. 그녀는 'Harry Potter' 시리즈의 작가입니다.
(3) 그녀는 몇 살입니까?
→ 그녀는 지금 50살입니다.
(4) 그녀는 어디 출신입니까?
→ 그녀는 영국 출신입니다.

WRAP-UP TEST

P.18

1 ⓑ   2 ⓒ   3 ⓑ
4 ⓑ   5 ⓐ   6 ⓐ
7 ⓑ   8 ⓒ
9 1) Jack and Bill are not my best
friends.
2) Were you angry at that time?
10 He was an actor.

1 그들은 매우 행복하다.
2 A 저 여자는 누구니?
B 그녀는 우리 이모, Ann이야.
3 Mack과 Mike는 전에 농부였다.
4 ⓐ 그들은 강하다.
ⓑ 그는 야구 선수가 아니다. (He'sn't → He isn't)
ⓒ 그것은 나의 잘못이 아니었다.
ⓓ 나는 학생이 아니다.
5 A Bill은 가수였나요?
B 네, 그렇습니다.
6 나는 학생이었다. (그때 / 2년 전에 / 지난 달)
7 ⓐ Mark 조종사가 아니다.
ⓑ 그들은 어제 동물원에 있었다. (are → were)
ⓒ 어제 본 영화 어땠니?
ⓓ 그녀는 제빵사입니까?
8 ⓐ 이것들은 무엇이니?
그것들은 책들이야.
ⓑ 지난 일요일에 너는 어디에 있었니?
나는 해변에 있었어.
ⓒ 너의 언니는 몇 살이니? (How → How old)
그녀는 17살이야.
ⓓ 영화가 언제 시작하니?
5시에.
9 1) Jack과 Bill은 나의 가장 친한 친구이다.
Jack과 Bill은 나의 가장 친한 친구가 아니다.
2) 너는 그때 화를 냈다.
너는 그때 화를 냈었니?

Unit 02

1 셀 수 있는 명사

Quick Test _____ P.20

1	a, girls	2	a, houses
3	a, books	4	an, oranges
5	an, apples	6	a, cats
7	a, pencils	8	a, lilies
9	a, strawberries	10	an, elephants
11	a, boys	12	a, foxes

EXERCISE _____ P.21

A   1   A   2   A   3   A   4   An
    5   A   6   A   7   An

B   1   A rose, Roses
    2   A ball, Balls
    3   A pineapple, Pineapples

C   1   A ladybug, Ladybugs
    2   An orange, Oranges,
    3   a cat, cats
    4   A fox, Foxes

2 셀 수 없는 명사

Quick Test _____ P.22

1   a - girl, house, strawberry
2   an - egg, airplane, envelope
3   ø - London, Asia, air

EXERCISE _____ P.23

A   1   Ø   2   An   3   Ø   4   An
    5   Ø   6   Ø   7   Ø

B   1   Jason   2   Korea   3   glass   4   baby
    5   some   6   Water

C   1   Soccer
    2   a cup of coffee
    3   France
    4   a carton of milk
    5   Juice

3 인칭/지시대명사

Quick Test _____ P.24

1	he	2	it
3	he	4	she
5	we	6	they
7	you	8	it

EXERCISE _____ P.25

A   1   This, He   2   This, She
    3   This, It   4   Those, They
    5   That, It   6   That, He
    7   Those, They

B   1   She   2   You
    3   It   4   He
    5   She   6   They

C   1   This, a book
    2   She, my sister
    3   This, a new student
    4   We, soccer players
    5   They, nice guys

R REVIEW TEST _____ P.26

A   1   Jack   2   birds
    3   A piece of bread   4   potato
    5   Seals   6   Vegetables
    7   cups of coffee

B   1   ⓐ   2   ⓐ   3   ⓑ   4   ⓓ
    5   ⓒ   6   ⓐ   7   ⓑ

A   1   Jack은 소년이다.
    2   두 마리의 새가 새장 안에 있다.
    3   접시 위에는 빵 한 조각이 있다.
    4   바구니 속에는 감자 한 개가 있다.
    5   바다표범은 수영을 참 잘한다.
    6   야채는 건강에 좋다.
    7   커피 두 잔 주세요.

B   1   사과는 몸에 좋다.
    2   서울은 한국의 수도이다.
    3   바닥에는 상자 세 개가 있다.
    4   그것은 초록 앵무새이다.
    5   열차에는 사람들이 타고 있다.
    6   설탕은 달다.
    7   시리얼 한 그릇이 나의 아침 식사이다.

F FURTHER STUDY

P.27

A 1 foxes   2 London
3 mammals   4 soldiers
5 daughters   6 glass

B (1) people (2) an (3) a (4) Sumi
(5) a (6) a (7) He (8) a
(9) She (10) an (11) These

A 1 A 우리 안에 두 마리의 여우가 있어.
    B 아니야, 여우 한 마리만 우리 안에 있어.
2 A 나는 한국 서울에서 왔어.
    B 나는 영국 런던에서 왔어.
3 A 고래는 물고기야.
    B 아니야, 그것들은 포유류야.
4 A Jack과 Jill은 군인이야.
    B 그래, 그들은 용감해.
5 A 이 소녀들은 제 딸들이에요.
    B 그래요? 그들은 무척 귀엽군요.
6 A 엄마, 저 정말 목말라요.
    B 여기 물 한 잔이 있단다.

B

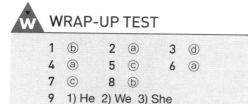

우리 가족은 6명이다. 나의 아버지는 영어 선생님이다. 나의 어머니는 요리사이다. Sumi는 나의 누나다. 그녀는 학생이다. 나의 형은 야구 선수다. 그는 LA에 있다. 내 여동생은 아기다. 그녀는 2개월이 됐다. 나는 초등학교 학생이다. 내 이름은 Jude이다. 이들이 나의 가족이다.

W WRAP-UP TEST

P.28

1 ⓑ   2 ⓐ   3 ⓓ
4 ⓐ   5 ⓒ   6 ⓐ
7 ⓒ   8 ⓑ
9 1) He 2) We 3) She
10 two cups of coffee

1 사과는 과일이다.
   그는 예술가이다.
5 ⓐ 그들은 내 가장 친한 친구들이다.
   ⓑ 뉴욕은 도시이다.
   ⓒ 개미는 곤충이다. (an insects → an insect)
   ⓓ 두 소녀들이 내 방에 있다.
6 (이것 / 저것 / 그것)은 내 가방이다. 그것은 크다.
7 ⓐ 병 속에 많은 물이 있다. (Many water → Much water)
   ⓑ 인생은 아름답다. (A life → Life)
   ⓒ Mark와 Jason은 기술자이다.
   ⓓ 그것들은 나의 책이다. (It → They)

---

8 A 이것은 내 차야.
   B 우와, 그것은 정말 멋지다.
9 1) 이 사람은 우리 오빠다. 그는 학생이다.
   2) Ann과 나는 가수이다. 우리는 유명하다.
   3) 우리 언니는 L.A.에 있다. 그녀는 피아니스트이다.
10 하나의 꽃병, 한 조각의 파이, 두 잔의 커피가 부엌 테이블 위에 있다.

Unit 03

1 인칭대명사의 주격과 목적격

Quick Test

P.30

1 He   2 You
3 She   4 We
5 It   6 him
7 you   8 her
9 us   10 it

EXERCISE

P.31

A 1 me, her   2 It
3 We   4 them
5 He   6 They
7 It

B 1 them   2 it
3 She   4 them
5 He

C 1 She was my classmate last year.
2 They drive it every day.
3 I like them very much.
4 It is her favorite sport.

2 인칭대명사의 소유격

Quick Test

P.32

1 my, mine   2 your, yours
3 his, his   4 her, hers
5 Its   6 their, theirs

EXERCISE

P.33

A 1 his   2 Yours
  3 its   4 girls'
  5 Jenny's   6 boys'
  7 Our

B 1 Mine   2 their
  3 His   4 hers
  5 mine   6 its

C 1 Her boyfriend is handsome.
  2 Is this his telephone number?
  3 Where is Carl's classroom?
  4 My bag is light. Yours is heavy.

R REVIEW TEST

P.34

A 1 ⓐ   2 ⓑ   3 ⓒ   4 ⓑ
  5 ⓐ   6 ⓓ   7 ⓒ

B 1 his   2 It
  3 We   4 hers
  5 their   6 their

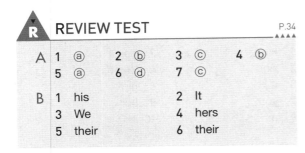

A 1 벌은 꿀을 먹는다. 그들은 그것을 매우 좋아한다.
  2 네 여자 친구가 문 앞에 있다.
  3 탁자 위에 1달러가 있어. 네 거니?
  4 오전에 나한테 전화해.
  5 나는 Helen을 좋아한다. 나는 그녀를 매일 만난다.
  6 우리 집까지는 5마일 거리다.
  7 그 의자의 다리는 헐겁다.

B 1 나는 그를 매일 본다. 하지만 나는 그의 이름을 모른다.
  2 이 손목시계는 500달러다. 그것은 비싸다.
  3 Jack과 나는 음악을 좋아한다. 우리는 종종 연주회에 간다.
  4 그녀의 셔츠는 빨간색이다. 이 푸른색 셔츠는 그녀의 것이 아니다.
  5 그들은 개를 기른다. 그것은 그들의 개다.
  6 우리 부모님은 모자를 많이 가지고 있다. 이것들은 그들의 모자다.

F FURTHER STUDY

P.35

A 1 My   2 its   3 her
  4 mine   5 them

B (1) My   (2) Her   (3) Her
  (4) They   (5) me   (6) we

A 1 A 네 전화번호를 알려 줄래?
    B 내 전화번호는 101-123-12340t.
  2 A 저 고양이를 봐! 정말 귀엽다!
    B 그래, 눈동자가 예쁘다.
  3 A Mike는 Sarah를 정말 사랑해.
    B 나도 알아. 그는 그녀를 정말 사랑해.
  4 A 내 공하고 방망이를 가져왔어.
    B 나도 내 것을 가져왔어.
  5 A 이 팬케이크는 아주 맛있구나.
    B 맞아, 난 그것들을 정말 좋아해.

B

안녕하세요, 여러분. 제 이름은 Shrek입니다. 제 부인을 소개하지요. 그녀의 이름은 Fiona예요. 그녀는 공주랍니다. 그녀의 부모님은 왕과 왕비예요. 그들은 예전에는 저에게 친절하게 대해 주지 않았지만 지금은 아주 친절하고 좋습니다. 그들은 저를 좋아해요. Fiona는 다른 사람들에게는 예뻐 보이지 않습니다. 그러나 그녀는 제게 세상에서 가장 아름다운 여자랍니다. Fiona와 저는 세 명의 자녀가 있고 숲에서 살아요.

W WRAP-UP TEST

P.36

1 ⓒ   2 ⓒ   3 ⓐ
4 ⓑ   5 ⓐ   6 ⓓ
7 It's → Its   8 ⓓ
9 theirs
10 1) He 2) Her 3) our 4) They

2 너와 Jenny는 테니스를 쳤니?
3 나는 톰을 잘 안다.
  그러나 그는 나를 알지 못한다.
4 ⓐ Ann은 우유를 좋아한다. 그녀는 그것을 매일 마신다.
  ⓑ 내게는 두 명의 조카가 있다. 나는 그들을 사랑한다.
    (they → them)
  ⓒ 그것들은 네 신발이 아니다.
  ⓓ Cindy와 나는 친구다. 우리는 옆집에 산다.
5 나는 그녀와 함께 인도로 여행을 가고 싶다.
6 이것이 네 핸드폰이니?
  ⓐ 아니, 그것은 그녀의 것이야.
  ⓑ 응, 그것은 내 거야.
  ⓒ 아니, 그것은 그의 것이야.
7 나는 고양이 한 마리를 가지고 있다. 그것은 아름다운 눈을 가졌다. 그것의 발톱은 날카롭다.
8 우리 집 근처에는 큰 공원이 하나 있다. Joe와 나는 주말이면 그곳에 간다. 항상 많은 사람들이 있다. 한 남자가 개를 산책시킨다. 한 어린아이가 자전거를 탄다. 한 여자가 풀밭에 누워 책을 읽고 있다. 이곳은 사람들에게 멋진 장소이다.
9 이것은 우리의 공이다. 저것은 그들의 공이다.
  그들의 것(theirs)
10 1) 우리 아버지는 농구선수이다.
    그는 키가 크다.

6

2) Mike는 한 여자를 만났다. 그녀의 이름은 Jessica이다.
3) 우리는 지금 막 기차에서 내렸다. 우리는 우리의 가방을 잃어버렸다.
4) 너의 조부모님은 어디 사시니? 그들은 Springfield에 사셔.

Unit 04

1 일반동사의 현재형

Quick Test _____ ▲ P.38

1	talks	2	does
3	likes	4	passes
5	watches	6	goes
7	plays	8	makes
9	speaks	10	runs
11	sings	12	dances
13	catches	14	flies
15	cries	16	buys

EXERCISE ▼ P.39

A 1 likes 2 helps 3 have 4 does
   5 write 6 visit 7 rises

B 1 cries, cry   2 barks, bark
   3 smiles, smile

C 1 She washes her face.
   2 He ties his shoes.
   3 Kids play in the sand.
   4 They do many activities.

2 의문문과 부정문

Quick Test _____ ▲ P.40

1 Do I know, I don't know
2 Do you know, You don't know
3 Does he know, He doesn't know
4 Does she know, She doesn't know
5 Do we know, We don't know
6 Do they know, They don't know

EXERCISE ▼ P.41

A 1 don't   2 Mary
   3 Do   4 live
   5 does   6 doesn't
   7 Do

B 1 Does, wear, Yes, does
   2 Does, wear, No, doesn't
   3 Do, have, Yes, do

C 1 Does Mike like kimchi?
   2 They don't go to school on Sundays.
   3 Does the toy store open at 10?
   4 My cat doesn't meow at night.

3 일반동사의 과거형

Quick Test _____ ▲ P.42

1	had	2	did
3	ran	4	cut
5	helped	6	came
7	made	8	went
9	washed	10	flew

EXERCISE ▼ P.43

A 1 enjoyed   2 did
   3 visited   4 eats
   5 cried   6 drove
   7 met

B 1 saw 2 flew 3 took 4 went
   5 told 6 gave

C 1 He washed his face this morning.
   2 She helped me a lot.
   3 I saw a horror movie last year.
   4 They came back in 1950.

4 의문문과 부정문

Quick Test _____ ▲ P.44

1 Did, meet   2 didn't wait
3 Did, send   4 didn't get up
5 Did, buy   6 didn't break
7 Did, come   8 didn't take

7

A 1 Did 2 didn't
  3 arrive 4 didn't
  5 didn't 6 didn't have
  7 Did

B 1 did, studied 2 did, took
  3 didn't, went

C 1 Kelly didn't have a sandwich for lunch.
  2 I didn't see Mark last night.
  3 Did you go to church last Sunday?
  4 Did Amy hurt her knee?

5 일반동사의 현재진행형

Quick Test ▲ P.46

1 reading 2 having
3 sitting 4 visiting
5 meeting 6 lying
7 coming 8 pulling
9 planning 10 making
11 giving 12 losing
13 swimming 14 studying
15 writing

EXERCISE ▼ P.47

A 1 have, are having 2 is smiling, smiles
  3 is sitting, sits 4 delivers, is delivering

B 1 cooks 2 are losing
  3 opens 4 is taking
  5 wins 6 is watching

C 1 Tony is smiling.
  2 He is sitting on the bench.
  3 He is waving to Sally.
  4 Sally is coming close to him.

6 의문문과 부정문

Quick Test ▲ P.48

1 is not following 2 Is, snowing
3 is not telling 4 Are, catching
5 am not calling 6 Is, ringing

A 1 are 2 are not
  3 Are 4 is not
  5 Is 6 am not
  7 are

B 1 Is, drawing, is
  2 Is, riding, isn't, riding, is, riding
  3 Are, washing, am, not, am, baking

C 1 They are not having a conversation.
  2 Is he lying on the floor?
  3 My sister is not watching TV.
  4 Is your uncle cooking a turkey?

R REVIEW TEST P.50

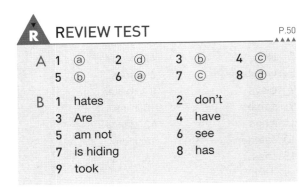

A 1 ⓐ 2 ⓓ 3 ⓑ 4 ⓒ
  5 ⓑ 6 ⓐ 7 ⓒ 8 ⓓ

B 1 hates 2 don't
  3 Are 4 have
  5 am not 6 see
  7 is hiding 8 has
  9 took

A 1 Mike는 비싼 차를 운전한다.
  2 나는 그것을 이해하지 못한다.
  3 그는 지금 딸을 업어 주고 있다.
  4 어젯밤에 개한테 먹이를 줬니?
  5 당신은 지금 차를 이동시키고 있습니까?
  6 그녀는 명절에는 주로 떡을 만든다.
  7 그 학생이 이번에는 신문에서 사진을 오리고 있습니다.
  8 그 비행기는 하루에 두 번 공항으로 날아간다.

B 1 그녀는 생강이 든 빵을 싫어한다.
  2 우리는 그 중국 식당에는 가지 않는다.
  3 지금 내 얘기를 듣고 있는 거니?
  4 어젯밤에 닭고기 수프를 먹었니?
  5 난 너한테 얘기하는 게 아냐.
  6 어제 뉴스에 나온 토네이도를 봤니?
  7 그 쥐는 지금 구멍 속에 숨어 있다.
  8 그의 집은 갈색 지붕으로 덮여 있다.
  9 지난 금요일에는 지하철을 타고 집에 갔다.

FURTHER STUDY

P.51

A   1   did   2   bought
    3   am not playing   4   am buying
    5   Are

B   (1) gave   (2) dreamed   (3) made
    (4) like   (5) enjoy

A   1   A 지난 주말에는 뭐했니?
        B 놀이 공원에 가서 롤러코스터를 탔어.
    2   A 오늘 너 아주 멋지구나! 그 멋진 드레스는 어디서 샀니?
        B 그것은 쇼핑몰에서 샀어.
    3   A Tom, 너 어디 있니? 여동생과 놀고 있는 거야?
        B 아니에요! 여동생과 놀고 있지 않아요. 그녀는 지금 자고 있어요.
    4   A 시장에서 무엇을 살 거니?
        B 계란과 메론 한 개를 살 거야.
    5   A 지금 떠나는 거야?
        B 아니, 우리는 2시간 후에 떠날 거야.

B

> Steven Spielberg는 미국의 유명한 영화감독이다. 그는 1946년 미국 오하이오 주에서 태어났다. 어느 날, 그의 아버지는 그에게 카메라를 주었다. 그 이후로 그는 영화감독이 되는 것을 꿈꿨다. 그의 첫 번째 영화는 The Last Gun이다. 1970년대와 1980년대에 Spielberg는 E.T, Jaws, Star Wars 영화를 만들었다. 그는 아카데미상을 세 번 탔다. 사람들은 그를 좋아하며 그의 영화를 즐긴다.

WRAP-UP TEST

P.52

    1   ⓐ   2   ⓓ   3   ⓑ
    4   ⓑ   5   ⓒ   6   ⓒ
    7   ⓒ
    8   1) She is not singing a song.
        2) Do they take piano lessons after
           school?
    9   1) finishes 2) teaches 3) setting
    10 I am making a kite.

2   그는 주로 바닥에서 잔다.
    그는 어제 영어를 공부했다.
3   마이크는 코미디 영화를 봤다.
    마이크는 코미디 영화를 보지 않았다.
4   ⓐ John은 일요일마다 교회에 간다.
    ⓑ 그 아기는 많이 운다. (crys → cries)
    ⓒ 그녀는 프라하에 산다.
    ⓓ 그는 큰 입을 가지고 있다. (말이 많다.)

5   그가 그녀의 이름을 아니?
    응, 그는 알아.
6   ⓐ 그녀는 지난 밤 비행기를 타고 런던으로 갔다. (flyed → flied)
    ⓑ 그는 학교에 걸어서 가나요? (Do → Does)
    ⓒ 우리는 좋은 시간을 보내고 있다.
    ⓓ 그들은 수업에 왔나요? (came → come)
7   그는 (어제 / 작년에 / 2년 전에) 좋은 차를 샀다.
8   1) 그녀는 노래를 부르고 있다.
       그녀는 노래를 부르고 있지 않다.
    2) 그들은 방과 후에 피아노 수업을 듣는다.
       그들은 방과 후에 피아노 수업을 듣나요?
9   1) 그는 5시에 수업이 끝난다.
    2) 그녀는 학교에서 영어를 가르친다.
    3) 그들은 지금 식탁을 차리고 있나요?
10 A 너는 지금 무엇을 하고 있니?
    B 나는 지금 연을 만들고 있어.

Unit 05

▼ 1   현재/과거/미래

Quick Test
P.54

1   runs, ran, will [be going to] run
2   studies, studied, will [be going to] study
3   travels, traveled, will [be going to] travel
4   goes, went, will [be going to] go
5   visits, visited, will [be going to] visit

EXERCISE
P.55

A   1   was   2   saw
    3   walk   4   is going to stay
    5   will change   6   works
    7   was

B   1   passed   2   call
    3   was   4   cut
    5   will [are going to] come
    6   sold

C   1   We are going to [will] go hiking
    2   He was really happy
    3   I will [am going to] give her nice flowers
    4   The man will [is going to] be in the office
    5   His friends went to the movies

2 will/be going to

▲ P.56

Quick Test

1 Will they go, They will not [won't] go
2 Is he going, He is not [isn't] going to

EXERCISE

▼ P.57

A 1 start 2 won't
 3 will not plant 4 Will she
 5 Is 6 Will he
 7 are not going to

B 1 is not going to sell
 2 Are you going to give
 3 is going to stay
 4 will bring
 5 will have

C 1 He is going to graduate from high school next year.
 2 Will you have dinner with me?
 3 We are going to go to Hawaii this summer.
 4 Won't you help me?

R REVIEW TEST

P.58

A 1 were 2 won't be
 3 will 4 won't be
 5 ran 6 will be
 7 grow 8 going to

B 1 ⓐ 2 ⓑ 3 ⓒ 4 ⓑ
 5 ⓓ 6 ⓐ 7 ⓓ

A 1 그들은 어제 바닷가에 있었다.
 2 Sam은 내일 바쁘지 않을 것이다.
 3 나는 그 대회에서 우승할 것이다.
 4 그녀는 며칠 동안 돌아오지 않을 것이다.
 5 Ben은 작년에 마라톤에 참가했다.
 6 Kelly는 오늘 오후에 박물관에 있을 것이다.
 7 나는 이번 봄에 토마토를 기를 것이다.
 8 그는 일곱 시에 축제에 갈 것이다.

B 1 Jim이 시험에 합격할까?
 2 나는 이번 주 일요일에 San Diego에 갈 것이다.
 3 그녀는 학교에 가지 않을 것이다. 그녀는 아프다.
 4 수업은 9시에 시작한다.
 5 그는 보고서를 쓰지 않을 것이다.
 6 우리는 다음 주 일요일에 생일 파티를 할 것이다.

7 네가 내 편지를 읽었니?

F FURTHER STUDY

P.59

A 1 will
 2 am going to [will] clean
 3 am going to [will] write
 4 are going to [will] visit
 5 will not [won't] be

B (1) am (2) left (3) stayed (4) went
 (5) won't [will not] forget (6) took
 (7) will [am going to] stay (8) will be
 (9) leaves (10) will [am going to] show

A 1 A 부탁 하나만 들어줄래?
  B 물론이야. 뭔데?
 2 A 네 방은 너무 지저분하구나.
  B 나도 알아. 이번 주말에 청소하려고 해.
 3 A 다음 주 월요일 저녁에 뭐 할 거니?
  B 나는 리포트를 쓸 거야.
 4 A 아이들은 오늘 오후에 공원에서 놀 건가요?
  B 아니오. 아이들은 2시에 조부모님을 뵈러 갈 거예요.
 5 A 오늘 아침 바닷가 날씨는 따뜻했나요?
  B 네. 그랬어요. 하지만 내일은 따뜻하지 않을 거예요.

B

Anne에게
나는 지금 런던으로 가는 기차를 타고 있어. 한 시간 전에 파리를 떠났어. 나는 파리에서 2주를 보냈어. 파리에서 아름다운 곳에 많이 갔는데 나는 그곳을 잊지 못할 거야. 사진도 많이 찍었어. 나는 런던에서 일주일 동안 머물 거야. 유감스럽게도 런던에서 머무는 시간은 너무 짧아. 나의 비행기는 15일에 떠날 거야. 몇 주 후에 내가 찍은 멋진 사진들을 너에게 보여 줄게.
사랑하는
Sarah가

W WRAP-UP TEST

P.60

1 ⓓ 2 ⓒ 3 ⓒ
4 ⓒ 5 ⓑ 6 share
7 ⓒ 8 is going to write
9 ⓑ
10 I will [am going to] go to the library.

1 어제는 바람이 불었다.
 오늘은 따뜻하다.
 내일은 추울 것이다.
3 ⓐ 나는 그를 파티에 초대하지 않을 것이다.
 ⓑ 너는 미팅에 참석할 거니?

ⓒ Simon은 지금 모자를 쓰고 있다. (is)
ⓓ 그녀는 이번 금요일에 그녀의 이모를 방문할 것이다.

4 ⓐ 너는 그녀와 함께 저녁을 먹을 거니?
   ⓑ 그는 그 차를 사지 않을 것이다.
   ⓒ 그녀는 숙제를 할 것이다. (will does → will do)
   ⓓ 너는 9시까지 일을 할 거니?

5 ⓐ 우리는 이번 주말에 우리 집을 페인트로 칠할 것이다.
   ⓑ Jack은 어제 시험에서 큰 실수를 했다. (makes → made)
   ⓒ 그녀는 피아노 치는 것을 즐긴다.
   ⓓ 공원에 큰 조각품이 있었다.

6 그는 남동생과 그의 방을 함께 쓰지 않을 것이다.
7 그는 내년이면 14살이 될 것이다.
8 그녀는 그녀의 할머니에게 편지를 쓸 것이다.
9 A 너는 (방과 후에 / 이번 주말에 / 내일) 무엇을 할 거니?
   B 나는 도서관에 갈 거야.

Unit 06

능력을 나타내는 조동사

Quick Test _____ ▲ P.62

1 Can she speak
   She cannot [can't] speak
   She will be able to speak
   She could speak
   She was able to speak

2 Can they eat
   They cannot [can't] eat
   They will be able to eat
   They could eat
   They were able to eat

EXERCISE   ▼ P.63

A 1 can   2 answer
   3 ride   4 park
   5 Was   6 cannot
   7 can

B 1 could solve   2 will be able to
   3 cannot [can't] find 4 able to book
   5 could not [couldn't] send
   6 is not able to call
   7 will be able to finish

C 1 She was able to sing well before.

2 Mary could not find her dog last night.
3 I can't see the moon right now.
4 We will be able to meet soon.

허가를 나타내는 조동사

Quick Test _____ ▲ P.64

1 (b)   2 (a)
3 (d)   4 (c)
5 (e)

EXERCISE   ▼ P.65

A 1 open   2 May   3 Can   4 turn
   5 Can   6 May   7 fly

B 1 Can, borrow
   2 Can, call
   3 Can, help
   4 Can, wait
   5 Can, have
   6 can, go

C 1 Can you order some food?
   2 You cannot go out and play.
   3 Would [Could] you say your name again?
   4 Could [Would] you (please) get me some
      lemonade?
   5 Can you show me your ID?

의무를 나타내는 조동사

Quick Test _____ ▲ P.66

1 조언   2 추측
3 불필요   4 의무

EXERCISE   ▼ P.67

A 1 go   2 not bring
   3 have to   4 to return
   5 may not   6 Do you have to
   7 watch

B 1 I will have to study hard
   2 She must not open
   3 Should I take
   4 They had to get on

11

C 1 You must not swim here.
2 You must open a bank account.
3 You should go home early.
4 She had to take care of her sister last night.
5 He must be sick.

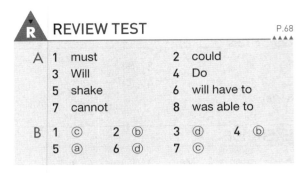

REVIEW TEST

A 1 must 2 could
3 Will 4 Do
5 shake 6 will have to
7 cannot 8 was able to

B 1 ⓒ 2 ⓑ 3 ⓓ 4 ⓑ
5 ⓐ 6 ⓓ 7 ⓒ

A 1 우리는 7시에 저녁 식사를 할 거야. 그러니까 너는 7시 전까지 집으로 와야 해.
2 나는 어제 막차를 탈 수 있었다.
3 제 컴퓨터를 고칠 수 있으세요?
4 그들은 계획을 세워야 합니까?
5 당신과 악수를 해도 될까요?
6 Doris는 파티 전에 옷을 갈아입어야 할 거야.
7 Steve는 영자 신문을 읽을 수 없다.
8 Erica는 어젯밤에 나를 데리러 올 수 있었다.

B 1 학교는 장발을 허용하지 않아. 너는 머리를 짧게 유지해야만 해.
2 그는 지갑을 잃어버렸어. 그래서 그는 어제 집까지 걸어와야 했어.
3 내일 내 여동생은 나와 바이올린을 연주하지 않을 거야.
4 내게 간식을 사줄 수 있니?
5 Charlie는 곧 일자리를 찾을 수 있을 거야.
6 제가 진찰을 받아야만 합니까?
7 제가 한 부 더 복사할 수 있어요.

FURTHER STUDY

A 1 shouldn't [must not / can't]
2 should [must / have to]
3 should [must / have to]
4 can [may / could]
5 should [must / have to]
6 can [will be able to]
7 must [should]
8 shouldn't [must not / can't]

A 1 A 여기서 담배를 피워도 될까요?
B 아니오, 여기서 담배를 피우면 안 됩니다.

2 A 여기서는 얼마나 빨리 차를 몰 수 있습니까?
B 당신은 시속 30마일 이하로 운전하셔야 합니다.
3 A 여기서 우회전을 해도 될까요?
B 아니오, 할 수 없습니다. 좌회전을 하셔야 합니다.
4 A 여기서 차를 운전해도 될까요?
B 아니오, 하지만 여기서는 자전거를 타셔도 됩니다.
5 A 여기서는 빨리 운전해도 됩니까?
B 아니오, 당신은 천천히 운전하셔야 합니다. 아이들이 이 근처에서 놀고 있습니다.
6 A 출구를 찾을 수가 없어요!
B 출구 표시를 따라가세요. 나가는 길을 찾으실 수 있을 거예요.
7 A 조심하세요! 표지판이 있어요.
B 아, 그렇군요. 사람들은 큰 개 때문에 조심해야 합니다.
8 A 나는 점심을 싸 왔어.
B 아, 저 표지판을 봐. 여기서 음식을 먹거나 음료수를 마시면 안 된대.

WRAP-UP TEST

1 ⓑ 2 ⓓ
3 must → have to 4 ⓒ
5 ⓓ 6 ⓐ 7 ⓒ
8 is able to 9 had to
10 have to

1 그들은 바이올린을 잘 연주할 수 있다.
이것을 입어봐도 될까요?
2 창문을 열어 주시겠어요?
3 당신은 당신의 신분증을 보안 요원에게 보여 줘야 할 것입니다.
4 ⓐ 너는 우산을 가져가야 한다.
ⓑ 우리는 영화를 보는 도중 핸드폰을 사용해선 안 된다.
ⓒ 그는 두 시간 후 이 책 읽기를 끝낼 수 있을 것이다. (will can → will be able to)
ⓓ 제가 거기에 10시 전에 도착해야 하나요?
5 ⓐ 당신은 높이 뛸 수 있나요? (능력)
ⓑ 그가 그의 차를 찾을 수 있나요? (능력)
ⓒ 그들이 게임을 이길 수 있나요? (능력)
ⓓ 이것을 도와주실 수 있나요? (요청)
6 A 나가서 놀아도 될까요?
B 응, 그래도 돼.
7 ⓐ 너는 강렬한 햇볕 아래에서는 모자를 써야 한다. (의무)
ⓑ 너는 도심가에서 조심해야 한다. (의무)
ⓒ 너는 장시간의 비행 후 몹시 피곤함이 틀림 없다. (추측)
ⓓ 너는 저녁을 먹기 전에 숙제를 해야 한다. (의무)
8 그는 말을 탈 수 있다. (can = be able to)
10 지난 밤, 나는 한 시에 잠에 들었다. 나는 늦게 일어났고 학교에 늦었다. 내일 나는 좀더 일찍 수업에 와야 할 것이다. (will have to)

Unit 07

1 형용사의 의미와 쓰임

Quick Test
P.72

1	small	2	dirty
3	hot	4	difficult
5	weak	6	full
7	short	8	young [new]

EXERCISE
P.73

A
1 cute, a cute   2 big, a big
3 small, small   4 fun, fun
5 happy, a happy   6 exciting, an exciting
7 honest, an honest

B
1 happy, sad   2 big, small
3 short, long

C
1 She is a pretty girl.
2 He is a kind doctor.
3 It is an old book.
4 Pigs are fat animals.

2 여러 가지 형용사

Quick Test
P.74

1	O	2	O
3	X	4	O
5	X	6	X
7	X	8	X

EXERCISE
P.75

A
1 This   2 Those
3 These   4 panda
5 candies 6 sweater
7 oranges

B
1 a few
2 a little
3 many

C
1 There are lots of books in the bookcase.
2 There is a little water in the pond.
3 These are interesting stories.
4 That teddy bear is cute.

R REVIEW TEST
P.76

A
1 lovely   2 clever girls
3 yellow   4 something red
5 These   6 real diamonds
7 any   8 rainy city

B
1 ⓑ   2 ⓑ   3 ⓒ   4 ⓓ
5 ⓐ   6 ⓓ   7 ⓒ

A
1 그녀는 사랑스럽다.
2 그들은 영리한 소녀들이다.
3 저것들은 노란 나비들이다.
4 그것은 빨간 것이었어.
5 이 쿠키들은 맛있다.
6 그것들은 진짜 다이아몬드이다.
7 항아리 속에는 잼이 하나도 없다.
8 시애틀은 비가 내리는 도시다.

B
1 뉴욕은 대도시이다.
2 그녀는 예쁘니?
3 차가운 음료수 좀 마실래요?
4 그는 정직한 소년이다.
5 통에 소금이 남아 있니?
6 그 운동화는 더럽다.
7 유리잔에는 우유가 조금 있다.

F FURTHER STUDY
P.77

A
1 was not sunny
2 is long, is beautiful
3 is dirty
4 is a short game, is not long
5 was warm
6 is cheap, is not expensive

B
(1) new   (2) large   (3) brown   (4) large
(5) blue   (6) very clean   (7)quiet

A
1 A 어제는 화창했니?
  B 아니. 화창하지 않았어.
2 A 이 사진 속에서 너의 어머니는 어느 분이니?
  B 머리가 길고 아름다운 분이셔.
3 A 네 방은 깨끗하니?
  B 아니. 지저분해.
4 A 이 비디오 게임은 길어?
  B 아니, 이것은 짧은 게임이야. 이것은 길지 않아.
5 A 오늘 아침에 추웠어?
  B 아니. 따뜻했어.
6 A 저것은 비싼 셔츠니?
  B 아니. 이것은 싼 거야. 이건 비싸지 않아.

B

아파트 임대

– 침실 하나
  새 침대, 큰 옷장
– 부엌
  회색 빛 탁자, 갈색 의자 2개
– 가구가 갖추어진 거실
  대형 TV, 아늑한 소파, 푸른색 카펫
– 욕실
  매우 깨끗함
– 기타
  조용한 이웃
정보가 더 필요하시면 전화주세요: 555-3258

여기 당신을 위한 완벽한 아파트가 있습니다. 침대 하나와 옷장 하나가 딸린 침실이 하나 있습니다. 침대는 새 것이고 옷장은 큽니다. 부엌에 있는 식탁은 회색으로 의자는 갈색입니다. 거실에는 모든 가구가 갖춰져 있습니다. 거실에는 대형 TV와 아늑한 소파가 있습니다. 카펫도 깔려 있습니다. 그것은 푸른색 카펫입니다. 욕실은 매우 깨끗합니다. 게다가 이웃도 조용합니다. 더 많은 정보를 원하시면 555-3258로 전화 주세요.

 WRAP-UP TEST   P.78

1	ⓓ	2	ⓓ	3	ⓑ
4	ⓒ	5	ⓒ	6	any
7	ⓑ	8	ⓐ	9	few apples
10	1) a big animal				
	2) an honest man				

1 이것들은 좋은 시계이다.
  저 시계는 좋다.
2 그녀는 (소녀이다 / 예쁘다 / 키가 큰 여자다).
3 그의 지갑에는 많은 돈이 있다.
4 그는 잘생긴 소년이다.
5 ⓐ 파리는 낭만적인 도시이다.
  ⓑ 이 다이아몬드는 진짜다.
  ⓒ 그녀는 친절한 간호사이다. (a kind nurse)
  ⓓ 저 거미들은 빠르다.
6 오븐 안에 케이크가 하나도 없다.
8 이것들은 멋진 엽서이다.
  ⓐ 이 엽서들은 멋지다.
9 A 사과나무에 사과가 몇 개 있니?
  B 사과나무에 사과가 거의 없어.
10 1) 코끼리는 동물이다. 코끼리는 크다.
  → 코끼리는 큰 동물이다.
  2) Jason은 남자다. Jason은 정직하다.
  → Jason은 정직한 남자다.

Unit 08

Quick Test   P.80

1	late	2	slowly
3	up	4	badly
5	far	6	hard

EXERCISE   P.81

A
1	well	2	very	3	then	4	pretty
5	too	6	so	7	near		

B
1	early	2	well
3	quietly	4	easily
5	carefully	6	happily

C 1 The book is quite interesting.
  2 Sadly, they lost the game.
  3 She talks very loudly.
  4 He speaks English well.

 2 부사의 형태

Quick Test   P.82

1	simply	2	cleanly
3	well	4	happily
5	largely	6	easily
7	gentle	8	careful
9	quick	10	smart
11	poor	12	strong

EXERCISE   P.83

A
1	friendly	2	kind
3	actually	4	happily
5	Suddenly	6	clearly
7	cheerfully		

B
1	really	2	loudly
3	brightly	4	gently
5	poorly	6	usually

C 1 He ran fast.
  2 The train left early.
  3 Luckily, the bird escaped the cage.
  4 He came late to the party.

3 빈도부사

Quick Test P.84

1 often rains
2 am never afraid
3 sometimes calls
4 are always
5 usually order
6 never walks

EXERCISE P.85

A
1 often goes
2 never tell
3 How
4 usually have
5 often makes
6 five times
7 often

B
1 often
2 always
3 sometimes
4 usually
5 never

C
1 How often does he fly a kite?
2 They sometimes bring leftovers home.
3 The class always gets good grades.
4 Susan is never late for work.
5 Brad often gets up early these days.

R REVIEW TEST P.86

A
1 late
2 he often
3 very
4 often
5 quickly
6 very
7 usually studies
8 loudly

B
1 ⓓ
2 ⓑ
3 ⓓ
4 ⓒ
5 ⓐ
6 ⓒ

A
1 그들은 파티에 늦게 왔다. 남아 있는 음식이 없었다.
2 그는 자주 아프니?
3 수학 시험은 너무 어려웠다.
4 그녀는 얼마나 자주 실수를 합니까?
5 그는 그의 생일 선물을 재빨리 풀었다.
6 그 소년은 매우 빨리 달렸다.
7 그녀는 대체로 열심히 공부한다.
8 군중이 시끄럽게 소리를 지르고 있다.

B
1 나는 Billy와 싸웠다. 나는 절대 그와 다시 이야기하지 않을
  것이다.
2 우리 아버지는 차를 빠르게 운전한다.
3 슬프게도 나는 강아지를 잃어버렸다.
4 그는 부상을 입은 아이에게 친절하게 말을 건넸다.
5 우리는 주말에 가끔 숲속을 거닌다.
6 그들은 얼마나 자주 여행을 합니까?

F FURTHER STUDY P.87

A
1 many
2 fast
3 always
4 really
5 never

B
(1) late
(2) always
(3) hard
(4) really
(5) Luckily
(6) Hopefully
(7) soon

A
1 A 너는 일주일에 몇 번 아이스크림을 먹니?
  B 아마 일주일에 세 번 정도.
2 A 어제 사고가 났어. 내가 차를 너무 빨리 몰았어.
  B 너는 정말 부주의한 운전자야.
3 A 나는 여름에 절대 바닷가에 가지 않아. 너는 어때?
  B 나는 여름이면 항상 바닷가에 가.
4 A 그는 정말 똑똑해. 그는 영어도 잘해.
  B 그는 정말 행운아구나.
5 A 너는 매일 수영하러 가니?
  B 아니, 수영은 절대 가지 않아. 나는 수영을 못하거든.

B

> 나에게는 나쁜 버릇이 많이 있다. 나는 매일 아침 늦게 일어난다.
> 그래서 아침식사를 늘 거른다. 나는 이따금씩 다른 아이들에게서
> 돈을 빌리고는 갚지 않는다. 공부도 열심히 하지 않는다. 나는 주
> 로 수업 중에 잠을 잔다. 나에겐 정말 변화가 필요하다. 다행히도
> 나에게는 좋은 부모님이 있다. 또 좋은 선생님들도 계시고 친구들
> 도 있다. 이제 나는 그들에게 도움을 요청하고 있다. 바라건대 그
> 들이 좋은 조언을 해 주면 좋겠다. 나는 곧 내 나쁜 버릇을 고치겠
> 다고 약속한다.

W WRAP-UP TEST P.88

1 ⓐ
2 ⓓ
3 ⓑ
4 ⓐ
5 ⓒ
6 ⓓ
7 ⓑ
8 1) brightly 2) happy 3) late
9 How often
10 Luckily

2 당신을 만나게 되어 (너무 / 정말 / 매우) 좋습니다.
3 그는 형편없는 요리사이다.
  그는 요리를 못한다.
4 그는 가끔 나에게 우편엽서를 보낸다.
5 ⓐ 그녀는 경제학을 열심히 공부한다.
  ⓑ 기차가 일찍 떠났다.
  ⓒ 그는 차를 빠르게 운전했다. (fastly → fast)
  ⓓ 주의 깊게 들어 주십시오.
6 ⓐ 그녀는 종종 나를 보고 웃는다.
  ⓑ 그곳에는 항상 많은 사람들이 있다.
  ⓒ Paul은 주로 일요일에 그의 방을 청소한다.
  ⓓ 그는 절대 외롭지 않다. (never is → is never)

8 1) 별들이 하늘에서 밝게 빛난다.
 2) 그녀는 친절한 여자다.
 3) 그는 오늘 아침 늦게 일어났다.

9 A 얼마나 자주 외식을 하니?
 B 나는 보통 일주일에 한 번 외식을 해

10 그는 시험을 통과했다. 그것은 행운이었다.
 운 좋게도, 그는 시험을 통과했다.

Unit 09

1 비교급/최상급의 의미와 형태

Quick Test _____ ▲ P.90

1 bigger, biggest   2 hotter, hottest
3 more beautiful, most beautiful
4 happier, happiest   5 more, most
6 better, best   7 faster, fastest
8 easier, easiest   9 worse, worst
10 wiser, wisest

EXERCISE ▼ P.91

A 1 prettier   2 hottest
 3 bigger   4 better
 5 worse   6 more
 7 oldest

B 1 lighter   2 worse
 3 the tallest   4 more
 5 the kindest   6 more interesting
 7 the most beautiful

C 1 Dogs are friendlier than cats.
 2 My room is the smallest in my house.
 3 Red shoes are more expensive than black shoes.
 4 You look better than yesterday.

2 비교 표현

Quick Test _____ ▲ P.92

1 그는 그녀만큼 나이가 많다.
2 Kelly는 John만큼 영화를 좋아하지는 않는다.

---

3 그의 점수는 그가 예상했던 것보다 훨씬 좋았다.
4 우리 할머니는 그 누구보다도 다정하다.
5 그는 우리 반에서 가장 힘 센 남자들 중 하나이다.

EXERCISE ▼ P.93

A 1 most   2 even
 3 clever   4 much
 5 not as   6 far
 7 cleaner

B 1 worse   2 better
 3 not as cold as   4 as fast as

C 1 My father is as angry as my mother.
 2 "I" is one of the shortest words in English.
 3 The KTX runs faster than any other train in Korea.
 4 You laugh much louder than your mother.

R REVIEW TEST ▲ P.94

A 1 braver   2 much
 3 well   4 most important
 5 girls   6 most
 7 heavier   8 a lot

B 1 ⓑ   2 ⓐ   3 ⓓ   4 ⓑ
 5 ⓑ   6 ⓒ   7 ⓓ

A 1 Tom은 Johnny보다 더 용감하다.
 2 나는 예전보다 훨씬 더 건강하다.
 3 그녀는 Alex Agassi만큼 테니스를 잘 친다.
 4 네 인생에서 무엇이 가장 중요하니?
 5 Jane은 우리 반에서 가장 귀여운 소녀 중 한 명이야.
 6 Cape Town은 세계에서 가장 아름다운 도시 중 하나야.
 7 이 가방은 내 것보다 무겁다.
 8 그 연극은 기대했던 것보다 훨씬 더 좋았다.

B 1 Gary는 Jim보다 더 힘이 세다.
 2 고양이는 여우만큼이나 영리하다.
 3 오렌지는 사과보다 훨씬 더 신선해 보인다.
 4 그의 목소리는 우리 반에서 가장 크다.
 5 아테네는 세계에서 가장 오래된 도시 중 하나다.
 6 당신은 제가 생각했던 것보다 훨씬 더 친절하군요.
 7 Warren은 우리 회사에서 가장 정직한 사람이야.

FURTHER STUDY P.95

A 1 earlier   2 more
   3 the prettiest   4 the most popular
   5 bigger than

B (1) faster   (2) stronger   (3) larger

A 1 A 일찍 도착하셨나요?
     B 아니요. 당신보다 5분 일찍 왔을 뿐입니다.
   2 A 나는 내 여동생만큼 책을 많이 읽지 않아.
     B 그녀는 너보다 책을 훨씬 더 많이 읽는구나.
   3 A 너희 반에 새로 온 학생을 봤니? 그녀는 예쁘니?
     B 물론이야. 그녀는 학교에서 가장 예쁜 소녀야.
   4 A 하와이는 인기가 많은 섬입니까?
     B 네, 세계에서 가장 인기가 많은 섬 중 하나입니다.
   5 A 뉴욕 시는 미국의 그 어느 도시보다 커.
     B 맞아. 그 나라에서 가장 큰 도시야.

B

교사:
좋아요, 여러분. 첫 번째 질문이에요. 한 번 듣고 생각해보세요. 열기와 냉기 중에 뭐가 더 빠르게 이동할 수 있을까요? 답은 열기예요. 열기는 냉기보다 빨리 이동해요. 왜냐고요? 여러분이 냉기를 잡을 수(감기에 걸릴 수) 있기 때문이에요. 무슨 말인지 이해가 되나요? 그러면 다음 질문을 해 보죠. 세상에서 가장 힘 센 생물은 무엇일까요? 바로 달팽이에요! 달팽이는 등에 자신의 집을 등에 지고 다닌답니다. 달팽이는 저보다도 힘이 세죠! 흥미롭지 않나요? 마지막 질문이에요. 세상에서 가장 큰 ant는 무엇일까요? 바로 elephant예요. elephant(코끼리)는 ant(개미)보다 훨씬 크죠. 물론 둘은 같은 생물은 아니지만 어쨌든 재미있는 농담이에요. 그렇죠?

 WRAP-UP TEST P.96

   1 ⓓ   2 ⓐ   3 ⓒ
   4 ⓑ   5 ⓐ   6 ⓓ
   7 ⓒ   8 not as fast
   9 worse
   10 it was the most boring movie

2 이 스카프는 저 스카프보다 더 비싸다.
   그녀는 그보다 더 유명하다.
3 ⓐ 나는 그가 가지고 있는 것보다 더 많은 책을 가지고 있다.
     (→ more)
   ⓑ 수학은 공부하기에 가장 어려운 과목이다. (→ the most difficult)
   ⓒ 그녀는 가족에서 가장 나이가 많은 아이이다.
   ⓓ 그 영화는 내가 기대했던 것보다 더 흥미로웠다. (→ more exciting)

4 그녀는 내가 생각했던 것보다 훨씬 더 예쁘다.
5 오렌지들이 신선하다. 사과들도 신선하다.
   ⓐ 오렌지들이 사과만큼 신선하다.
6 ⓐ James가 우리 반에서 가장 키가 큰 남자이다.
   ⓑ 우리 반에 어떤 남자도 James만큼 크진 않다.
   ⓒ James는 우리 반에서 그 어떤 남자보다도 키가 크다.
   ⓓ James는 내 친구보다 키가 크다.
8 비행기는 기차보다 빠르다.
   = 기차는 비행기만큼 빠르지 않다.

9-10
A 그 영화는 최악이었어.
B 정말? 네가 생각했던 것보다 더 별로였니?
A 아니. 그것은 가장 지루한 영화였어.
B 난 그것을 보지 말아야겠다.

Unit 10

1 ▼ 목적어를 가지는 동사

Quick Test P.98

1 him, the truth   2 coffee
3 X   4 me, nice flowers
5 me, a Christmas card   6 a big fish
7 X   8 your homework

EXERCISE P.99

A 1 him, the ball
   2 X
   3 the woman
   4 a letter
   5 the boat
   6 X
   7 them, the news

B 1 for me
   2 to my relatives
   3 the picture
   4 chocolates

C 1 She showed me his pictures.
   2 Mary bought us tickets for the concert.
   3 My uncle opened a Taekwondo gym.
   4 The carpenter built a doghouse for my dog.
   5 The coach guaranteed a victory.

② 보어를 가지는 동사

Quick Test

P.100

1	the president	2	angry
3	soft	4	beautiful
5	ready	6	white
7	exciting	8	sorry
9	roommates	10	mad
11	John	12	good

EXERCISE

P.101

A
1	good	2	him to say
3	sweet	4	my dog Tom
5	oily	6	her sad
7	famous		

B
1 sounds, wonderful
2 made, me, surprised
3 wish, you, a merry Christmas
4 feel, very tired
5 want, them, ready
6 tastes, spicy

C
1 She became a web designer.
2 People call him a genius.
3 The idea sounds interesting.
4 The movie made me smile.

R REVIEW TEST

P.102

A
1	makes	2	lied to me
3	me stories	4	busy
5	quiet	6	me a picture
7	lent me		

B
1 ⓒ	2 ⓓ	3 ⓑ	4 ⓒ
5 ⓒ	6 ⓒ	7 ⓓ	

A
1 Philip은 항상 나를 화나게 한다.
2 내 아들은 어제 나에게 거짓말을 했다.
3 나의 할아버지는 나에게 그의 어린 시절 이야기를 해 주셨다.
4 그 남자는 그때 바빠 보였다.
5 청중은 공연 중에 조용했다.
6 그는 나에게 그의 사진을 보여 주었다.
7 그는 나에게 돈을 빌려 주었다.

B
1 ⓐ 그녀는 나에게 엽서를 보냈다. / ⓑ 그녀는 그에게 편지를 보냈다. / ⓓ 그녀는 그에게 소포를 보냈다.
2 ⓐ Mary와 Tom은 파티에 도착했다. / ⓑ Mary와 Tom은 일찍 도착했다. / ⓒ Mary와 Tom은 늦게 도착했다.
3 ⓐ 그들은 친근해 보였다. / ⓒ 그들은 아파 보였다. / ⓓ 그들은 건강해 보였다.
4 ⓐ 그의 친구는 추위를 느꼈다. / ⓑ 그의 친구는 고마워했다. / ⓓ 그의 친구는 슬퍼했다.
5 ⓐ 그녀는 도서관에서 나에게 영어를 가르쳤다. / ⓑ 그녀는 도서관에서 영어를 나에게 가르쳐 주었다. / ⓓ 그녀는 도서관에서 나를 가르쳤다.
6 ⓐ 나는 그것에 대해 그녀에게 말했다. / ⓑ 나는 그에게 가라고 했다. / ⓓ 나는 경찰관에게 내 이름을 말했다.
7 ⓐ 저에게 택시를 불러 주세요. / ⓑ 저녁 때 전화해 주세요. / ⓒ 다시 전화해 주세요.

F FURTHER STUDY

P.103

A
1	look	2	gave
3	rises	4	good
5	open		

B
(1) I flew in the sky
(2) They tasted sweet
(3) The clouds gave me some rain
(4) I lay on the clouds
(5) They called me an angel

A
1 A 와, 그 드레스를 입으니 아름다워 보여. 파티에 가니?
　 B 응, 내 친구가 나를 위해 생일 파티를 열어 준대.
2 A 그 멋있는 운동화는 어디서 났어?
　 B 우리 엄마가 크리스마스 선물로 주셨어.
3 A 해는 동쪽에서 떠서 서쪽으로 진다.
　 B 그러면 달은?
4 A 그는 매우 좋은 친구야.
　 B 그래, 맞아. 그는 종종 내 숙제를 도와주기도 해.
5 A 창문을 열어 두세요. 실내는 덥습니다.
　 B 죄송합니다만, 밖은 너무 추워요.

B

지난 밤 나는 새처럼 날 수 있는 꿈을 꾸었다. (1) 나는 하늘을 날아다녔다. 나는 배가 고파서 구름을 먹었다. (2) 그것들은 솜사탕처럼 달콤한 맛이 났다. 내 얼굴은 더러웠다. (3) 구름이 나에게 비를 조금 내려 주어 나는 얼굴을 씻었다. 나는 잠이 와서 (4) 구름 위에 누었다. 그것들은 아주 푹신푹신했다. 구름과 달과 별들은 나의 친구들이었다. (5) 그들은 나를 천사라 불렀다. 갑자기 해가 떴다. 내 날개가 사라지고 나는 땅 위로 떨어졌다. 그리고 나는 잠에서 깼다.

P.104

1 ⓑ　　2 ⓒ　　3 ⓒ
4 ⓓ　　5 ⓐ　　6 ⓑ
7 My friends call me Jimmy.
8 1) She gave a pen to him.
　　2) My teacher asked a question of me.
9 She teaches us English.
10 ⓑ

1 나는 실수를 했다.
　그녀는 그녀의 아들을 조종사로 만들었다.
2 Alex는 그들에게 두 통의 편지를 보냈다.
3 그녀는 (사랑스러워 / 다정해 / 예뻐) 보인다.
4 ⓐ Mike는 유명해졌다.
　ⓑ 그는 나에게 흥미로운 이야기를 해 주었다.
　ⓒ 나는 그녀의 전화번호를 잊어버렸다.
　ⓓ 너는 항상 나를 행복하게 만든다. (→ happy)
5 ⓐ 그는 정각에 공항에 도착했다. (→ arrived at the airport)
　ⓑ 그들은 축구 경기에서 이겼다.
　ⓒ Jim은 열심히 일하는 사람이다.
　ⓓ 그 책을 제게 건네주세요.
6 우리 아빠가 나에게 자전거를 사 주었다.
8 1) 그녀는 그에게 펜을 주었다.
　　2) 우리 선생님이 나에게 질문을 했다.
9-10
Barbara는 내가 가장 좋아하는 선생님이다. 그녀는 우리에게 영어를
가르쳐 준다. 그녀는 대학에서 수학을 공부했지만, 영어 선생님이 되었
다. 그녀는 우리를 향해 항상 웃는다.

Unit 11

1 명령문

Quick Test
P.106

1 Open
2 Be
3 Don't
4 Don't
5 Be

EXERCISE
P.107

A 1 Be
　2 Watch
　3 Don't
　4 or
　5 and
　6 not
　7 Be

B 1 Give
　2 watch
　3 have
　4 Take
　5 Be

C 1 Let's meet at six.
　2 Study hard, and you will pass the test.
　3 Don't swim in this river.
　4 Let's not go out tonight.
　5 Don't make any noise.

2 감탄문

Quick Test
P.108

1 What
2 What
3 How
4 What
5 How
6 What
7 How
8 How
9 How
10 What

EXERCISE
P.109

A 1 What
　2 How
　3 a wonderful world
　4 honest
　5 eyes
　6 funny
　7 joyful

B 1 old　2 cute　3 nice

C 1 huge animals (they are)
　2 bad news (it is)
　3 an old church (it is)
　4 a strong man (he is)

19

3 부가/선택의문문

Quick Test
▲P.110

1 isn't it	2 aren't they
3 won't she	4 does he
5 wasn't it	6 isn't he
7 doesn't he	8 doesn't it
9 don't you	10 isn't it

EXERCISE
▼P.111

A
1 isn't it	2 was he
3 didn't you	4 don't understand
5 What	6 can't
7 Who	

B
1 Who	2 Which
3 When	4 Did
5 Is	

C
1 You like green tea, don't you?
2 They were in Africa last year, weren't they?
3 The computer won't work, will it?
4 They could see Mary, couldn't they?

R REVIEW TEST
P.112 ▲▲▲▲

A
1 Don't		2 go	
3 or		4 What	
5 How		6 isn't he	
7 did you		8 Which	

B
1 ⓒ	2 ⓑ	3 ⓓ	4 ⓑ
5 ⓑ	6 ⓐ	7 ⓓ	

A
1 너무 화내지 마.
2 방과 후에 쇼핑하러 가자.
3 나를 따라 와, 그렇지 않으면 넌 길을 잃을 거야.
4 멋진 드레스를 갖고 있구나!
5 이거 정말 맛있다!
6 Patrick은 그녀에게 사과를 할 거야, 그렇지 않니?
7 넌 이것을 복사하지 않았어, 그렇지?
8 우유랑 주스 중에 어떤 것을 더 좋아해?

B
1 너 잠시 동안 기다릴 수 있지, 그렇지 않니?
2 그의 점수에 대해서는 얘기하지 말자.
3 그는 정말 입이 크구나!
4 다이아몬드와 에메랄드 중에 뭐가 더 단단하지?
5 시험지를 열어 보지 마시오.
6 그는 정말 어리석어 보이는구나!
7 전화를 받아 주세요.

F FURTHER STUDY
P.113 ▲▲▲▲

A
1 be		2 will you	
3 How		4 Let's	
5 and		6 or	

B
(1) Let's	(2) didn't	(3) Let's not
(4) call	(5) hotter	

A 1 A 저는 전화 통화를 하고 있어요. 조용히 해 주세요.
　　B 미안해요. 조용히 할게요.
2 A 그녀는 또 약속을 어겼어. 이번이 다섯 번째야.
　　B 너 그녀를 용서하지 않을 거지, 그렇지?
3 A 엄마, 저 배고파요. 뭐든지 먹을 수 있을 것 같아요.
　　B 정말 배가 고픈가 보구나! 기다려 봐. 엄마가 먹을 것을 가져다 줄게.
4 A 휴가 때 무엇을 하고 싶니, 아들아?
　　B 캠핑 가요, 아빠.
5 A 이 게임은 어떻게 하는 거야?
　　B 노래 제목을 맞추면 상을 타는 거야.
6 A 큰 개를 원해, 작은 개를 원해?
　　B 나는 아파트에서 살기 때문에 작은 개를 원해.

B

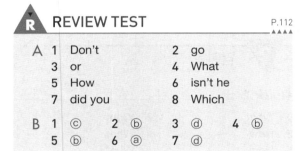

A	여름 방학이 다가오고 있어. 올해는 어디로 가고 싶어?
B	아시아에 가 보고 싶어. 발리는 어때?
A	음, 나는 이집트에 가고 싶어. 이집트로 가자.
B	넌 2년 전에 거기 갔잖아, 아니야?
A	응, 그래도 피라미드를 또 보고 싶어. 발리는 가지 말자.
B	좋아. 여행사에 전화해서 비행기 표를 예약해 줘.
A	고마워.
B	그런데 이집트와 발리 중에 어디가 더 더워?
A	내 생각엔 이집트.

W WRAP-UP TEST
P.114 ▲▲▲▲

1 ⓑ	2 ⓒ	3 ⓐ
4 ⓑ	5 ⓐ	6 going → go
7 ⓒ		

8 1) Do not [Don't] open the door.
　 2) Be proud of yourself.
9 1) a nice dream you have!
　 2) high the mountain is!
10 or

1 산책하러 가자.
2 ⓐ 이 얼마나 작은 세상인가! (What)
　 ⓑ 너는 진짜 큰 눈을 가졌구나! (What)
　 ⓒ 그녀는 얼마나 아름다운가! (How)
　 ⓓ 너는 얼마나 행복한 소녀인가! (What)

3 지금 일어나라, 그렇지 않으면 너는 늦을 것이다.
열심히 일하라, 그러면 당신은 성공할 것이다.

4 조심해!

5 ⓐ Barbara는 우리와 함께 머무를 것이다, 그렇지 않니?
ⓑ Jane은 선생님이 아니야, 그렇지? (→ is she?)
ⓒ Smith 씨는 그녀를 만날 수 없었어, 그렇지? (→ could he?)
ⓓ 그는 그것을 이해하지 못했어, 그렇지? (→ did he?)

6 밖에 비가 오고 있어. 낚시하러 가지 말자.

7 ⓐ 화내지 마.
ⓑ 제발 도와주세요.
ⓒ 돈을 낭비하지 마세요. (Doesn't → Don't)
ⓓ 그 개로부터 떨어져!

8 〈보기〉 너는 숙제를 해야 한다.
숙제를 해라.
1) 너는 문을 열어서는 안 된다.
문을 열지 마라.
2) 너는 네 자신을 자랑스럽게 여겨야 한다.
네 스스로를 자랑스럽게 여겨라.

9 1) 너는 진짜 멋진 꿈을 가지고 있다.
너는 멋진 꿈을 가지고 있구나!
2) 그 산은 매우 높다.
그 산은 매우 높구나!

10 너는 어떤 것을 더 좋아하니, 장미 아니면 백합?

Unit 12

1 명사적 쓰임

Quick Test _____ ▲ P.116

1 목적어   **2** 주어
3 보어   **4** 주어
5 목적어   **6** 보어

EXERCISE _____ ▼ P.117

A **1** to see   **2** knitting
   3 smoking   **4** to fly
   5 to be   **6** opening
   7 having

B **1** driving   **2** To collect
   3 eating   **4** to listen

C **1** She enjoys baking cakes.
   2 My goal is finishing the work by 9.
   3 To write books is my job. [My job is to write books.]
   4 He needs to see a doctor.
   5 His hobby is growing unusual plants. [Growing unusual plants is his hobby.]

2 형용사적/부사적 쓰임

Quick Test _____ ▲ P.118

1 그는 마실 물을 좀 샀습니다.
2 그녀는 건강해지기 위해 수영을 합니다.
3 영어를 공부할 시간입니다.
4 당신을 만나게 되어 행복합니다.
5 저에게 무언가 말씀하실 것이 있나요?
6 나는 선물을 사기 위해 쇼핑을 갔습니다.

EXERCISE _____ ▼ P.119

A **1** to do   **2** to read
   3 to hear   **4** to see
   5 to do   **6** in order to
   7 time to

B **1** to pour   **2** to hear
   3 to work   **4** to play
   5 to go   **6** to pick up

C 1 Miami is a good place to visit.
2 I called her to have a lunch with her.
3 It's time to wake up.
4 John has a report to finish this afternoon.

 REVIEW TEST   P.120
▲▲▲▲

A 1 to help   2 Watching
3 to pay   4 to study
5 hiking   6 to go
7 in order to   8 To pass

B 1 ⓒ   2 ⓑ   3 ⓐ   4 ⓓ
5 ⓒ   6 ⓑ   7 ⓓ

A 1 우리는 가난한 사람들을 돕기를 원했다.
2 영화 보기는 내 취미 중 하나다.
3 여기 지불하실 계산서가 있습니다.
4 영문법은 (공부하기에) 재미있다.
5 나는 숲속에서 걷는 것을 즐긴다.
6 집에 갈 시간이다.
7 그는 고객을 만나기 위해 사무실에서 나왔다.
8 시험에 합격하는 것은 매우 어렵다.

B 1 야구는 재미있다.
2 우리 아버지는 담배를 끊으셨다.
3 일찍 일어나는 것이 내게는 힘들다.
4 그녀는 귀신을 보고 충격을 받았다.
5 지도를 읽는 것이 나에게는 어렵다.
6 소방관이 그 여자를 구하기 위해 집으로 뛰어 들어갔다.
7 실수를 한 그녀를 용서해야 할 때다.

 FURTHER STUDY   P.121
▲▲▲▲

A 1 to see   2 to drink
3 closing   4 to interview
5 to pack

B (1) to see   (2) to do   (3) to watch
(4) to show   (5) to go   (6) to leave

A 1 A 오랜만이야! 어떻게 지내?
B 안녕, Jack. 다시 보게 되어 반갑구나.
2 A 엄마, 저 목말라요. 마실 것이 필요해요.
B 냉장고 안에 시원한 물이 있단다.
3 A 너무 추워요. 창문을 닫아도 될까요?
B 물론이지요. 어서 닫으세요.
4 A 그녀는 왜 오는 거죠?
B 그녀는 면접관이에요. 사람들을 면접하기 위해 오는 겁니다.
5 A Steve, 가족 휴가를 위해 짐을 싸야 할 시간이다.
B 알았어요, 엄마. 제 가방은 어디 있죠?

B
어제 나는 Sea World에 갔다. 그곳에는 볼만한 동물들이 많았고 할 것도 많았다. 처음에는 바다표범 관에 갔다. 바다표범을 보고 있으면 즐겁다. 내가 가장 좋아하는 일은 고래에게 먹이를 주는 것이었다. 고래가 물에서 뛰어오르면서 물이 튀었다. 관중에 물이 튀었다. 나는 가족에게 보여줄 사진을 많이 찍었다. 마침내 집에 가야 할 시간이 됐다. 나는 떠나고 싶지 않았다. 나는 Sea World에서 즐거운 시간을 보냈다!

 WRAP-UP TEST   P.122
▲▲▲▲

1 ⓓ   2 ⓑ   3 ⓓ
4 ⓒ   5 ⓒ   6 ⓑ
7 to see → seeing
8 My job is to teach students math.
9 ⓑ   10 to be [being]

1 시험을 통과하는 것이 내 목표이다.
2 그녀는 좋은 점수를 받기 위해 열심히 공부했다.
3 ⓐ 자전거를 타는 것은 재미있다.
ⓑ 나는 해야 할 두 개의 과제가 있다.
ⓒ 그녀는 담배 피우는 것을 끊었다.
ⓓ 나의 취미는 사진을 찍는 것이다.
4 나는 신문을 읽는 것을 (마쳤다 / 즐겼다 / 좋아한다).
5 A 문을 좀 열어도 괜찮을까요?
B 물론이죠.
6 이 가게는 신선한 과일들을 사기에 좋은 장소이다.
ⓐ 쇼핑을 가는 것은 내가 가장 좋아하는 활동이다. (주어; 명사적 쓰임)
ⓑ 나는 옷을 갈아입을 시간이 필요하다. (명사 수식; 형용사적 쓰임)
ⓒ 그는 그녀를 다시 보게 되어서 기뻤다. (~해서; 부사적 쓰임)
ⓓ 우리는 영어를 배우는 것을 좋아한다. (목적어; 명사적 쓰임)
7 그들은 어젯밤 마술 쇼를 보는 것을 매우 즐겼다.

9-10
A 넌 뭐가 되고 싶니?
B 내 꿈은 우주비행사가 되는 거야.
A 우주비행사! 우와...
B 그래. 나는 정말로 화성으로 여행을 가고 싶어.

22

Unit 13

1 장소 전치사 1

EXERCISE
P.125

A 1 on   2 under
  3 by [next to]   4 by [next to]
  5 on   6 in front of
  7 between, and

B 1 by [beside / next to]
  2 behind
  3 across from
  4 across from
  5 by [next to / beside]

2 장소 전치사 2

Quick Test
P.126

1 on   2 in
3 at   4 on
5 in   6 at, in

EXERCISE
P.127

A 1 on   2 in   3 in   4 in
  5 at   6 at   7 on

B 1 on the school bus
  2 in the garden
  3 at the bus stop

C 1 James is at the party.
  2 Tom is in France.
  3 My cat is on the roof.
  4 Dan is on the plane.

3 There is/are

Quick Test
P.128

1 Is there, there is, there isn't
2 Are there, there are, there aren't

EXERCISE
P.129

A 1 is   2 are not
  3 Was there   4 There
  5 is   6 Is there
  7 There are

B 1 there is, There is
  2 Are there, No, There is
  3 Are there, Yes, there are, There are

C 1 There is a car in front of the house.
  2 There are five kittens in the basket.
  3 Is there a bank next to the post office?
  4 Is there a spoon in the drawer?

R REVIEW TEST
P.130

A 1 in   2 on
  3 There   4 Where
  5 across from   6 There are
  7 Where were   8 There isn't

B 1 ⓐ   2 ⓓ   3 ⓒ   4 ⓑ
  5 ⓐ   6 ⓓ   7 ⓑ

A 1 Steve는 미시건에 있다.
  2 John과 Mike는 런던으로 가는 비행기를 탔다.
  3 우리 집 앞에는 큰 개가 있다.
  4 우체국은 어디입니까?
  5 백화점은 빵집 맞은편에 있습니다.
  6 교실에 7명의 학생이 있다.
  7 그 쌍둥이 소년들은 어젯밤 어디 있었습니까?
  8 그 도시에는 이탈리아 식당이 없다.

B 1 그들은 지금 회의 중이다.
  2 10년 전 이곳에는 큰 영화관이 있었다.
  3 내 양말이 어디 있지?
  4 그 건물 옆에는 도로가 없다.
  5 TV 가이드가 어디 있지?
  6 강 옆에는 오솔길이 하나 있다.
  7 Ben은 견학을 갔니?

F FURTHER STUDY
P.131

A 1 is, across from
  2 where, next to [by / beside]
  3 behind

B (1) on   (2) in front of
  (3) on   (4) by [next to / beside]

23

A 1 A 실례합니다. 지하철역이 어디죠?
   B 지하철역은 은행 맞은편에 있습니다.
 2 A 죄송하지만, 은행은 어디죠?
   B 은행은 경찰서 옆에 있습니다.
 3 A 아, 경찰서 앞에 도서관이 있나요?
   B 아닙니다. 도서관은 경찰서 뒤편에 있습니다.
   A 대단히 감사합니다.

B

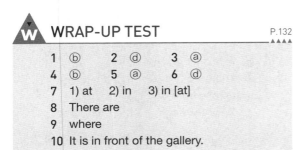

여기는 나의 방이다. 내 방에는 침대, 책상, 몇 권의 책, 그리고 커튼이 있는 큰 창문이 있다. 벽에는 시계가 있다. 책상 앞에는 의자가 있다. 책상 위에는 몇몇 권의 책이 있다. 창문을 봐라! 그것은 문 옆에 있다. 나는 내 방이 정말 좋다.

WRAP-UP TEST P.132

1 ⓑ   2 ⓓ   3 ⓐ
4 ⓑ   5 ⓐ   6 ⓓ
7 1) at   2) in   3) in [at]
8 There are
9 where
10 It is in front of the gallery.

1 멋진 그림이 벽에 걸려 있었다.
  아이들은 스쿨버스를 타고 있다.
2 성 옆에 큰 나무가 있다.
3 장난감 군인들은 상자 (뒤에 / 안에 / 위에) 있다.
4 ⓐ 너의 배낭은 탁자 아래에 있다.
  ⓑ 동물원에 캥거루가 있나요?
  ⓒ 5번가에는 도서관이 없다.
  ⓓ 은행은 서점 옆에 있다.
6 ⓐ 우리 언니들은 서울에 있다.
  ⓑ Jay는 수업 중이다.
  ⓒ 그들은 차 안에 있었다.
  ⓓ 새들이 지붕 위에 있다.
7 1) Brian은 집에 있다.
  2) 약국에 사람들이 많다.
  3) Jamie는 극장에 있다.
9-10
A 실례합니다. 도서관이 어디에 있죠?
B 그것은 미술관 앞에 있어요.

Unit 14

1 시간 전치사 1

Quick Test P.134

1 in   2 on
3 in   4 at

EXERCISE P.135

A 1 on   2 in   3 at   4 on
  5 at   6 in   7 on

B 1 at   2 on   3 on   4 in
  5 in

C 1 The movie was over at midnight.
  2 He graduated in 2014.
  3 Fred has an appointment in the morning.
  4 I will meet him at this time tomorrow.

2 시간 전치사 2

EXERCISE P.137

A 1 before   2 from
  3 during   4 around
  5 from   6 before
  7 for

B 1 at, on   2 at, on
  3 on   4 from, to, on

C 1 I was so nervous before the test.
  2 They lay on the beach for five hours.
  3 What did you do during spring break?
  4 The office is closed from Monday to Wednesday.

3 기타 전치사

Quick Test P.138

1 with   2 for
3 by   4 of
5 among

EXERCISE

▼ P.139

A 1 with 2 for
  3 between 4 by
  5 without 6 with
  7 among

B 1 about 2 among
  3 by 4 with
  5 for 6 of

C 1 I am going to pay by credit card.
  2 This picture is for Craig.
  3 I read an article about seals.
  4 The plane arrived without my luggage.

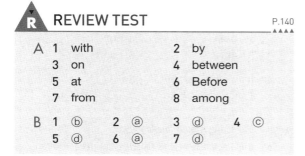

REVIEW TEST

P.140 ▲▲▲▲

A 1 with 2 by
  3 on 4 between
  5 at 6 Before
  7 from 8 among

B 1 ⓑ 2 ⓐ 3 ⓓ 4 ⓒ
  5 ⓓ 6 ⓐ 7 ⓓ

A 1 그녀는 친구와 함께 쇼핑하러 갔다.
  2 너는 비행기를 타고 로마에 갔니?
  3 우리는 보통 휴일에는 일하지 않는다.
  4 나는 9시와 11시 사이에 체육관에 갔다.
  5 6시에 내게 모닝콜을 해 줘.
  6 사고가 나기 전에 그는 술을 많이 마셨다.
  7 그 버스는 새벽 5시부터 자정까지 운행한다.
  8 그녀는 학교의 학생들 중에서 가장 뛰어나다.

B 1 그녀는 한 시간 동안 똑같은 노래를 불렀다.
  2 우리는 4시부터 9시까지 수다를 떨었다.
  3 그 연사는 그녀의 새 소설에 대해 이야기 했다.
  4 은행은 국경일에 문을 닫는다.
  5 내 친구들은 강아지와 함께 놀았다.
  6 그는 정오에 그들을 만날 것이다.
  7 그는 여름 방학 동안 그림을 많이 그렸다.

FURTHER STUDY

P.141 ▲▲▲▲

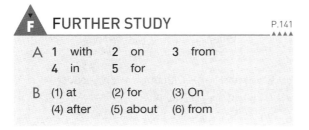

A 1 with 2 on 3 from
  4 in 5 for

B (1) at (2) for (3) On
  (4) after (5) about (6) from

A 1 A 너 혼자서 극장에 갔니?
    B 친구들과 함께 갔어.
  2 A 추수감사절에는 뭐 했어?
    B 가족들과 풍성한 저녁식사를 했어.
  3 A 유럽에는 얼마나 있었어?
    B 6월부터 8월까지 그곳에 있었어.
  4 A 나는 주로 지하 주차장에 내 차를 주차시켜.
    B 나도 그곳에 내 차를 주차하는데.
  5 A 저를 위해 멋있는 모자를 골라 주세요.
    B 이것이 너한테 잘 어울리겠네.

B

> 우리 수업은 늘 오전 9시에 시작한다. 우리는 12시에 점심을 먹는다. 우리는 한 시간 동안 점심 식사를 한다. 월요일에는 점심 식사 후에 미술 수업이 있다. 화요일에는 10시에 역사 수업이 있다. 우리는 역사 시간에 남북전쟁에 대해 공부한다. 목요일에는 1시부터 3시까지 체육수업이 있다. 우리는 이번 달에 수영을 배우고 있다. 많은 교과목 중에서 내가 가장 좋아하는 것은 영어다. 다행히 나는 매일 영어 수업을 듣는다.

WRAP-UP TEST

P.142 ▲▲▲▲

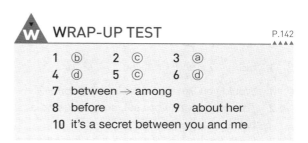

  1 ⓑ 2 ⓒ 3 ⓐ
  4 ⓓ 5 ⓒ 6 ⓓ
  7 between → among
  8 before 9 about her
  10 it's a secret between you and me

1 쇼는 7시에 시작한다.
  나는 Sue와 함께 이집트에 갔다.
  그녀는 그녀의 엄마를 위해 케이크를 만들었다.
2 그는 그 책을 다섯 시간 동안 읽었다.
3 나는 아침에 신문을 읽는다.
  그녀는 1992년에 태어났다.
  겨울에는 눈이 많이 온다.
4 ⓐ 10시쯤에 그가 당신에게 전화를 했어요.
  ⓑ 나는 어제 오전 10시부터 저녁 8시까지 잤다.
  ⓒ 그녀는 마술에 관한 이야기를 쓰고 있다.
  ⓓ 너는 거기에 버스를 타고 갔니?
5 ⓐ 그녀는 방과 후에 피아노를 연습한다.
  ⓑ 그들은 방학 동안 일본에 머물렀다.
  ⓒ 너는 백발 머리의 그 남자를 보았니?
  ⓓ 나는 마우스 없이 컴퓨터를 사용한다.
6 ⓐ 우리는 일요일에 학교에 가지 않는다.
  ⓑ 그들은 금요일 밤에 파티를 한다.
  ⓒ 그녀는 생일날에 멋진 드레스를 받았다.
  ⓓ 나는 내일 이 시간에 미팅이 있다.
7 나는 많은 색깔 중에서 빨간 모자를 샀다.
9-10
A 너 그녀에 대한 소식을 들었니?
B 아니. 뭔데?

A 그녀가 수학 시험에서 D를 받았어.
B 정말? 그거 정말 안됐다.
A 어쨌든, 그것은 너와 나만 아는 비밀이야.

Unit 15

1 and/but/or/so

Quick Test ▲P.144

1 and   2 but
3 or   4 so
5 and   6 but

EXERCISE ▲P.145

A 1 but   2 or   3 so   4 and
   5 or   6 so   7 so

B 1 but   2 and   3 so   4 or

C 1 Would you like hot coffee or iced coffee?
   2 There was nothing to eat, so we ordered a pizza.
   3 I met him before, but I couldn't remember his name.
   4 Mary can play the violin and the cello.
   5 Henry looks weak, but he is very strong.

2 기타 접속사

Quick Test ▲P.146

1 When   2 after
3 Before   4 Since [Because]
5 If

EXERCISE ▲P.147

A 1 If   2 Since
   3 When   4 before
   5 After   6 because
   7 If

B 1 When   2 Since
   3 after   4 before

C 1 I was late for school because I got up late. [Because I got up late, I was late for school.]
2 If you do your best, you can get a good result.
3 Jenny takes ballet lessons after she finishes school.
4 We had an accident since Ken drove too fast. [Since Ken drove too fast, we had an accident.]
5 I will tell him when he comes home. [When he comes home, I will tell him.]

R REVIEW TEST ▲P.148

A 1 and   2 When
   3 If   4 Since
   5 but   6 or
   7 after   8 and

B 1 ⓒ   2 ⓓ   3 ⓐ   4 ⓑ
   5 ⓒ   6 ⓑ   7 ⓓ

A 1 내가 유리컵을 떨어뜨려서 깨졌어.
2 할머니는 우리와 계실 때 재미있는 이야기를 들려주었다.
3 밖에 나가고 싶지 않으면 집에 있어도 된다.
4 그녀는 지갑을 잃어버렸기 때문에 표를 살 수가 없었다.
5 나는 쇼핑몰에 갔지만 아무것도 사지 않았다.
6 너는 생일 선물을 원하니, 아니면 용돈을 원하니?
7 나는 수업이 끝난 후에 가끔 1마일을 뛴다.
8 나는 어제 공원에서 삼촌과 숙모를 만났다.

B 1 그는 일찍 일어났지만 회사에 늦었다.
2 나는 살이 쪘을 때 다이어트를 했다.
3 그는 유성을 본 후에 우주비행사가 되기로 결심했다.
4 레모네이드를 드시겠어요? 아니면, 차를 드시겠어요?
5 그들은 표가 없어서 TV로 경기를 봤다.
6 제가 이 의자에 앉아도 될까요?
7 그녀는 초록색 드레스를 입었고 하얀 모자를 썼으며 오렌지색 스카프를 둘렀다.

F FURTHER STUDY ▲P.149

A 1 or   2 Before
   3 When   4 and
   5 but

B (1) and   (2) but   (3) because
   (4) so   (5) after

A 1 A 우리는 농구를 할 거야. 너도 할 거야, 안 할 거야?
   B 농구를 하기에는 너무 더워서 난 빠질래.
  2 A 불은 다 껐니?
   B 물론이야. 나오기 전에 모든 불을 껐어.
  3 A 그를 언제 봤습니까?
   B 제가 주차하고 있을 때 그가 거리를 뛰어가고 있었습니다.
  4 A 나는 수학 시간이 가장 좋아.
   B 내가 가장 좋아하는 과목은 과학이랑 영어야.
  5 A Kelly는 좋은 사람이라고 생각하지 않니?
   B 그렇게 생각하지 않아. 그녀에게 말을 걸었지만 그녀는
     대답하지 않았어.

B

Jim Carrey는 유명한 코미디언이자 배우다. 그는 재미있고 행복
해 보이지만 그의 삶은 그렇게 행복하지 않았다. 어렸을 때 그의
집은 가난했기 때문에 그는 공장에서 일을 해야 했다. 그가 유명
한 코미디언이 되겠다고 결심한 후에 그는 미국으로 갔다. 당시에
그는 가난했고, 그래서 그는 작은 차 안에서 살았다. 그에게는 돈
도 없었기 때문에 하루에 하나의 햄버거만 먹어야 했다. 결국 그는
1995년에 Dumb and Dumber에 출연한 후 유명해졌다.

 WRAP-UP TEST   P.150

    1 ⓒ   2 ⓑ   3 ⓐ
    4 ⓓ   5 ⓑ   6 ⓑ
    7 Because [Since]   8 but
    9 ⓒ
    10 Because [Since] I couldn't sleep

1 그녀는 아름다웠지만 불친절했다.
2 그는 열심히 공부하지 않아서 시험에 떨어졌다.
3 서둘러, 그러면 너는 기차를 탈 수 있을 거야.
  Mike와 나는 민속 음악 클럽에 가입했다.
4 ⓐ 나는 아팠기 때문에 병원에 갔다.
  ⓑ 우리는 저녁식사를 한 후에 콘서트에 갔다.
  ⓒ 너는 밖에 나가고 싶니, 아니면 집에 있고 싶니?
  ⓓ 나는 돈이 없었기 때문에 그 가방을 살 수 없었다.
    (Before → Because [Since])
5 ⓐ 너는 언제 집에 왔니?
  ⓑ 네가 일어나면, 나에게 전화를 해 줄래? (~할 때)
  ⓒ 너는 언제 잠자리에 드니?
  ⓓ 우리 언제 다시 만날까?
6 만약 네가 지금 바쁘다면, 나중에 내가 다시 전화할게.
7 그들은 버스를 놓쳐서 택시를 탔다.
  = 그들은 버스를 놓쳤기 때문에 택시를 탔다.
8 우리는 박물관에 갔다. 박물관은 닫혀 있었다.
  우리는 박물관에 갔지만 닫혀 있었다.

9-10
A 너는 그 비명소리를 들었을 때 무엇을 하고 있었니?
B 나는 잠을 잘 수 없었기 때문에 잡지를 읽고 있었어.

Unit 01

▼1 be동사의 현재형

P. 2~3

A
1 are   2 aren't   3 isn't   4 are
5 is   6 am   7 are   8 is

B
1 is not [isn't]   2 is not [isn't]
3 are not [aren't]   4 am not
5 are not [aren't]

C
1 Vincent is not [isn't] a dentist.
2 We are writers.
3 They are my grandparents.
4 He is a soldier.
5 She is a ballerina.
6 It is not a magazine.

내신 FOCUS

A 1 is   2 O   3 O
    4 am not   5 O
B 1 ⓑ   2 ⓒ
C 1 ⓐ   2 ⓓ
D 1 He is an engineer.
    2 They are not nurses.
    3 Jason is a good boy.
    4 You are not a pilot.

▼2 be동사의 과거형

P. 4~5

A
1 was   2 was   3 was
4 weren't   5 were   6 wasn't
7 were

B
1 am, was   2 is, was   3 is, was
4 are, were   5 are, were

C
1 It was not my fault.
2 They were fire fighters.
3 I was a patient.
4 We were not musicians.
5 He was a reporter.
6 She was not a dancer.

내신 FOCUS

A 1 were, are   2 was, is
    3 was, is   4 were, are
B 1 ⓒ   2 ⓓ
C 1 ⓐ   2 ⓒ
D 1 We were students last year.
    2 It was a puppy six months ago.
    3 I was not a photographer.
    4 They were good people.

▼3 be동사의 일반 의문문

P. 6~7

A
1 Is, is   2 Are, am not
3 Are, are   4 Is, isn't
5 Was, was   6 Were, weren't
7 Were, were

B
1 Are, they aren't, are
2 Is, he is
3 Are, I am
4 Is, she isn't, is

C
1 Harry and Sally are college students.
Are they college students?
Yes, they are.
No, they aren't.
2 It was my bike.
Was it your bike?
Yes, it was.
No, it wasn't.

내신 FOCUS

A 1 she isn't   2 he was
  3 they are   4 I wasn't

B 1 ⓑ   2 ⓑ

C 1 ⓒ   2 ⓓ

D 1 Is Angela tall? / No, she isn't.
  2 Are you a liar? / No, I'm not.
  3 Are they cooks? / Yes, they are.
  4 Was it true? / No, it wasn't.

▼4 be동사의 의문사 의문문

P. 8~9

A
1 Who, is, is   2 What, is, is
3 When, is, is   4 Where, were, were
5 How old, are, am   6 How, was, was
7 What time, is, is

B
1 - (c)   2 - (g)   3 - (f)   4 - (a)
5 - (d)   6 - (b)   7 - (e)

C
1 Who is that girl? / She is my cousin.
2 What's your name? / My name is Steven.
3 When is the math class? / It is at three.
4 Where is your sister? / She is in the library.
5 How was the movie? / It was exciting.

내신 FOCUS

A 1 How   2 Where   3 Who
  4 What   5 When

B 1 ⓐ   2 ⓒ

C 1 ⓐ   2 ⓓ

D 1 How old is he?
    He is 21 years old.
  2 Where is the teacher?
    She is in the teachers' room.
  3 How was the dinner?
    It was nice.
  4 When is the concert?
    It is in the afternoon.

▼1 셀 수 있는 명사

P. 10~11

A
1 A   2 A   3 An
4 An   5 A   6 A
7 A

B
1 Pandas   2 Iguanas   3 turtles
4 Sharks   5 Oranges   6 Exams

C
1 A dragonfly, Dragonflies
2 An eggplant, Eggplants
3 A donkey, Donkeys
4 A tulip, Tulips
5 A mango, Mangoes [Mangos]

내신 FOCUS

A 1 eggs   2 roses   3 men
  4 people   5 potatoes 6 toys
  7 cities   8 elephants

B 1 ⓐ   2 ⓓ

C 1 ⓑ   2 ⓒ

D 1 dogs   2 A peach
  3 Pens   4 a baby

▼2 셀 수 없는 명사

P. 12~13

A
1 Ø   2 Ø   3 Ø
4 Ø   5 A   6 Ø
7 A

B
1 China   2 bottle   3 Emma
4 Mr. Smith 5 London

C
1 Damon   2 a country
3 a piece [slice] of apple pie
4 an island 5 some coffee

A 1 Ø, a, a   2 Ø, Ø, a
   3 Ø, Ø   4 Ø, Ø

B 1 ⓒ   2 ⓑ

C 1 ⓑ   2 ⓓ

D 1 Canada   2 Jason
   3 a glass of milk

3 인칭/지시대명사

P. 14~15

A
1 This, He   2 These, They
3 This, It   4 These, They
5 That, He   6 Those, They
7 That, It

B
1 She   2 It   3 He
4 You   5 They   6 They
7 We

C
1 That   2 These   3 It
4 We   5 You

내신 FOCUS

A 1 These   2 That
   3 They   4 She

B 1 ⓓ   2 ⓓ

C 1 ⓓ   2 ⓐ

D 1 They   2 These
   3 That, He   4 This

Unit 03

1 인칭대명사의 주격과 목적격

P. 16~17

A
1 her   2 They   3 We
4 me   5 him   6 It
7 She

B
1 him   2 it   3 her
4 us   5 me

C
1 She is kind to us.
2 He listens to them every day.
3 I bought it ten years ago.
4 I don't believe him.
5 They love me.

내신 FOCUS

A 1 They   2 He
   3 her   4 They

B 1 ⓓ   2 ⓐ

C 1 ⓐ   2 ⓒ

D 1 I know them.
   2 They invited me.
   3 She doesn't like it.
   4 They are very cute.

2 인칭대명사의 소유격

P. 18~19

A
1 their   2 mine   3 her
4 Peter's   5 girls'   6 our
7 my parents'

B
1 Her   2 his   3 my
4 theirs   5 Its   6 your

C
1 his address   2 our shoes, theirs
3 her father's company   4 your key
5 Its color

내신 FOCUS

A 1 mine   2 ours   3 yours
   4 hers   5 his   6 theirs

B 1 ⓐ   2 ⓓ

C 1 ⓑ   2 ⓓ

D 1 His grandmother is 90 years old.
   2 My answer is wrong.
   3 I visited their farm last year.
   4 This is my daddy's guitar.

Unit 04

 1 일반동사의 현재형

P. 20~21

A
1 reads   2 wear   3 walks
4 fly   5 practice   6 sets
7 works

B
1 makes, make   2 goes, go
3 swims, swim   4 bites, bite
5 dances, dance

C
1 He jumps rope.
2 She misses her family.
3 We catch a cold.
4 My brother eats a hamburger.
5 My sister enjoys music class.

내신 FOCUS

A 1 has   2 studies   3 goes
   4 walks   5 pushes   6 does
   7 mixes   8 plays

B 1 ⓐ   2 ⓑ

C 1 ⓐ   2 ⓒ

D 1 He loves animals.
   2 Kids play in the sand.
   3 Sam learns English.
   4 She does her homework.

 2 의문문과 부정문

P. 22~23

A
1 don't   2 doesn't   3 Do
4 does   5 Do   6 do
7 doesn't

B
1 Does, doesn't   2 Do, do
3 Does, does   4 Does, does
5 Does, doesn't

C
1 Do they come from Brazil?
2 Ann doesn't drink Coke.
3 Do kids sing Christmas carols?
4 He doesn't tell a lie.
5 Where do you buy books?

내신 FOCUS

A 1 Does, drives   2 Do, open

B 1 ⓒ   2 ⓒ

C 1 ⓑ   2 ⓒ

D 1 Does the toy store close at five?
   2 I don't drink much water.
   3 Where does your aunt live?
   4 He doesn't write a novel.

3 일반동사의 과거형

P. 24~25

A
1 went   2 barked   3 caught
4 rides   5 moved   6 swam
7 makes

B
1 washed   2 bought   3 saw
4 brought   5 raised   6 knocked

C
1 I knew the answer.
2 He shut the door ten minutes ago.
3 My sister left home this morning.
4 He met her ten years ago.
5 They held a party last night.

내신 FOCUS

A　1　sat　　2　sang　　3　put
　　4　went　　5　helped　　6　left
　　7　slept　　8　thought

B　1　ⓒ　　2　ⓓ

C　1　ⓒ　　2　ⓓ

D　1　She studied science yesterday.
　　2　I saw a horror movie last weekend.
　　3　They met Jim this afternoon.
　　4　John had pizza and Coke last night.

4　의문문과 부정문

P. 26~27

A　1　didn't　　2　Did　　3　didn't
　　4　don't　　5　Did　　6　Did
　　7　Did

B　1　didn't, caught　　2　did, sold
　　3　didn't, taught　　4　did, won

C　1　They didn't sit on the grass.
　　2　Did you put toys into the box?
　　3　We didn't live in China then.
　　4　Did Matt order a tuna sandwich?
　　5　Did the boy break the window?

내신 FOCUS

A　1　don't, didn't
　　2　Does, Did

B　1　ⓐ　　2　ⓑ

C　1　ⓓ　　2　ⓑ

D　1　Did you study science yesterday?
　　2　They did not [didn't] go to the park last weekend.
　　3　Did she take a trip last summer?
　　4　He did not [didn't] come home two days ago.

5　일반동사의 현재진행형

P. 28~29

A　1　go, are going　　2　reads, is reading
　　3　is wearing, wears　　4　ties, is tying
　　5　have, am having

B　1　is taking　　2　bites　　3　is sleeping
　　4　has　　5　visits

C　1　Cathy is riding a horse now.
　　2　A cat is running to the kitchen.
　　3　We are watching a sad movie.
　　4　He is pushing a shopping cart.
　　5　The kids are playing hide-and-seek.

내신 FOCUS

A　1　lying　　2　sitting　　3　putting
　　4　closing　　5　telling　　6　eating
　　7　making　　8　running

B　1　ⓒ　　2　ⓑ

C　1　ⓒ　　2　ⓒ

D　1　It is snowing now.
　　2　A cat is running after a mouse.
　　3　I go to church every Sunday.
　　4　He is having a good time with her.

6　의문문과 부정문

P. 30~31

A　1　is not　　2　is　　3　Are
　　4　am not　　5　are　　6　are not
　　7　Are

B　1　A: making　　B: am, making
　　2　A: hitting　　B: isn't
　　3　A: drinking　　B: aren't, drinking
　　4　A: writing　　B: is

C　1　Is Ted listening to classical music?
　　2　They are not playing baseball.
　　3　Are you painting a fence?
　　4　Is she staying in an expensive hotel?

내신 FOCUS

A 1 are not having   2 doesn't love
   3 Are you looking   4 Do they like

B 1 ⓒ   2 ⓐ

C 1 ⓒ   2 ⓓ

D 1 What are you doing now?
   2 The boy is not sleeping.
   3 Are they waiting for me?
   4 She is not sitting on the sofa.

Unit 05

1 현재 / 과거 / 미래

P. 32~33

A
1 were   2 goes
3 will wash   4 left
5 is going to move   6 closes
7 will serve

B
1 hit   2 graduate
3 paid   4 spends
5 will [be going to] play   6 went

C
1 will [are going to] be
2 began
3 will [are going to] visit
4 covered
5 will [is going to] repair

내신 FOCUS

A 1 won, will [be going to] win
   2 drank, will [be going to] drink
   3 told, will [be going to] tell
   4 caught, will [be going to] catch
   5 kept, will [be going to] keep
   6 studied, will [be going to] study
   7 lost, will [be going to] lose
   8 met, will [be going to] meet

B 1 ⓐ   2 ⓓ

C 1 ⓒ   2 ⓑ

D 1 She lived in London two years ago.
   2 My brother works for a bank.
   3 He was happy to receive her letter.
   4 Steve will [is going to] stay in Rome next month.

2 will / be going to

P. 34~35

A
1 leave   2 not
3 will not buy   4 Will
5 Are   6 not going to

B
1 is not going to give
2 Will she pick
3 will not [won't] play
4 are going to go out
5 will take a walk

C
1 My sister is going to enter the university next year.
2 I will paint my room green.
3 We are going to take a taxi.
4 The fireworks festival will end on Friday night.

내신 FOCUS

A 1 She will not [won't] show him her vacation pictures.
     Will she show him her vacation pictures?
   2 Tom is not going to visit his uncle this weekend.
     Is Tom going to visit his uncle this weekend?

B 1 ⓑ   2 ⓐ

C 1 ⓑ   2 ⓒ

D 1 They will [are going to] arrive next weekend.
   2 He will [is going to] come home before 9.
   3 What will you [are you going to] do tomorrow?

Unit 06

1 능력을 나타내는 조동사

P. 36~37

A
1 can
2 knit
3 paly
4 Were
5 finish
6 will be able to
7 was not

B
1 could not sleep
2 is not able to use
3 is not able to talk
4 was able to book
5 will be able to fix
6 able to win
7 be able to go

C
1 I could not meet my aunt last night.
2 He can save twenty dollars every week.
3 Terry will be able to pass the driving test.
4 Kevin was not able to use chopsticks.

내신 FOCUS

A 1 find   2 make
    3 be able to   4 not

B 1 ©   2 ⓓ

C 1 ©   2 ⓐ

D 1 He will be able to win the contest next year.
   2 Can you [Are you able to] ride a bike with one hand?
   3 I could not [was not able to] send the file yesterday.

2 허가를 나타내는 조동사

P. 38~39

A
1 May   2 hold   3 Can   4 turn
5 May   6 Can   7 move

B
1 use   2 tell   3 leave
4 make   5 borrow   6 pick

C
1 You cannot [can't] bring your pet in the building.
2 Can I ride a bike in this park?
3 Can [Could / Would] you fill out this form?
4 Could [Would] you take me home, please?
5 Can you bring me a drink?

내신 FOCUS

A 1 Can [Could / Will / Would]
   2 Can [Could / May]
   3 Can [Could / Will / Would]
   4 Can [Could / May]

B 1 ©   2 ⓓ

C 1 ⓓ   2 ⓑ

D 1 Can [Could / May] I have a cup of coffee?
   2 Can [Could / Will / Would] you call a taxi?
   3 Can [Could / May] I take a picture with you?
   4 Can [Could / Will / Would] you wait for a moment?

3 의무를 나타내는 조동사

P. 40~41

A
1 keep   2 have to
3 not take   4 Should I
5 Do we have to   6 park

B
1 I must not go
2 Do you have to have a passport
3 He had to cancel
4 They will have to read

C
1 You should pay attention in class.
2 There must be something wrong.
3 She doesn't have to worry about her son.
4 He had to stay home last weekend.
5 She must be very happy.

내신 FOCUS

A 1 You must not stay at home.
    Do you have to stay at home?
   2 We should not bring our lunch.
    Should we bring our lunch?

B 1 ⓒ   2 ⓑ
C 1 ⓑ   2 ⓐ
D 1 I must [should / have to] study hard to pass the test.
  2 You should [must] not be late for class.
  3 Must they [Do they have to] wear school uniforms?
  4 He must be tired.

Unit 07

 형용사의 의미와 쓰임

P. 42~43

A
1 tall, a tall
2 pretty, a pretty
3 big, big
4 talkative, a talkative
5 interesting, an interesting
6 nice, nice
7 delicious, delicious

B
1 safe   2 new   3 weak
4 exciting   5 easy

C
1 He is an honest man.
2 It is a sweet apple.
3 She is a lazy worker.
4 Cheetahs are fast animals.
5 They are rich people.

내신 FOCUS

A 1 Something warm
  2 was hot
  3 a good tennis player
  4 a romantic city
B 1 ⓐ   2 ⓑ
C 1 ⓓ   2 ⓑ
D 1 My hair is long.
  2 A watermelon is a round fruit.

3 This is something fun.
4 Polar bears are not small animals.

2 여러 가지 형용사

P. 44~45

A
1 This   2 Those   3 These
4 river   5 trees   6 picture

B
1 are a lot of cookies
2 is not any milk
3 is little juice
4 are a few students

C
1 There is a little money in my piggy bank.
2 This is a wild flower.
3 These cars are expensive.
4 There are many bananas in the basket.
5 This game is exciting.

내신 FOCUS

A 1 This   2 book   3 little
  4 any   5 These   6 watches
  7 many [lots of / a lot of]   8 a few
B 1 ⓓ   2 ⓒ
C 1 ⓑ   2 ⓓ
D 1 This movie is scary.
  2 These rings are expensive.
  3 There are a few [some] birds in the cage.
  4 How much milk is there in the bottle?

Unit 08

1 부사의 의미와 쓰임

P. 46~47

A
1 so 2 soon 3 very 4 too
5 quite 6 too 7 really

B
1 well 2 Sadly 3 kindly
4 quietly 5 Luckily 6 brightly

C
1 The movie is very boring.
2 She drives her car fast.
3 The boy is very tall.
4 I don't know them well.

내신 FOCUS

A 1 very, well 2 really, slowly
3 quite 4 too

B 1 © 2 ⓐ

C 1 © 2 ⓐ

D 1 I study English hard.
2 He speaks loudly.
3 They went to sleep early last night.
4 The weather was really cold.

2 부사의 형태

P. 48~49

A
1 carefully 2 wisely 3 really
4 easily 5 Strangely 6 beautifully
7 badly

B
1 clearly 2 softly 3 strongly
4 heavily 5 hard 6 kindly

C
1 She walks slowly.
2 Surprisingly, he didn't come to the party.
3 The repairman repaired my bike easily.
4 They sang a song loudly [loud].
5 I came back home late.

내신 FOCUS

A 1 well 2 fast 3 gently
4 nicely 5 badly 6 luckily
7 really 8 easily

B 1 ⓐ 2 ©

C 1 ⓑ 2 ⓑ

D 1 They lived happily.
2 I make money easily.
3 The train left early.
4 He played the music loudly [loud].

3 빈도부사

P. 50~51

A
1 is always 2 usually walk
3 three times 4 often
5 sometimes makes 6 How

B
1 always 2 sometimes
3 never 4 often
5 usually

C
1 They usually eat out on weekends.
2 How often do you go to a French restaurant?
3 He is never angry at me.
4 I am sometimes busy.
5 Jenny always has a cup of coffee in the morning.

내신 FOCUS

A 1 She sometimes goes hiking.
2 He is never tired.
3 They are always friendly.
4 Susan often has a party.

B 1 ⓑ 2 ⓐ

C 1 ⓐ 2 ©

D 1 How often do you meet him?
2 They usually have lunch in the cafeteria.
3 I walk my dog three times a week.
4 He is always happy.

Unit 09

1 비교/최상급의 의미와 형태

P. 52~53

A
1 better   2 taller   3 kindest
4 cheapest   5 thinner   6 biggest
7 heavier

B
1 more tired   2 cleverer   3 better
4 best   5 funnier   6 more
7 fastest

C
1 The Vatican is the smallest country in the world.
2 Your health is more important than money.
3 She has the sweetest voice in the choir.
4 The weather is sunnier than yesterday.

내신 FOCUS

A 1 cuter, cutest   2 louder, loudest
   3 busier, busiest   4 more, most
   5 worse, worst   6 older, oldest
   7 stronger, strongest   8 fewer, fewest
   9 shorter, shortest
   10 more famous, most famous
   11 better, best   12 prettier, prettiest

B 1 ⓒ   2 ⓑ

C 1 ⓓ   2 ⓑ

D 1 My gift is more costly than his.
   2 My room is the biggest in the house.
   3 The weather is worse than yesterday.
   4 This building is the tallest in our city.

2 비교 표현

P. 54~55

A
1 a lot   2 much money
3 not as   4 highest
5 more   6 handsome
7 much

B
1 faster   2 worse
3 as beautiful as   4 as expensive as

C
1 An e-mail is much faster than postal mail.
2 Picasso is one of the most famous painters.
3 The Antarctic is colder than any other place on earth.
4 Your hands are as dirty as mine.

내신 FOCUS

A 1 more handsome, as handsome as
   2 lighter, heavier

B 1 ⓓ   2 ⓐ

C 1 ⓐ   2 ⓑ

D 1 You are a lot smarter than she.
   2 Kelly doesn't like movies as much as Tom.
   3 Jim is one of the tallest boys in my class.

Unit 10

1 목적어를 가지는 동사

P. 56~57

A
1 x   2 o
3 x   4 o
5 x

B
1 brought good news to me
2 made a nice bed for me
3 asked a difficult question of me
4 got two movie tickets for my parents
5 told her secrets to me

C
1 He sent roses to his wife.
2 Jenny often writes a letter to her grandmother.
3 Mark was standing under the tree.
4 They are planning their spring break trip.
5 Jim bought her a diamond ring.

A 1 Jenny
  2 him, a birthday gift
  3 two apple trees
  4 dinner
B 1 ⓒ   2 ⓑ
C 1 ⓐ   2 ⓒ
D 1 The history class starts at 11 in the morning.
  2 He sent her a package last month.
  3 I saw frogs in the pond.
  4 The student wrote a letter to his teacher.

 2 보어를 가지는 동사

P. 58~59

A
1 very difficult   2 great
3 her cat Fluffy   4 popular
5 me laugh   6 sick   7 red

B
1 keep the door open
2 looks very healthy
3 found her class interesting
4 feel sorry
5 makes me angry
6 seems very friendly
7 look nice

C
1 He believes his girlfriend is pretty.
2 He became a great doctor.
3 They feel very hungry.
4 She made her son a pianist.

A 1 comfortable   2 open
  3 Piglet   4 sad
B 1 ⓐ   2 ⓑ
C 1 ⓒ   2 ⓐ
D 1 People call him a genius.
  2 The cake seems very sweet.
  3 We chose him as our leader.
  4 They were very happy.

Unit 11

1 명령문

P. 60~61

A
1 Be   2 Don't   3 or   4 and
5 have   6 Do   7 not

B
1 go   2 turn   3 raise   4 be
5 Take   6 open

C
1 Let's study English grammar.
2 Don't forget to call me.
3 Let's not drink Coke.
4 Turn right, and you will see the bank.
5 Please be quiet. [Be quiet, please.]

A 1 Drink lots of water.
  2 Don't make a noise.
  3 Let's make plans for the next month.
  4 Let's not go to a Japanese restaurant.
  5 Be nice to your friends.
B 1 ⓑ   2 ⓐ
C 1 ⓓ   2 ⓓ
D 1 Answer the question, please. [Please answer
     the question.]
  2 Let's take a break.
  3 Be careful!
  4 Take the pill, and you will feel better.

2 감탄문

P. 62~63

A
1 What   2 How   3 talkative
4 a small fish 5 flowers   6 exciting
7 pretty

B
1 expensive   2 boring   3 tall   4 kind

C

1 terrible the accident was
2 a sweet dream it was
3 beautiful eyes she has
4 fast my computer is

내신 FOCUS

A 1 What 2 What 3 How
 4 What 5 How 6 How
 7 What 8 How

B 1 ⓒ 2 ⓐ

C 1 ⓓ 2 ⓒ

D 1 What a nice sister you have!
 2 What sad news it is!
 3 What a funny story it is!
 4 How beautiful she is!

▼3 부가/선택의문문

P. 64~65

A

1 could they 2 will she 3 aren't we
4 does she 5 Which 6 weren't you
7 Who

B

1 Which 2 Who 3 Did
4 Is 5 Where

C

1 You can find a way home, can't you?
2 He didn't catch a cold, did he?
3 Billy couldn't get an A on the test, could he?
4 The copy machine is out of order, isn't it?

내신 FOCUS

A 1 can't you
 2 won't they
 3 doesn't he
 4 Which

B 1 ⓒ 2 ⓒ

C 1 ⓑ 2 ⓑ

D 1 Which flies faster, a butterfly or a bee?
 2 You ordered a tuna sandwich, didn't you?
 3 Damon cannot ride a bike, can he?
 4 Susan will come to the party, won't she?

Unit 12

▼1 명사적 쓰임

P. 66~67

A

1 to believe 2 to collect
3 to have 4 waiting
5 reading 6 to go

B

1 being a pop singer
2 to study French last year
3 to read cartoons
4 To get up early

C

1 They like taking a walk.
2 She gave up keeping a diary every day.
3 My dream is traveling to space.
4 He wants to meet you.
5 Her favorite activity is to play basketball.

내신 FOCUS

A 1 lying [to lie]
 2 spending
 3 buying [to buy]
 4 to put

B 1 ⓒ 2 ⓑ

C 1 ⓓ 2 ⓑ

D 1 I like seeing [to see] movies.
 2 She finished writing an essay.
 3 Reading [To read] the Harry Potter books is
  exciting.
 4 Do you want to be a movie star?

▼2 형용사적/부사적 쓰임

P. 68~69

A

1 to be 2 to meet 3 in order to
4 to eat 5 to play 6 to have
7 to do

B

1 see 2 stay 3 study
4 give 5 change 6 help

C
1 I am sorry to disturb you.
2 We have a test to take on Thursday.
3 I came here to join this club.
4 It is time to go home.

내신 FOCUS

A 1 이야기할
  2 빌리기 위해서
  3 그것을 들으니
  4 세탁할

B 1 ⓐ   2 ⓒ

C 1 ⓒ   2 ⓓ

D 1 I need something to drink.
  2 He was surprised to hear the news.
  3 She went to the bakery to buy some bread.
  4 It's time to say good-bye.

Unit 13

 1 장소 전치사 1

P. 70~71

A
1 under   2 in front of
3 beside   4 between

B
1 in   2 under   3 in front of
4 between   5 behind

C
1 My car key is in the drawer.
2 The station is across from the post office.
3 Your jacket was on the sofa.
4 The ice cream shop is next to the toy store.

내신 FOCUS

A 1 next to [by / beside]   2 on
  3 behind   4 between
  5 across from   6 under
  7 in front of   8 in

B 1 ⓒ   2 ⓐ

C 1 ⓓ   2 ⓑ

D 1 The dental clinic is next to [by / beside] the bank.
  2 My cat is under the desk.
  3 Is the bookstore across from the library?
  4 My bag is behind the chair.

2 장소 전치사 2

P. 72~73

A
1 on   2 in   3 on
4 at   5 in   6 at

B
1 on the roof   2 in the aquarium
3 on the flight   4 in the parking lot

C
1 They are at the meeting.
2 My brother is in the army.
3 Tim and Joy are on the street.
4 Your dog is at the door.
5 We are on the train.

내신 FOCUS

A 1 at   2 on   3 in
  4 in   5 at   6 on

B 1 ⓑ   2 ⓒ

C 1 ⓒ   2 ⓓ

D 1 She is in my car.
  2 He is on the stage.
  3 They are at the bus stop.
  4 We are on the school bus.

3 There is/are

P. 74~75

A
1 There   2 was   3 Is there
4 are not   5 is   6 There is

B
1 There are not [aren't] books on the desk.

2 Is there a toilet in the store?

3 There was not [wasn't] a restaurant on the 5th Street 10 years ago.

4 Were there frogs in the pond?

5 There are not [aren't] spoons on the table.

C

1 There is not a TV in my house.

2 There are two boys under the tree.

3 Is there a park across from the museum?

4 There is a cinema between the mall and the bank.

내신 FOCUS

A 1 Is there a ball in the basket?

   2 There are not [aren't] students in the class.

B 1 ⓑ   2 ⓐ

C 1 ⓑ   2 ⓓ

D 1 There is a car in front of the house.

   2 Is there a soccer ball on the floor?

   3 There were gift boxes on the table.

   4 There is a post office next to the store.

Unit 14

1 시간 전치사 1

P. 76~77

A

1 in   2 on   3 in

4 at   5 on   6 At

7 in

B

1 in   2 at

3 in   4 on

C

1 I don't have any class on Fridays.

2 Valentine's Day is in February.

3 What did you have at lunchtime?

4 We eat a turkey on Thanksgiving Day.

내신 FOCUS

A 1 in   2 at   3 on

B 1 ⓓ   2 ⓐ

C 1 ⓐ   2 ⓑ

D 1 He always goes skiing in winter.

   2 We have a party on Christmas Eve.

   3 Where did you go at lunchtime?

   4 She always has a cup of tea in the afternoon.

2 시간 전치사 2

P. 78~79

A

1 from   2 Before   3 for

4 after   5 during   6 around

7 to

B

1 after   2 for   3 during

4 from   5 around   6 before

C

1 He was not in his office from four to six.

2 The concert was over around five.

3 My father washed the dishes after dinner.

4 I mowed the lawn for two hours yesterday.

내신 FOCUS

A 1 after   2 for   3 before

   4 during   5 around   6 from, to

B 1 ⓒ   2 ⓑ

C 1 ⓓ   2 ⓓ

D 1 We went to the movies after school.

   2 She has classes from two to seven.

   3 We do our homework before dinner.

   4 He swam for one hour.

3 기타 전치사

P. 80~81

A

1 with   2 about   3 for

4 by   5 between   6 without

7 of

B
1 for   2 about   3 by
4 of   5 with   6 among

C
1 The movie is about Napoleon.
2 We had a break between two tests.
3 I moved my bed without any help.
4 She often goes to school by bike.
5 George built a house for his parents.

내신 FOCUS

A 1 with   2 between   3 about
  4 for   5 among   6 without

B 1 ⓑ   2 ⓒ

C 1 ⓒ   2 ⓒ

D 1 I bought a Christmas gift for my wife.
  2 She always talks about her new boyfriend.
  3 There is a problem with his computer.

Unit 15

 and/but/or/so

P. 82~83

A
1 and   2 so   3 and
4 or   5 so   6 but
7 or

B
1 or   2 and
3 so   4 but

C
1 Would you like to have some apple pie or cherry pie?
2 My grandfather is old but healthy.
3 They practiced hard, so they won the football game.
4 My sister and my brother enjoy singing.
5 I hurried to go to the airport, but I missed my flight.

내신 FOCUS

A 1 and   2 or
  3 so   4 but

B 1 ⓑ   2 ⓒ

C 1 ⓒ   2 ⓒ

D 1 He was tired, so he went to bed early.
  2 Let's buy ice cream or pudding for dessert.
  3 I went swimming yesterday, but my sister didn't go.
  4 She ordered a hamburger and orange juice.

▼2 기타 접속사

P. 84~85

A
1 When   2 Since   3 because
4 before   5 If   6 After
7 If

B
1 After   2 When   3 If
4 because   5 before

C
1 before we arrived
2 because it was slippery
3 If we walk to school
4 when I was waiting
5 Since he has a bad cold

내신 FOCUS

A 1 날씨가 추울 때
  2 4년의 대학 생활 후
  3 내가 만약 표를 구하면
  4 길을 건너기 전에
  5 나는 점심을 먹지 않았기 때문에

B 1 ⓒ   2 ⓑ

C 1 ⓓ   2 ⓒ

D 1 when I get home
  2 so I opened the window
  3 After she finished her homework
  4 If the weather is nice

Memo

The Grammar

Starter

Concise & Core Grammar
불필요하고 잘 사용하지 않는 문법은 배제하고 핵심적인 부분만을 간결하고 정확하게 예문 중심으로 이해할 수 있도록 구성

Sentence Expansion
기초 문법을 기반으로 문장을 완성, 확장해 가는 학습 방법 적용

A Variety of Question Types
문법 포인트 확인 · 기초 문법 문제 · 응용 문제 · 리뷰 테스트 · 문법 확장 문제 · 종합 문제

Preparation for School Tests
다양한 문제 유형을 통해 내신 대비는 물론 말하기 및 쓰기 실력 향상

Grammar Summary
배운 학습 내용을 차트 및 표로 정리하여 쉽게 암기할 수 있도록 구성

Workbook
내신 대비 및 서술형 평가 대비를 위한 충분한 분량의 문제가 수록된 워크북 제공

www.nexusEDU.kr
넥서스 초 · 중 · 고등 사이트

www.nexusbook.com
넥서스 홈페이지

The Grammar

Nexus Contents Development Team

Starter

Workbook

NEXUS Edu

The Grammar

Nexus Contents Development Team

Starter

Workbook

NEXUS Edu

Unit 01

1 be동사의 현재형

A 다음 중 가장 알맞은 것을 고르시오.

1 They am / are / is good actresses.

2 You amn't / aren't / isn't a mailman.

3 He amn't / aren't / isn't a taxi driver.

4 You am / are / is a banker.

5 She am / are / is a mother.

6 I am / are / is a carpenter.

7 We am / are / is fortune-tellers.

8 It am / are / is a butterfly.

B 다음 주어진 단어를 이용하여 문장을 완성하시오.

1 She _____ (is, not) a student. She's a math teacher.

2 A penguin _____ (is, not) a fish. It is a bird.

3 Roses and lilies _____ (are, not) vegetables. They're flowers.

4 I _____ (am, not) a gardener. I'm a baker.

5 Mark and I _____ (are, not) bad. We are kind.

C 다음 주어진 단어를 이용하여 문장을 완성하시오.

1 Vincent는 치과의사가 아니다. (Vincent, a dentist)

→ _____

2 우리는 작가이다. (we, writers)

→ _____

3 그들은 나의 조부모님이다. (they, my grandparents)

→ _____

4 그는 군인이다. (he, a soldier)

→ _____

5 그녀는 발레리나이다. (she, a ballerina)

→ _____

6 그것은 잡지가 아니다. (it, a magazine)

→ _____

A 다음 밑줄 친 부분이 어법상 옳으면 ○, 틀리면 바르게 고쳐 쓰시오.

1 She <u>am</u> a pretty ballerina. _____

2 They're <u>mailmen</u>. _____

3 He <u>isn't</u> old. _____

4 I <u>amn't</u> a bad boy. _____

5 It <u>is not</u> a bird. _____

B 다음 빈칸에 알맞은 말을 고르시오.

1 It _____ my textbook.

ⓐ are   ⓑ is   ⓒ am   ⓓ not is

2 They _____ her grandparents.

ⓐ am not   ⓑ is   ⓒ are   ⓓ am

C 다음 중 어법상 옳지 않은 문장을 고르시오.

1 ⓐ She and I am students.
   ⓑ My puppies are very cute.
   ⓒ We're hungry.
   ⓓ He is not a nice boy.

2 ⓐ She's my teacher.
   ⓑ They are his bags.
   ⓒ My books aren't easy.
   ⓓ You is very polite.

D 다음 주어진 단어를 이용하여 문장을 완성하시오.

1 그는 엔지니어이다. (he, an engineer)
   → _____

2 그들은 간호사가 아니다. (they, nurses)
   → _____

3 Jason은 착한 소년이다. (Jason, a good boy)
   → _____

4 너는 비행사가 아니다. (you, a pilot)
   → _____

2 be동사의 과거형

A 다음 중 가장 알맞은 것을 고르시오.

1 I was / were a little boy then.

2 He was / were a good boy before.

3 Rome was / were a kingdom at that time.

4 You wasn't / weren't my classmate last year.

5 They was / were small last time.

6 It wasn't / weren't sunny yesterday.

7 We was / were short two years ago.

B 다음 빈칸에 알맞은 말을 넣어 문장을 완성하시오.

1 I _____ 15 years old this year.　　I _____ 14 years old last year.

2 He _____ a baseball player now.　　He _____ a basketball player before.

3 Mr. Johnson _____ rich now.　　Mr. Johnson _____ not rich then.

4 They _____ popular now.　　They _____ not popular two years ago.

5 You _____ tall now.　　You _____ short last year.

C 다음 주어진 단어를 이용하여 문장을 완성하시오.

1 그것은 내 잘못이 아니었다. (it, my fault)

　　→ _____

2 그들은 소방관이었다. (they, fire fighters)

　　→ _____

3 나는 환자였다. (I, a patient)

　　→ _____

4 우리는 음악가가 아니었다. (we, musicians)

　　→ _____

5 그는 기자였다. (he, a reporter)

　　→ _____

6 그녀는 무용수가 아니었다. (she, a dancer)

　　→ _____

A 다음 빈칸에 알맞은 be동사를 쓰시오.

1 My shoes ＿＿＿＿＿＿ new last month.   They ＿＿＿＿＿＿ old now.

2 He ＿＿＿＿＿＿ a baker 5 years ago.   He ＿＿＿＿＿＿ a cook now.

3 The coffee ＿＿＿＿＿＿ hot an hour ago.   It ＿＿＿＿＿＿ cold now.

4 We ＿＿＿＿＿＿ actors before.   We ＿＿＿＿＿＿ movie directors now.

B 다음 빈칸에 알맞은 말을 고르시오.

1 She ＿＿＿＿＿＿ a good student now.

ⓐ were not   ⓑ was not   ⓒ is   ⓓ are

2 They ＿＿＿＿＿＿ angry yesterday.

ⓐ is not   ⓑ are   ⓒ wasn't   ⓓ weren't

C 다음 중 어법상 옳지 않은 문장을 고르시오.

1 ⓐ You are a little boy five years ago.
  ⓑ It was very windy last night.
  ⓒ He is not my best friend now.
  ⓓ They weren't at home yesterday.

2 ⓐ She was very sick last night.
  ⓑ They aren't friendly today.
  ⓒ It weren't cold yesterday.
  ⓓ I was not his teacher last year.

D 다음 주어진 단어를 이용하여 문장을 완성하시오.

1 우리는 작년에 학생이었다. (we, students, last year)
  → ＿＿＿＿＿＿＿＿＿＿＿＿＿＿＿＿＿＿＿＿＿＿＿＿

2 그것은 여섯 달 전에는 강아지였다. (it, a puppy, six months ago)
  → ＿＿＿＿＿＿＿＿＿＿＿＿＿＿＿＿＿＿＿＿＿＿＿＿

3 나는 사진 작가가 아니었다. (I, a photographer)
  → ＿＿＿＿＿＿＿＿＿＿＿＿＿＿＿＿＿＿＿＿＿＿＿＿

4 그들은 좋은 사람들이었다. (they, good people)
  → ＿＿＿＿＿＿＿＿＿＿＿＿＿＿＿＿＿＿＿＿＿＿＿＿

3 be동사의 일반 의문문

A 다음 중 가장 알맞은 것을 고르시오.

1 Am / Are / Is he a golfer?   Yes, he am / are / is .

2 Am / Are / Is you a teacher?   No, I am not / are not .

3 Am / Are / Is they home?   Yes, they am / are / is .

4 Am / Are / Is it your car?   No, it aren't / isn't .

5 Was / Were she fat?   Yes, she was / were .

6 Was / Were they strangers?   No, they wasn't / weren't .

7 Was / Were Jason and Peter on the bus?   Yes, they was / were .

B 다음 주어진 문장을 참고하여 문장을 완성하시오.

> 1. Jim and John are bankers.   2. He is a fisherman.
> 3. You are a swimmer.   4. Susan is a painter.

1 A: _____ Jim and John painters?   B: No, _____. They _____ bankers.

2 A: _____ he a fisherman?   B: Yes, _____.

3 A: _____ you a swimmer?   B: Yes, _____.

4 A: _____ Susan a dancer?   B: No, _____. She _____ a painter.

C 다음 주어진 단어를 이용하여 문장을 완성하시오.

1 Harry와 Sally는 대학생입니다. (Harry and Sally, college students)

→ _____

그들은 대학생입니까?   → _____

네, 그렇습니다.   → _____

아니오, 그렇지 않습니다.   → _____

2 그것은 내 자전거였습니다. (it, my bike)

→ _____

그것은 당신의 자전거였습니까?   → _____

네, 그랬었습니다.   → _____

아니오, 그렇지 않았습니다.   → _____

6

A 다음 빈칸에 알맞은 말을 쓰시오.

1 Is Tina your math teacher?   No, _____.

2 Was John your English teacher?   Yes, _____.

3 Are they new jeans?   Yes, _____.

4 Were you a good runner?   No, _____.

B 다음 빈칸에 알맞은 말을 고르시오.

1 A: Were you a good student last year?   B: No, I _____.

   ⓐ am not   ⓑ was not   ⓒ were not   ⓓ not was

2 A: Are they happy today?   B: Yes, they _____.

   ⓐ is   ⓑ are   ⓒ am   ⓓ were

C 다음 중 어법상 옳지 <u>않은</u> 문장을 고르시오.

1 ⓐ Is she a secretary?
   ⓑ Were you at home last weekend?
   ⓒ Is your dog is a bulldog?
   ⓓ Are those your shoes?

2 ⓐ Is it her book bag?
   ⓑ Are Bill and Sarah friends?
   ⓒ Was his house big?
   ⓓ Were designers they?

D 다음 주어진 단어를 이용하여 문장을 완성하시오.

1 A: Angela는 키가 크니? (Angela, tall)   → _____
   B: 아니, 그렇지 않아.   → _____

2 A: 너는 거짓말쟁이니? (you, a liar)   → _____
   B: 아니야, 그렇지 않아.   → _____

3 A: 그들은 요리사니? (they, cooks)   → _____
   B: 응, 그래.   → _____

4 A: 그것이 사실이었니? (it, true)   → _____
   B: 아니, 그렇지 않았어.   → _____

Unit 01

4 be동사의 의문사 의문문

A 다음 중 가장 알맞은 것을 고르시오.

1 Who / What | is / are | she? She | is / are | my daughter.

2 What / Who | is / are | this? It | is / are | an apple pie.

3 What / When | is / are | the movie? It | is / are | at 7 o'clock.

4 Who / Where | was / were | my gloves? They | was / were | in your closet.

5 How / How old | is / are | you? I | am / are | 14 years old.

6 How / What | was / were | she? She | was / were | fine.

7 What / What time | is / are | it now? It | is / are | 10:30.

B 다음 질문에 알맞은 답변을 찾아 연결하시오.

1 How tall is your brother? • (a) My birthday is July 7th.

2 What is this? • (b) She is in the garden.

3 What day is today? • (c) He is 5 feet tall.

4 When is your birthday? • (d) He is Johnny Depp.

5 Who is he? • (e) He is great.

6 Where is Mom? • (f) It is Sunday.

7 How is your grandfather? • (g) It is my cell phone.

C 다음 주어진 단어를 이용하여 문장을 완성하시오.

1 A: 저 소녀는 누구입니까? (that girl) → _____

   B: 그녀는 내 사촌입니다. (she, my cousin) → _____

2 A: 당신의 이름은 무엇입니까? (your name) → _____

   B: 내 이름은 Steven입니다. (my name, Steven) → _____

3 A: 수학 시간은 언제입니까? (the math class) → _____

   B: 3시입니다. (it, at three) → _____

4 A: 당신의 여동생은 어디에 있습니까? (your sister) → _____

   B: 그녀는 지금 도서관에 있습니다. (she, in the library) → _____

5 A: 영화는 어땠습니까? (the movie) → _____

   B: 그것은 재미있었습니다. (it, exciting) → _____

A 다음 대답을 보고 빈칸에 알맞은 의문사를 고르시오.

1 A: What / How is he? B: He is fine.

2 A: Where / Who are you? B: I'm in the bathroom.

3 A: Who / What are they? B: They are movie stars.

4 A: What / How is it? B: It is my pet.

5 A: When / What is the party? B: The party is at 9:00.

B 다음 빈칸에 알맞은 말을 고르시오.

1 What are _____?

ⓐ these ⓑ it ⓒ she ⓓ he

2 What is _____?

ⓐ I ⓑ they ⓒ it ⓓ we

C 다음 중 어법상 옳지 않은 문장을 고르시오.

1 ⓐ Who is his name?
   ⓑ Where is my wallet?
   ⓒ When is the show?
   ⓓ How are you?

2 ⓐ A: Who is that boy? B: He is my brother.
   ⓑ A: Where were you last night? B: I was in the library.
   ⓒ A: What are these? B: These are pencils.
   ⓓ A: How are they? B: They are 10 years old.

D 다음 주어진 단어를 이용하여 문장을 완성하시오.

1 A: 그는 몇 살입니까? (he, old) → _____

   B: 21살입니다. (he, 21 years old) → _____

2 A: 선생님께서는 어디에 계십니까? (the teacher) → _____

   B: 교무실에 계십니다. (she, in the teachers' room) → _____

3 A: 저녁식사는 어떠셨습니까? (the dinner) → _____

   B: 좋았습니다. (it, nice) → _____

4 A: 콘서트는 언제입니까? (the concert) → _____

   B: 오후에 있습니다. (it, in the afternoon) → _____

셀 수 있는 명사

A 다음 중 가장 알맞은 것을 고르시오.

1 A / An parrot is a bird.

2 A / An lily is a flower.

3 A / An elephant is an animal.

4 A / An onion is a vegetable.

5 A / An pine is a tree.

6 A / An spider is an insect.

7 A / An pear is a fruit.

B 다음 주어진 조건에 맞도록 빈칸에 알맞은 말을 넣어 문장을 완성하시오.

1 A panda is cute.   (복수) → _____ are cute.

2 An iguana is a lizard.   (복수) → _____ are lizards.

3 My pet is a turtle.   (복수) → My pets are _____ .

4 A shark is scary.   (복수) → _____ are scary.

5 An orange is my favorite.   (복수) → _____ are my favorites.

6 An exam is in March.   (복수) → _____ are in March.

C 다음 주어진 단어를 이용하여 지시문에 맞게 문장을 완성하시오.

1 dragonfly

(단수) → _____ is an insect.   (복수) → _____ are insects.

2 eggplant

(단수) → _____ is good for health.   (복수) → _____ are good for health.

3 donkey

(단수) → _____ is a diligent animal. (복수) → _____ are diligent animals.

4 tulip

(단수) → _____ is my favorite.   (복수) → _____ are my favorites.

5 mango

(단수) → _____ is sweet.   (복수) → _____ are sweet.

A 다음 명사의 복수형을 쓰시오.

1 an egg → _____   5 a potato → _____

2 a rose → _____   6 a toy → _____

3 a man → _____   7 a city → _____

4 a person → _____   8 an elephant → _____

B 다음 빈칸에 알맞은 말을 고르시오.

1 _____ are my favorite snacks.

ⓐ Candies   ⓑ A candy   ⓒ Candyes   ⓓ An candy

2 _____ are busy on Sundays.

ⓐ An church   ⓑ Churchs   ⓒ A church   ⓓ Churches

C 다음 중 어법상 옳지 <u>않은</u> 문장을 고르시오.

1 ⓐ Penguins are birds.
  ⓑ A puppies is very cute.
  ⓒ Eggs are good for health.
  ⓓ An umbrella is a useful thing.

2 ⓐ Tigers are cats.
  ⓑ A boat is in the sea.
  ⓒ An apple is an fruit.
  ⓓ Plates and cups are dishes.

D 다음 지시문에 맞게 문장을 완성하시오.

1 My pet is a dog.   (복수) → My pets are _____.

2 Peaches are sweet fruits. (단수) → _____ is a sweet fruit.

3 A pen is useful.   (복수) → _____ are useful.

4 My sisters are babies.   (단수) → My sister is _____.

2 셀 수 없는 명사

A 다음 중 가장 알맞은 것을 고르시오.

1 A / An / Ø French is an interesting language.

2 A / An / Ø Alex is an astronaut.

3 A / An / Ø Hope is a good thing.

4 A / An / Ø Greece is a beautiful country.

5 A / An / Ø cup of coffee is here.

6 A / An / Ø Africa is a big continent.

7 A / An / Ø slice of pizza is my favorite snack.

B 다음 빈칸에 알맞은 말을 골라 문장을 완성하시오.

Word Bank	China	Emma	London	bottle	Mr. Smith

1 _____ is a country in Asia.

2 Here is a _____ of Coke.

3 My aunt's name is _____.

4 _____ is kind.

5 _____ is a big city.

C 다음 주어진 단어를 이용하여 문장을 완성하시오.

1 Damon은 용감한 소년이다. (Damon)

_____ is a brave boy.

2 필리핀은 나라의 이름이다. (country)

The Philippines is the name of _____.

3 내가 가장 좋아하는 디저트는 한 조각의 사과 파이이다. (apple pie)

My favorite dessert is _____.

4 하와이는 섬이다. (island)

Hawaii is _____.

5 커피를 조금 마실 수 있을까요? (coffee)

Can I get _____, please?

A 다음 빈칸에 알맞은 an, a, Ø를 쓰시오.

1 _____ Tom is _____ movie star. He is _____ man.

2 _____ Bali is a city. _____ Indonesia is _____ country.

3 _____ Sugar is sweet, and _____ salt is salty.

4 _____ Life is short. _____ Happiness is in us.

B 다음 빈칸에 알맞은 말을 고르시오.

1 _____ is my teacher.

   ⓐ A Mark   ⓑ mark   ⓒ Mark   ⓓ An Mark

2 _____ is my favorite.

   ⓐ An glass of juice   ⓑ A glass of juice   ⓒ Glasses of juice   ⓓ Glass of juice

C 다음 중 어법상 옳지 <u>않은</u> 문장을 고르시오.

1 ⓐ London is a city in the U.K.
   ⓑ Two milks are on the table.
   ⓒ Japanese is easy.
   ⓓ Water is essential.

2 ⓐ A piece of pie is on a plate.
   ⓑ A slice of cheese is on my hamburger.
   ⓒ Dan is my boyfriend.
   ⓓ Lemon is sour.

D 다음 주어진 단어를 이용하여 문장을 완성하시오.

1 Canada는 북미에 있는 나라이다. (Canada)

   _____ is a country in North America.

2 Jason은 우리 오빠다. (Jason)

   _____ is my brother.

3 여기에 한 잔의 우유가 있다. (milk)

   Here is _____.

Unit 02

3 Unit 인칭/지시대명사

A 다음 중 가장 알맞은 것을 고르시오.

1 This / These is Jim. He / She / It is my uncle.

2 This / These are Leo and Susan. He / She / They are my brother and sister.

3 This / These is my laptop. He / She / It is old.

4 This / These are scissors. He / They / It are sharp.

5 That / Those is Raymond. He / We / It is a police officer.

6 That / Those are my pets. They / She / It are a cat and a dog.

7 That / Those is my bike. He / She / It is new.

B 다음 빈칸에 알맞은 말을 넣어 문장을 완성하시오.

1 Cindy is my best friend. _____ is in Paris.

2 This is my book. _____ is interesting.

3 Randy is my son. _____ is seven years old.

4 You and Matt are my friends. _____ are nice.

5 These dogs are young. _____ are puppies.

6 Ginny and Kim are scientists. _____ are smart.

7 You and I are classmates. _____ are good students.

C 다음 빈칸에 알맞은 말을 넣어 문장을 완성하시오.

1 저것은 시계이다.

→ _____ is a clock.

2 이 사람들이 내 사촌들이다.

→ _____ are my cousins.

3 그것은 내 컵이다.

→ _____ is my cup.

4 우리는 행복하다.

→ _____ are happy.

5 너는 훌륭한 화가이다.

→ _____ are a great artist.

A 빈칸에 알맞은 말을 고르시오.

1 This / These are my favorite computer games.

2 That / Those is a pancake.

3 Jack and Jill are my neighbors. They / We are very kind.

4 Susan is in Italy. She / He is an opera singer.

B 다음 빈칸에 알맞은 말을 고르시오.

1 Mangos and melons are fruits. _____ are on my plate.

ⓐ It   ⓑ That   ⓒ This   ⓓ They

2 A roller coaster is in the amusement park. _____ is fun.

ⓐ This   ⓑ She   ⓒ He   ⓓ It

C 다음 중 어법상 옳지 않은 문장을 고르시오.

1 ⓐ This is a pen, and that is a pencil.
   ⓑ She is in the kitchen.
   ⓒ You are police officers.
   ⓓ Those is my sister.

2 ⓐ He are my brother.
   ⓑ Those are my farm animals.
   ⓒ These are cookies, and those are brownies.
   ⓓ You and I are ready.

D 다음 빈칸에 알맞은 말을 넣어 문장을 완성하시오.

1 그들은 시인이다.

   → _____ are poets.

2 이것들은 백합꽃들이다.

   → _____ are lilies.

3 저 분이 Jim이다. 그는 나의 할아버지이다.

   → _____ is Jim. _____ is my grandfather.

4 이 사람은 새로운 학생이야.

   → _____ is a new student.

인칭대명사의 주격과 목적격

A 다음 중 가장 알맞은 것을 고르시오.

1 Larry saw she / her in the park.

2 I have two dogs. They / Them are my good friends.

3 Caroline and I had a good time. We / Us went to an amusement park.

4 My grandparents love I / me a lot.

5 I was at Alex's birthday party. I gave he / him a soccer ball.

6 They bought a big house. It / They has a swimming pool.

7 Beth is my daughter. She / Her always helps me.

B 다음 빈칸에 알맞은 말을 넣어 문장을 완성하시오.

1 That boy is David. I met _____ in Chess Club.

2 I like milk. I drink _____ every morning.

3 Clare is in Africa. I write _____ a letter once a month.

4 We love Uncle Jim. He visits _____ every summer.

5 I usually get up late. Mom always wakes _____ up.

C 다음 주어진 단어를 이용하여 문장을 완성하시오.

1 Susan은 우리 선생님입니다. 그녀는 우리에게 친절합니다. (is, kind to us)

Susan is our teacher. _____

2 Tom은 팝송을 좋아합니다. 그는 매일 그것들을 듣습니다. (listens to, every day)

Tom likes pop songs. _____

3 나는 멋진 시계를 가지고 있습니다. 나는 그것을 10년 전에 샀습니다. (bought, 10 years ago)

I have a nice watch. _____

4 내 남동생은 거짓말을 합니다. 나는 그를 믿지 않습니다. (don't believe)

My brother tells lies. _____

5 Jason과 Cathy는 나의 친구입니다. 그들은 나를 사랑합니다. (love)

Jason and Cathy are my friends. _____

A 다음 빈칸에 알맞은 말을 쓰시오.

1 Tim and Jake like music. _____ went to the concert last night.

2 Billy is a boy. _____ is tall.

3 I met Jane yesterday. I met _____ at the bus stop.

4 Elise and Ashley like books. _____ buy many books.

B 다음 빈칸에 알맞은 말을 쓰시오.

1 Brian and Jim like soccer. _____ are on the playground.

ⓐ Them   ⓑ He   ⓒ Him   ⓓ They

2 She and _____ play with a ball.

ⓐ I   ⓑ them   ⓒ her   ⓓ him

C 다음 중 어법상 옳지 않은 문장을 고르시오.

1 ⓐ A stranger talked to we.

  ⓑ I don't like Mike. I hate him.

  ⓒ The soup smells good. I like it.

  ⓓ She needs me.

2 ⓐ This lock needs a key. I lost it.

  ⓑ They are wonderful paintings.

  ⓒ Him is in the house.

  ⓓ Sue and Ken are my cousins. They are fun.

D 다음 주어진 단어를 이용하여 문장을 완성하시오.

1 Steve과 Greg는 학생이다. 나는 그들은 안다. (know)

  → Steve and Greg are students. _____

2 그들은 나를 그들의 결혼식에 초대했다. (invited)

  → _____ to their wedding.

3 그는 레몬을 좋아한다. 그녀는 그것을 좋아하지 않는다. (doesn't like)

  → He likes a lemon. _____

4 Beth와 나는 강아지를 좋아한다. 그것들은 매우 귀엽다. (very cute)

  → Beth and I like puppies. _____

Unit 03

2 인칭대명사의 소유격

A 다음 중 가장 알맞은 것을 고르시오.

1 I met them before. I forgot they / their / them names.

2 Your shirt is red. This is me / my / mine .

3 His cell phone is broken. He uses her / she phone.

4 Peter / Peter's mother is a movie star.

5 She went to a girl's / girls' high school.

6 They kicked us / our / ours ball.

7 I often drive my parents' / my parent's car.

B 다음 빈칸에 알맞은 말을 넣어 문장을 완성하시오.

1 I have a girlfriend. _____ hair is long and blond.

2 He lost his cell phone. Is this _____?

3 I called you. You didn't answer _____ call.

4 They are very rich. This boat is also _____.

5 We have a cat. _____ fur is gray.

6 Mike saw you. You were taking a walk with _____ mother.

C 다음 주어진 단어를 이용하여 문장을 완성하시오.

1 너는 그의 주소를 아니? (address)

→ Do you know _____?

2 이것들은 우리의 신발이 아니야. 그것들은 그들의 것이야. (shoes)

→ These are not _____. They are _____.

3 그녀는 그녀 아빠의 회사에서 일한다. (father's company)

→ She works at _____.

4 내가 테이블 위에 네 열쇠를 두었어. (key)

→ I put _____ on the table.

5 그는 모자를 쓰고 있다. 그것의 색깔은 녹색이다. (color)

→ He is wearing a cap. _____ is green.

내신 FOCUS

A 다음 빈칸에 알맞은 소유대명사를 쓰시오.

1 I - my - _____   **3** you - your - _____   **5** he - his - _____

2 we - our - _____   **4** she - her - _____   **6** they - their - _____

B 다음 빈칸에 알맞은 말을 고르시오.

1 Hermione and Ron are _____ best friends.

ⓐ Harry's   ⓑ Harry   ⓒ Harrys'   ⓓ Harry of

2 My brother's gift was Lego blocks. _____ was a storybook.

ⓐ My   ⓑ I   ⓒ Me   ⓓ Mine

C 다음 중 어법상 옳지 <u>않은</u> 문장을 고르시오.

1 ⓐ This is not mine.

ⓑ It's wing is big and wide.

ⓒ Are these your soccer shoes?

ⓓ His paintings are about the stories of the Bible.

2 ⓐ It's our turn.

ⓑ This is not my bike.

ⓒ Bill's car is behind my motorcycle.

ⓓ There are three girl's dresses on the table.

D 다음 주어진 단어를 이용하여 문장을 완성하시오.

1 그의 할머니는 아흔 살이다. (grandmother, is, 90 years old)

→ _____

2 내 대답은 틀렸어. (answer, is, wrong)

→ _____

3 나는 작년에 그들의 농장을 방문했다. (visited, farm, last year)

→ _____

4 이것은 우리 아빠의 기타야. (is, my daddy, guitar)

→ _____

1 일반동사의 현재형

A 다음 중 가장 알맞은 것을 고르시오.

1 James │read / reads│ the newspaper.

2 People │wear / wears│ clothes.

3 She │walk / walks│ in the park.

4 Birds │fly / flies│ in the sky.

5 We │practice / practices│ baseball.

6 The sun │set / sets│ in the west.

7 My father │work / works│ at a hospital.

B 다음 빈칸에 알맞은 말을 골라 어법에 맞도록 문장을 완성하시오.

Word Bank	go	dance	swim	bite	make

1 A baker _____ bread.　　Bakers _____ bread.

2 A student _____ to school.　　Students _____ to school.

3 A fish _____ in the sea.　　Fish _____ in the sea.

4 A mosquito _____ people.　　Mosquitoes _____ people.

5 A ballerina _____ ballet.　　Ballerinas _____ ballet.

C 다음 주어진 단어를 이용하여 문장을 완성하시오.

1 그는 줄넘기를 한다. (he, jump, rope)

→ _____

2 그녀는 그녀의 가족을 그리워한다. (she, miss, her family)

→ _____

3 우리는 감기에 걸렸다. (we, catch, a cold)

→ _____

4 내 남동생은 햄버거를 먹는다. (brother, eat, a hamburger)

→ _____

5 내 여동생은 음악 시간을 즐긴다. (my sister, enjoy, music class)

→ _____

A 다음 동사의 3인칭 단수형을 쓰시오.

1 have - _____   3 go - _____   5 push - _____   7 mix - _____

2 study - _____   4 walk - _____   6 do - _____   8 play - _____

B 다음 빈칸에 알맞은 말을 고르시오.

1 They _____ Stephen Hawking well.

ⓐ know   ⓑ are know   ⓒ knows   ⓓ knowes

2 I _____ the boxes to the car.

ⓐ carries   ⓑ carry   ⓒ carrie   ⓓ carrys

C 다음 중 어법상 옳지 않은 문장을 고르시오.

1 ⓐ They watches fantasy movies.
   ⓑ Mike speaks a little French.
   ⓒ My hair reaches my hips.
   ⓓ I have a flower shop.

2 ⓐ David has a new video game.
   ⓑ I do my homework after school.
   ⓒ She want something sweet.
   ⓓ They open their books.

D 다음 주어진 단어를 이용하여 문장을 완성하시오.

1 그는 동물들을 사랑한다. (he, love, animals)
   → _____

2 꼬마들이 모래사장에서 논다. (kids, play, in the sand)
   → _____

3 Sam은 영어를 배운다. (Sam, learn, English)
   → _____

4 그녀는 그녀의 숙제를 한다. (she, do, her homework)
   → _____

Unit 04

2 의문문과 부정문

A 다음 중 가장 알맞은 것을 고르시오.

1 I don't / doesn't have a bike.

2 Sue don't / doesn't watch horror movies.

3 Do / Does they play football?

4 How do / does he go to school?

5 Do / Does you study Chinese?

6 What do / does you do on weekends?

7 He don't / doesn't like spicy food.

B 다음 빈칸에 알맞은 말을 넣어 문장을 완성하시오.

1 A: _____ Harry go to the gym?   B: No, he _____. He doesn't like to exercise.

2 A: _____ Jerry and Tom always fight?   B: Yes, they _____. They don't like each other.

3 A: _____ your school have a rule?   B: Yes, it _____. It has five rules.

4 A: _____ she teach math?   B: Yes, she _____. She's a good teacher.

5 A: _____ your brother live in London?   B: No, he _____. He lives in Paris.

C 다음 주어진 단어를 이용하여 문장을 완성하시오.

1 그들은 브라질 출신입니까? (they, come, from Brazil)

→ _____

2 Ann은 콜라를 마시지 않습니다. (Ann, drink, Coke)

→ _____

3 꼬마들이 크리스마스 캐롤을 부릅니까? (kids, sing, Christmas carols)

→ _____

4 그는 거짓말을 하지 않습니다. (he, tell, a lie)

→ _____

5 너는 어디서 책을 사니? (where, you, buy, books)

→ _____

A 다음 빈칸에 알맞은 말을 쓰시오.

1 _____ she drive a car?   Yes, she does. She _____ a red car.

2 _____ banks open at eight?   No, they _____ at nine.

B 다음 빈칸에 알맞은 말을 고르시오.

1 I _____ the newspaper.

ⓐ doesn't read   ⓑ is not read   ⓒ don't read   ⓓ read not

2 He _____ on the soccer team.

ⓐ don't play   ⓑ is not play   ⓒ doesn't play   ⓓ play not

C 다음 중 어법상 옳지 않은 문장을 고르시오.

1 ⓐ They don't listen to rock music.
  ⓑ Does she sells books?
  ⓒ I don't understand them.
  ⓓ Do I know you?

2 ⓐ I don't have any cousins.
  ⓑ Does he go swimming often?
  ⓒ She don't make pancakes.
  ⓓ Do you want a green sweater?

D 다음 주어진 단어를 이용하여 문장을 완성하시오.

1 그 장난감 가게는 5시에 문을 닫습니까? (the toy store, close, at five)

→ _____

2 나는 물을 많이 마시지 않습니다. (drink, much, water)

→ _____

3 네 이모는 어디에 사시니? (where, your aunt, live)

→ _____

4 그는 소설을 쓰지 않습니다. (he, write, a novel)

→ _____

Unit 04

3 일반동사의 과거형

A 다음 중 가장 알맞은 것을 고르시오.

1 She go / goes / went to Australia last month.

2 Their dog bark / barks / barked all night long last night.

3 The policeman catch / catches / caught the robber yesterday.

4 My son ride / rides / rode a bike to school every day.

5 They move / moves / moved to New York last year.

6 Kelly swim / swims / swam in this lake before.

7 Sam make / makes / made pancakes every morning.

B 다음 주어진 단어를 이용하여 문장을 완성하시오.

1 She _____ (wash) the dishes yesterday.

2 Rick _____ (buy) a digital camera last year.

3 I _____ (see) Jim at that time.

4 My uncle _____ (bring) sandwiches last night.

5 We _____ (raise) five dogs two years ago.

6 Jane _____ (knock) on the door three times.

C 다음 주어진 단어를 이용하여 문장을 완성하시오.

1 나는 답을 알고 있었다. (I, know, the answer)

→ _____

2 그는 10분 전에 문을 닫았다. (he, shut, the door, ten minutes ago)

→ _____

3 내 여동생은 오늘 아침에 집을 떠났다. (my sister, leave, home, this morning)

→ _____

4 그는 그녀를 10년 전에 만났다. (he, meet, her, ten years ago)

→ _____

5 어젯밤에 그들은 파티를 열었다. (they, hold, a party, last night)

→ _____

A 다음 동사의 과거형을 쓰시오.

1 sit - _____   3 put - _____   5 help - _____   7 sleep - _____

2 sing - _____   4 go - _____   6 leave - _____   8 think - _____

B 다음 빈칸에 알맞은 말을 고르시오.

1 They _____ cookies yesterday.

   ⓐ maked   ⓑ were make   ⓒ made   ⓓ make

2 Dan _____ for my father last year.

   ⓐ were work   ⓑ work   ⓒ was worked   ⓓ worked

C 다음 중 어법상 옳지 <u>않은</u> 것을 고르시오.

1 ⓐ They wore colorful shirts.

   ⓑ She tried the noodles yesterday.

   ⓒ She readed a Harry Potter book last month.

   ⓓ You knew nothing about me last year.

2 ⓐ You owned a blue car once.

   ⓑ We did our homework together yesterday.

   ⓒ She came here a week ago.

   ⓓ He lives in India last summer.

D 다음 주어진 단어를 이용하여 문장을 완성하시오.

1 그녀는 어제 과학을 공부했다. (she, study, science, yesterday)

   → _____

2 나는 지난 주말에 공포 영화를 한 편 보았다. (I, see, a horror movie, last weekend)

   → _____

3 그들은 오늘 오후에 Jim을 만났다. (they, meet, Jim, this afternoon)

   → _____

4 John은 어젯밤에 피자와 콜라를 먹었다. (John, have, pizza and Coke, last night)

   → _____

Unit 04

4 의문문과 부정문

A 다음 중 가장 알맞은 것을 고르시오.

1 I don't / didn't / was not call him this morning.

2 Does / Did / Was he lose his way to the river yesterday?

3 They don't / didn't / was not sell their car last month.

4 We don't / didn't / was not take a walk every day.

5 Do / Did / Were James and Linda come home last night?

6 Does / Did / Was it rain a lot last year?

7 Does / Did / Was Sandy find her key at that time?

B 다음 빈칸에 알맞은 말을 넣어 문장을 완성하시오.

1 A: Did your father catch a big fish?

B: No, he _____. He _____ a small fish.

2 A: Did they sell their house?

B: Yes, they _____. They _____ their house last month.

3 A: Did she teach English at school?

B: No, she _____. She _____ math.

4 A: Did they win the soccer game?

B: Yes, they _____. They _____ the game, 3 to 1.

C 다음 주어진 단어를 이용하여 문장을 완성하시오.

1 그들은 잔디에 앉지 않았다. (they, sit, on the grass)

→ _____

2 너는 장난감을 상자에 넣었니? (you, put, toys, into the box)

→ _____

3 그때 우리는 중국에 살지 않았다. (we, live, in China, then)

→ _____

4 Matt는 참치 샌드위치를 주문했니? (Matt, order, a tuna sandwich)

→ _____

5 그 소년이 창문을 깼니? (the boy, break, the window)

→ _____

26

A 다음 빈칸에 알맞은 동사형태를 고르시오.

1 I don't / didn't usually eat meat.   I don't / didn't eat the steak last night.

2 Does / Did she go jogging every day?   Does / Did she go jogging yesterday?

B 다음 빈칸에 알맞은 말을 고르시오.

1 _____ your teacher ask some questions in class?

ⓐ Did   ⓑ Do   ⓒ Was   ⓓ Was did

2 You _____ late this time.

ⓐ doesn't arrive   ⓑ didn't arrive   ⓒ arrived not   ⓓ do arrive not

C 다음 중 어법상 옳지 않은 문장을 고르시오.

1 ⓐ Did Mandy bring some cookies?
  ⓑ The baby cried a lot last night.
  ⓒ I slept for 12 hours yesterday.
  ⓓ She didn't passed the exam.

2 ⓐ They did not go skiing last weekend.
  ⓑ Did David left before seven?
  ⓒ I didn't tell him my opinion.
  ⓓ Did you do your homework?

D 다음 주어진 단어를 이용하여 문장을 완성하시오.

1 너는 어제 과학을 공부했니? (you, study, science, yesterday)
  → _____

2 그들은 지난 주말에 공원에 가지 않았다. (they, go, to the park, last weekend)
  → _____

3 그녀는 지난 여름에 여행을 갔었니? (she, take a trip, last summer)
  → _____

4 그는 이틀 전에 집에 들어오지 않았다. (he, come, home, two days ago)
  → _____

5 일반동사의 현재진행형

A 다음 중 가장 알맞은 것을 고르시오.

1 They usually | go / are going | to the library after school.

They | go / are going | to the library now.

2 My father | reads / is reading | the newspaper every morning.

My father | reads / is reading | the newspaper now.

3 Look at the baby! She | wears / is wearing | sunglasses.

She often | wears / is wearing | sunglasses.

4 The runner always | ties / is tying | his shoes before the race.

He | ties / is tying | his shoes now.

5 I always | have / am having | hot coffee in the morning.

I | have / am having | hot coffee now.

B 다음 주어진 단어를 이용하여 문장을 완성하시오.

1 Smile! He _____ (be, take) your picture.

2 My dog always _____ (bite) my shoes.

3 The baby _____ (be, sleep) right now.

4 Jenny usually _____ (have) breakfast.

5 She _____ (visit) her grandparents every weekend.

C 다음 주어진 단어를 이용하여 문장을 완성하시오.

1 Cathy는 말을 타고 있는 중이다. (Cathy, ride a horse, now)

→ _____

2 고양이가 부엌으로 뛰어가고 있다. (a cat, run, to the kitchen)

→ _____

3 우리는 슬픈 영화를 보고 있는 중이다. (we, watch, a sad movie)

→ _____

4 그는 쇼핑 카트를 밀고 있다. (he, push, a shopping cart)

→ _____

5 아이들이 술래잡기를 하고 있다. (the kids, play, hide-and-seek)

→ _____

A 다음 동사를 –ing형으로 바꾸시오.

1 lie - _____   3 put - _____   5 tell - _____   7 make - _____

2 sit - _____   4 close - _____   6 eat - _____   8 run - _____

B 다음 빈칸에 알맞은 말을 고르시오.

1 He usually _____ a cake for my birthday.

ⓐ is buying   ⓑ bought   ⓒ buys   ⓓ buy

2 Oh, look! The girl _____ at me.

ⓐ smile   ⓑ is smiling   ⓒ smiles   ⓓ was smile

C 다음 중 어법상 옳지 <u>않은</u> 것을 고르시오.

1 ⓐ The dog is barking now.
   ⓑ She sells the best hot dogs.
   ⓒ They doing a crossword puzzle.
   ⓓ We are staying in Rome.

2 ⓐ The students are raising their hands.
   ⓑ Listen! The bell is ringing now.
   ⓒ I usually is listening to this radio station.
   ⓓ The boy is playing a new video game.

D 다음 주어진 단어를 이용하여 문장을 완성하시오.

1 지금 눈이 내리고 있어. (it, snow, now)

→ _____

2 고양이가 쥐를 쫓고 있어. (a cat, run after, a mouse)

→ _____

3 나는 일요일마다 교회에 간다. (I, go to church, every Sunday)

→ _____

4 그는 그녀와 좋은 시간을 보내고 있다. (he, have, a good time, with her)

→ _____

Unit 04

6 의문문과 부정문

A 다음 중 가장 알맞은 것을 고르시오.

1 Nora is not / do not / does not cooking now.

2 Where is / do / does he going?

3 Is / Are / Do they looking at me?

4 I am not / is not / do not reading your diary.

5 What is / are / do the kids doing in the yard?

6 Ann and Jane is not / are not / do not taking a nap now.

7 Is / Are / Do you setting the table?

B 다음 빈칸에 알맞은 말을 골라 문장을 완성하시오.

Word Bank	drink	make	write	hit

1 A: Are you _____ a cake for him?

   B: Yes, I _____. I am _____ a strawberry cake.

2 A: Is he _____ the ball?

   B: No, he _____. He is catching the ball.

3 A: Are they _____ soda pop?

   B: No, they _____. They are _____ water.

4 A: Is she _____ a poem?

   B: Yes, she _____. She is a great poet.

C 다음 주어진 단어를 이용하여 문장을 완성하시오.

1 Ted는 클래식 음악을 듣고 있니? (Ted, listen to, classical music)

   → _____

2 그들은 야구를 하고 있지 않다. (they, play baseball)

   → _____

3 너는 울타리에 페인트를 칠하고 있니? (you, paint a fence)

   → _____

4 그녀는 지금 비싼 호텔에 머물고 있니? (she, stay, in an expensive hotel)

   → _____

A 다음 밑줄 친 부분을 바르게 고치시오.

1 They <u>do not having</u> a big party.   → _____

2 She <u>is not love</u> him.   → _____

3 <u>Do you looking</u> for the box?   → _____

4 <u>Are they like</u> Justin?   → _____

B 다음 빈칸에 알맞은 말을 고르시오.

1 _____ a good time with your aunt?

   ⓐ Do you having   ⓑ Are you have   ⓒ Are you having   ⓓ Are having you

2 _____ a taxi now.

   ⓐ I'm not catching   ⓑ I'm not catch   ⓒ I do not catch   ⓓ I am catching not

C 다음 중 어법상 옳지 <u>않은</u> 문장을 고르시오.

1 ⓐ I'm not studying. I'm reading a book.
   ⓑ Dinner's ready. Are you coming?
   ⓒ Do your brother and you watching TV?
   ⓓ She isn't writing a letter to her cousin.

2 ⓐ The woman is standing by the elevator.
   ⓑ The boat is arriving at the dock.
   ⓒ She is taking care of her brother.
   ⓓ Is you waiting for me?

D 다음 주어진 단어를 이용하여 문장을 완성하시오.

1 너는 지금 무엇을 하고 있니? (what, you, do, now)
   → _____

2 그 소년은 잠을 자고 있지 않다. (the boy, sleep)
   → _____

3 그들이 나를 기다리고 있니? (they, wait, for me)
   → _____

4 그녀는 소파에 앉아 있지 않다. (she, sit, on the sofa)
   → _____

Unit 05

1 현재/과거/미래

A 다음 중 가장 알맞은 것을 고르시오.

1 They will be / are / were at my birthday party last night.

2 She often will go / goes / went swimming after school.

3 He will wash / washes / washed his car tomorrow.

4 The train for Busan will leave / leaves / left a minute ago.

5 My family is going to move / moves / moved to the countryside next month.

6 The bank always close / closes / will close at 4.

7 The waiter will serve / serves / served our meals soon.

B 다음 주어진 단어를 이용하여 문장을 완성하시오.

1 He _____ (hit) a home run at the last game.

2 They will _____ (graduate) from middle school next year.

3 Mike _____ (pay) 100 dollars for the bike yesterday.

4 She _____ (spend) lots of time with her child.

5 We _____ (play) beach volleyball tomorrow.

6 I _____ (go) horseback riding with my uncle last weekend.

C 다음 밑줄 친 부분을 지시문에 맞게 고쳐 문장을 완성하시오.

1 Jim and Sara <u>are</u> here.

(미래) → Jim and Sara _____ here soon.

2 The show <u>begins</u> at 10 and 12.

(과거) → The show _____ half an hour ago.

3 We <u>visited</u> the Picasso Museum yesterday.

(미래) → We _____ the Picasso Museum tomorrow.

4 Snow <u>covers</u> the top of the mountain.

(과거) → Snow _____ the top of the mountain last year.

5 He <u>repaired</u> the broken tap.

(미래) → He _____ the broken tap tomorrow.

A 다음 동사의 과거형과 미래형을 쓰시오.

1 _____ - win - _____   5 _____ - keep - _____

2 _____ - drink - _____   6 _____ - study - _____

3 _____ - tell - _____   7 _____ - lose - _____

4 _____ - catch - _____   8 _____ - meet - _____

B 다음 빈칸에 알맞은 말을 고르시오.

1 It _____ snowy and cold yesterday.

ⓐ was   ⓑ will be   ⓒ is   ⓓ is going to be

2 She _____ tomorrow's meeting.

ⓐ attended   ⓑ attends   ⓒ attend   ⓓ will attend

C 다음 중 어법상 옳지 <u>않은</u> 문장을 고르시오.

1 ⓐ We will visit you this afternoon.
  ⓑ I drink a glass of milk every day.
  ⓒ We are going to go to the festival last Sunday.
  ⓓ They won the game two weeks ago.

2 ⓐ Kenny is going to buy a car.
  ⓑ She will has a salmon sandwich.
  ⓒ Alice wore the red dress last night.
  ⓓ He feeds his dogs and cats every morning.

D 다음 주어진 단어를 이용하여 문장을 완성하시오.

1 그녀는 2년 전에 London에 살았다. (she, live, in London, two years ago)

→ _____

2 우리 오빠는 은행에서 일한다. (my brother, work for, a bank)

→ _____

3 그는 그녀의 편지를 받아서 매우 행복했다. (he, happy, to receive her letter)

→ _____

4 Steve는 다음 달에 로마에서 머무를 것이다. (Steve, stay, in Rome, next month)

→ _____

2 will/be going to

A 다음 중 가장 알맞은 것을 고르시오.

1 The train will │ leave / leaves │ in ten minutes.

2 She will │ don't / not │ believe you.

3 They │ will not buy / will buy not │ some snacks.

4 │ Will / Is │ he make a speech tonight?

5 │ Will / Are │ Mary and Jim going to get married in May?

6 Tom is │ not going to / going not to │ go to the exhibition.

B 다음 주어진 단어를 이용하여 문장을 완성하시오.

1 Sammy will give a present to his mom. (be going to, not)

→ Sammy _____ a present to his mom.

2 Is she going to pick you up at seven? (will)

→ _____ you up at seven?

3 He plays football after school every day. (will, not)

→ He _____ football after school tomorrow.

4 They go out on Friday night. (be going to)

→ They _____ this Friday night.

5 I take a walk before dinner. (will)

→ I _____ before dinner.

C 다음 우리말과 같은 뜻이 되도록 주어진 단어를 배열하시오.

1 우리 누나는 내년에 대학교에 입학할 것이다. (is going to / enter / my sister / next year / the university)

→ _____

2 나는 내 방을 녹색으로 칠할 거야. (paint / will / I / green / my room)

→ _____

3 우리는 택시를 타고 갈 거야. (take a taxi / are going to / we)

→ _____

4 그 불꽃축제는 금요일 저녁에 끝날 것이다. (end / will / the fireworks festival / on Friday night)

→ _____

A 다음을 괄호 안의 지시문에 맞게 고쳐 쓰시오.

1 She will show him her vacation pictures.

(부정문) → _____

(의문문) → _____

2 Tom is going to visit his uncle this weekend.

(부정문) → _____

(의문문) → _____

B 다음 빈칸에 알맞은 말을 고르시오.

1 Sam will _____ home this Sunday.

ⓐ gets   ⓑ get back   ⓒ got back   ⓓ going to get back

2 I'm _____ the ferry home.

ⓐ not going to ride   ⓑ going to not ride   ⓒ not to go to ride   ⓓ not ride

C 다음 중 어법상 옳지 않은 문장을 고르시오.

1 ⓐ My uncle will buy a big house next month.

ⓑ He is going to cooks a turkey this Thanksgiving.

ⓒ Are you going to clean your room?

ⓓ He won't lose the game.

2 ⓐ She'll not go to the beach with us in the afternoon.

ⓑ We are going to go to the festival on Friday.

ⓒ I will don't have time this afternoon.

ⓓ Is she going to keep our secret?

D 다음 주어진 단어를 이용하여 문장을 완성하시오.

1 그들은 다음 주말에 도착할 예정이야. (they, arrive, next weekend)

→ _____

2 그는 집에 9시 전에 들어올 거야. (he, come home, before 9)

→ _____

3 너 내일 뭐할 거니? (what, do, tomorrow)

→ _____

1 능력을 나타내는 조동사

A 다음 중 가장 알맞은 것을 고르시오.

1 He can / cans drive a bus.

2 Mandy could knit / knits this sweater easily.

3 Can Sarah play / plays chess?

4 Were / Could they able to get there by train?

5 I could finish / finished writing my essay on time.

6 We will can / will be able to speak Chinese soon.

7 She was not / could don't able to catch the flight.

B 다음 주어진 단어를 이용하여 문장을 완성하시오.

1 I _____ (can, not, sleep) well last night.

2 Betty _____ (be able to, not, use) her computer.

3 He _____ (be able to, not, talk) to you right now.

4 She _____ (be able to, book) the flight tickets yesterday.

5 The repairman _____ (be able to, fix) my car tomorrow.

6 Were they _____ (be able to, win) the baseball game?

7 Will John _____ (be able to, go) to Japan next summer?

C 다음 우리말과 같은 뜻이 되도록 주어진 단어를 배열하시오.

1 나는 어젯밤에 우리 이모를 만나지 못했다. (meet / could / I / not / my aunt / last night)

→ _____

2 그는 매주 20달러씩 저금할 수 있다. (twenty dollars / save / he / can / every week)

→ _____

3 Terry는 운전면허시험에 통과할 수 있을 거야. (Terry / pass / be able to / the driving test / will)

→ _____

4 Kevin은 젓가락을 사용할 수 없었다. (was / use / able to / Kevin / not / chopsticks)

→ _____

A 다음 밑줄 친 부분을 바르게 고치시오.

1 I could <u>found</u> my door key. → _____

2 She can <u>makes</u> all kinds of Italian food. → _____

3 They will <u>can</u> plant the trees tomorrow. → _____

4 I can <u>don't</u> understand his class. → _____

B 다음 빈칸에 알맞은 말을 고르시오.

1 Alex could _____ the math questions.

ⓐ solved   ⓑ solves   ⓒ solve   ⓓ to solve

2 Harry _____ Japanese well.

ⓐ is to able read   ⓑ able to read   ⓒ is able read   ⓓ is able to read

C 다음 중 어법상 옳지 않은 문장을 고르시오.

1 ⓐ He cannot give us an answer now.
   ⓑ The kid can operate a computer well.
   ⓒ Does he able to sing well?
   ⓓ I could see the ocean from my hotel room.

2 ⓐ Could he makes a kite?
   ⓑ They will be able to meet us soon.
   ⓒ I cannot read the story in Chinese.
   ⓓ He can give us an answer now.

D 다음 주어진 단어와 조동사를 이용하여 문장을 완성하시오.

1 그는 내년에 그 대회에서 우승할 수 있을 것이다. (he, will, win, the contest, next year)
   → _____

2 너는 한 손으로 자전거를 탈 수 있니? (you, ride a bicycle, with one hand)
   → _____

3 나는 어제 그 파일을 보낼 수가 없었다. (I, send, the file, yesterday)
   → _____

Unit 06

2 허가를 나타내는 조동사

A 다음 중 가장 알맞은 것을 고르시오.

1 May / Would I ask your age?

2 Can you hold / holds this bag for a second?

3 Can / May you lend me five dollars?

4 Would you please turns / turn on the light?

5 May / Would I watch TV?

6 Can / May you give me a ride to my office?

7 Can you move / moves these chairs to the hall?

B 다음 빈칸에 알맞은 말을 골라 문장을 완성하시오.

Word Bank	use	leave	tell	borrow	make	pick

1 I lost my cell phone. Can I _____ yours for a moment?

2 I think I am lost. Could you _____ me the way to the train station?

3 Oh, she is out. May I _____ her a message?

4 Mom, I'm hungry. Could you _____ me a sandwich?

5 I don't have any sugar. Can I _____ some?

6 Can you _____ up my laundry from the dry cleaner?

C 다음 지시문에 맞게 문장을 다시 쓰시오.

1 You can bring your pet in the building. (부정문으로)

→ _____

2 I can ride a bike in this park. (의문문으로)

→ _____

3 Fill out this form. (의문문으로)

→ _____

4 Can you take me home? (매우 예의 바르게)

→ _____

5 Could you bring me a drink? (허물 없는 표현으로)

→ _____

A 다음 빈칸에 알맞은 말을 쓰시오.

1 _____ you close the door? (문 좀 닫아 주시겠어요?)

2 _____ I use your pen? (제가 당신의 펜을 써도 될까요?)

3 _____ you help me? (저 좀 도와주시겠어요?)

4 _____ I go now? (저 이제 가도 되나요?)

B 다음 빈칸에 알맞은 말을 고르시오.

1 _____ I have some more bread?

ⓐ Will   ⓑ Would   ⓒ Can   ⓓ Do

2 Would _____ the guestbook?

ⓐ sign you please   ⓑ please you sign   ⓒ you sign please   ⓓ you please sign

C 다음 중 어법상 옳지 <u>않은</u> 문장을 고르시오.

1 ⓐ Could you open the window?
  ⓑ You cannot go there alone.
  ⓒ May I stay here tonight?
  ⓓ Would you are my friend?

2 ⓐ Will you stand up, please?
  ⓑ Could you says your name again?
  ⓒ May I leave my bag here?
  ⓓ Can you get me a pen and some paper?

D 다음 주어진 단어와 조동사를 이용하여 문장을 완성하시오.

1 제가 커피 한 잔 마셔도 될까요? (I, have, a cup of coffee)

→ _____

2 택시 한 대만 불러 주시겠어요? (you, call a taxi)

→ _____

3 제가 당신과 사진을 찍어도 될까요? (I, take a picture, with you)

→ _____

4 잠시만 기다려 주시겠어요? (you, wait for a moment)

→ _____

의무를 나타내는 조동사

Unit 06
3

A 다음 중 가장 알맞은 것을 고르시오.

1 He should keeps / keep his promise.

2 We will must / have to arrive there before nine.

3 You should not take / don't take a picture inside the museum.

4 Should I / Do I should call her back?

5 Do we must / Do we have to go home now?

6 He must not parks / park his car here.

B 다음 주어진 조건에 맞게 고쳐 문장을 완성하시오.

1 I must go to bed now. (부정문으로)

→ _____ to bed now.

2 You must have a passport to travel abroad. (의문문으로)

→ _____ to travel abroad?

3 He must cancel the soccer game. (과거시제로)

→ _____ the soccer game.

4 They must read the instructions carefully. (미래시제로)

→ _____ the instructions carefully.

C 다음 우리말과 같은 뜻이 되도록 주어진 단어를 배열하시오.

1 너는 수업에 집중해야 한다. (pay attention / should / you / in class)

→ _____

2 무언가 잘못된 것이 틀림없어. (be / something / there / must / wrong)

→ _____

3 그녀는 자신의 아들을 걱정할 필요가 없다. (have to / she / worry / about her son / doesn't)

→ _____

4 지난 주말에 그는 집에 있어야만 했다. (stay / home / had to / he / last weekend)

→ _____

5 그녀는 정말 행복할 거야. (very happy / she / be / must)

→ _____

A 다음을 괄호 안의 지시에 따라 바꿔 쓰시오.

1 You must stay at home.　　　　　→ (부정문) _____

　　　　　　　　　　　　　　　　　→ (의문문) _____

2 We should bring our lunch.　　　→ (부정문) _____

　　　　　　　　　　　　　　　　　→ (의문문) _____

B 다음 빈칸에 알맞은 말을 고르시오.

1 You _____ go home now. It's late.

　ⓐ can　　　　　　ⓑ will　　　　　　ⓒ should　　　　　　ⓓ may

2 _____ call my mother today?

　ⓐ Do you must　　ⓑ Do you have to　　ⓒ Did you had to　　ⓓ Must you

C 다음 중 어법상 옳지 <u>않은</u> 문장을 고르시오.

1 ⓐ You must follow the school rules.

　ⓑ Mandy must to do the dishes after dinner.

　ⓒ You should not forget to call Jim.

　ⓓ Do I have to make a reservation?

2 ⓐ Danny will must pay his bills tomorrow.

　ⓑ She shouldn't leave without an umbrella.

　ⓒ Drivers must obey the traffic laws.

　ⓓ You must not forget the ticket.

D 다음 주어진 단어와 조동사를 이용하여 문장을 완성하시오.

1 나는 시험에 통과하기 위해서 공부를 열심히 해야 한다. (I, study hard, to pass the test)

　→ _____

2 너는 수업 시간에 늦어서는 안 된다. (you, be late, for class)

　→ _____

3 그들은 교복을 반드시 입어야 합니까? (they, wear, school uniforms)

　→ _____

4 그는 피곤한 것임에 틀림없다. (he, be tired)

　→ _____

Unit 07
1

형용사의 의미와 쓰임

A 다음 중 가장 알맞은 것을 고르시오.

1 A giraffe is a tall / tall .

A giraffe is a tall / tall animal.

2 A butterfly is a pretty / pretty .

A butterfly is a pretty / pretty insect.

3 Whales are a big / big .

Whales are a big / big mammals.

4 She is a talkative / talkative .

She is a talkative / talkative woman.

5 It is an interesting / interesting .

It is an interesting / interesting comic book.

6 They are a nice / nice .

They are a nice / nice neighbors.

7 Oranges are a delicious / delicious .

Oranges are a delicious / delicious fruits.

B 다음 빈칸에 알맞은 말을 골라 문장을 완성하시오.

Word Bank	new	safe	weak	easy	exciting

1 A snake is dangerous. It is not _____.

2 Athens is an old city. It is not a _____ city.

3 They are strong people. They are not _____ people.

4 The movie was boring. It was not _____.

5 The math test is difficult. It was not _____.

C 다음 주어진 두 문장을 하나의 문장으로 완성하시오.

1 He is a man. He is honest.

→ _____

2 It is an apple. It is sweet.

→ _____

3 She is a worker. She is lazy.

→ _____

4 Cheetahs are animals. Cheetahs are fast.

→ _____

5 They are people. They are rich.

→ _____

A 다음 빈칸에 괄호 안의 단어를 알맞게 배열하시오.

1 (warm, something), **please.**   → _____

2 **The milk** (hot, was).   → _____

3 **Pete was** (good, a, tennis player).   → _____

4 **Paris is** (city, romantic, a).   → _____

B 다음 빈칸에 알맞은 말을 고르시오.

1 She is _____.

　ⓐ hungry　　　　ⓑ a hungry　　　　ⓒ girl　　　　ⓓ hungry girl

2 This is _____.

　ⓐ a big　　　　ⓑ a big ball　　　　ⓒ a ball big　　　　ⓓ an big ball

C 다음 중 어법상 옳지 <u>않은</u> 문장을 고르시오.

1 ⓐ She is the best student.
　ⓑ My room is clean.
　ⓒ Is this cheesecake delicious?
　ⓓ It's fresh an orange.

2 ⓐ That is a red rose.
　ⓑ Is it new something?
　ⓒ A mouse is a small animal.
　ⓓ Are they sweet?

D 다음 주어진 단어를 이용하여 문장을 완성하시오.

1 내 머리는 길다. (my hair, long)
　→ _____

2 수박은 둥근 과일이다. (watermelon, round, fruit)
　→ _____

3 이것은 무언가 재미있는 거야. (this, something, fun)
　→ _____

4 북극곰은 작은 동물이 아니다. (polar bears, small, animals)
　→ _____

2 여러 가지 형용사

A 다음 중 가장 알맞은 것을 고르시오.

1 This / These box is heavy.

2 That / Those shoes are new.

3 This / These cups are clean.

4 This river / rivers is long and wide.

5 Those tree / trees are tall.

6 That picture / pictures is beautiful.

B 다음 주어진 단어를 이용하여 문장을 완성하시오.

1 Are there any cookies in the jar?

   There _____ (a lot of) in the jar.

2 Is there any milk in the cup?

   There _____ (not, any) in the cup.

3 How much juice is there in the bottle?

   There _____ (little) in the bottle.

4 How many students are there on the playground?

   There _____ (a few) on the playground.

C 다음 우리말과 같은 뜻이 되도록 주어진 단어를 배열하시오.

1 내 돼지 저금통에는 돈이 조금 있다. (money / there is / in my piggy bank / a little)

   → _____

2 이것은 야생화이다. (is / wild / a / this / flower)

   → _____

3 이 자동차들은 비싸다. (cars / are / expensive / these)

   → _____

4 바구니 안에 바나나가 많이 있다. (bananas / there are / many / in the basket)

   → _____

5 이 게임은 흥미롭다. (game / exciting / is / this)

   → _____

A 다음 밑줄 친 부분을 바르게 고치시오.

1 Those melon is fresh. → _____ 5 This skirts are short. → _____

2 That books is thick. → _____ 6 These watch are expensive. → _____

3 I have few money. → _____ 7 I have much caps. → _____

4 There is not some salt. → _____ 8 Are there a little bananas? → _____

B 다음 빈칸에 알맞지 않은 것을 고르시오.

1 _____ oranges are sour.

ⓐ These   ⓑ Those   ⓒ Some   ⓓ This

2 There are _____ balls in the box.

ⓐ a lot of   ⓑ many   ⓒ any   ⓓ some

C 다음 중 어법상 옳지 않은 문장을 고르시오.

1 ⓐ This bird is pretty.
   ⓑ How much people are in your family?
   ⓒ There was little water in the bowl.
   ⓓ Are these pants cheap?

2 ⓐ These socks are clean.
   ⓑ Are there many books on your desk?
   ⓒ Is this cake delicious?
   ⓓ There are not some coins in my pocket.

D 다음 주어진 단어를 이용하여 문장을 완성하시오.

1 이 영화는 무서워. (this movie, scary)

   → _____

2 이 반지들은 비싸. (these rings, expensive)

   → _____

3 새장에는 새가 몇 마리 들어 있다. (there are, birds, in the cage)

   → _____

4 병에는 우유가 얼만큼 들어 있습니까? (how much, there, in the bottle)

   → _____

부사의 의미와 쓰임

A 다음 중 가장 알맞은 것을 고르시오.

1 They were so / many happy with the news.

2 The movie starts soon / near .

3 The Harry Potter books are very / well interesting.

4 It is raining too / lots of heavily.

5 The picture is quite / too beautiful.

6 They are playing the drum hard / too loudly.

7 She spoke really / many fast.

B 다음 빈칸에 알맞은 말을 골라 문장을 완성하시오.

Word Bank	brightly	sadly	well	kindly	luckily	quietly

1 My mom is a chef. She cooks _____.

2 _____, he failed the test.

3 They _____ told me the way to the museum.

4 She always talks _____.

5 _____, Jack found ten dollars on the street.

6 The sun shines _____.

C 다음 우리말과 같은 뜻이 되도록 주어진 단어를 배열하시오.

1 그 영화는 너무 지루해. (boring / the movie / very / is)
   → _____

2 그녀는 차를 빠르게 운전한다. (fast / drives / she / her car)
   → _____

3 그 소년은 정말 키가 크다. (tall / the boy / is / very)
   → _____

4 나는 그들을 잘 모른다. (well / know / don't / them / I)
   → _____

A 다음 문장에서 부사를 찾아 밑줄을 그으시오.

1 He swims very well.

2 He talks really slowly.

3 She is quite good at skiing.

4 The coffee was too hot.

B 다음 빈칸에 알맞은 말을 고르시오.

1 I am _____ angry.

  ⓐ many   ⓑ much   ⓒ very   ⓓ a lot

2 Did you get up _____ this morning?

  ⓐ early   ⓑ heavily   ⓒ well   ⓓ clearly

C 다음 중 어법상 옳지 않은 문장을 고르시오.

1 ⓐ They are very talkative.
  ⓑ July is coming soon.
  ⓒ She dressed nice.
  ⓓ Please stand up.

2 ⓐ The bed is too hardly.
  ⓑ He is quite strong.
  ⓒ Finally, she finished the report.
  ⓓ He wrote the letter then.

D 다음 우리말과 같은 뜻이 되도록 주어진 단어를 배열하시오.

1 나는 열심히 영어 공부를 한다. (hard / study / English / I)

  → _____

2 그는 시끄럽게 말한다. (loudly / speaks / he)

  → _____

3 그들은 어제 일찍 잠자리에 들었다. (early / went to sleep / they / last night)

  → _____

4 날씨가 너무 추웠다. (really / the weather / cold / was)

  → _____

부사의 형태

A 다음 중 가장 알맞은 것을 고르시오.

1 She crossed the street careful / carefully .

2 My son always acts wise / wisely .

3 Zoe's class is real / really interesting.

4 He passed the driving test easy / easily .

5 Strange / Strangely , I saw him five times today.

6 They decorated their house beautiful / beautifully .

7 My back hurt bad / badly .

B 다음 빈칸에 알맞은 말을 골라 문장을 완성하시오.

Word Bank	softly	kindly	hard	strongly	heavily	clearly

1 I don't understand it _____.

2 He whispered to me _____.

3 They _____ believe in God.

4 It snowed _____.

5 He works _____.

6 Mike _____ carried my heavy bag.

C 다음 주어진 단어를 이용하여 문장을 완성하시오.

1 그녀는 천천히 걷는다. (she, walks)

→ _____

2 놀랍게도, 그는 파티에 오지 않았다. (he, didn't come, to the party)

→ _____

3 그 수리공은 내 자전거를 쉽게 고쳤다. (the repairman, repaired, my bike)

→ _____

4 그들은 시끄럽게 노래를 불렀다. (they, sang a song)

→ _____

5 나는 집에 늦게 돌아왔다. (I, came back, home)

→ _____

A 다음 빈칸에 부사형을 쓰시오.

1 good - _____   3 gentle - _____   5 bad - _____   7 real - _____

2 fast - _____   4 nice - _____   6 lucky - _____   8 easy - _____

B 다음 빈칸에 알맞은 말을 고르시오.

1 She danced _____.

   ⓐ beautifully   ⓑ good   ⓒ pretty   ⓓ nice

2 He held her hand _____.

   ⓐ well   ⓑ very   ⓒ tightly   ⓓ thinly

C 다음 중 어법상 옳지 <u>않은</u> 문장을 고르시오.

1 ⓐ Sara has a lovely doll.
   ⓑ I got up lately and missed the bus.
   ⓒ Please speak slowly.
   ⓓ Rick is doing poorly in school.

2 ⓐ Mary leaves soon.
   ⓑ Beth drove her car fastly.
   ⓒ The man hardly ate the sandwich.
   ⓓ She plays the piano very well.

D 다음 주어진 단어를 이용하여 문장을 완성하시오.

1 그들은 행복하게 살았다. (they, lived)

   → _____

2 나는 돈을 쉽게 번다. (I, make money)

   → _____

3 열차는 일찍 떠났다. (the train, left)

   → _____

4 그는 음악을 크게 틀었다. (he, played the music)

   → _____

3 빈도부사

A 다음 중 가장 알맞은 것을 고르시오.

1 She is always / always is happy.

2 I usually walk / walk usually to school.

3 I borrow DVDs three time / three times a month.

4 How sometime / often do you go to a movie?

5 Sharon makes sometimes / sometimes makes mistakes.

6 What / How many times a month do you visit your grandparents?

B 다음 빈칸에 알맞은 말을 골라 문장을 완성하시오.

Word Bank	sometimes	never	usually	often	always

1 I call her seven days a week.　　　　　I _____ call her.

2 She visits him two times a week.　　　She _____ visits him.

3 They always get up early.　　　　　　They _____ sleep late.

4 It is foggy four days a week.　　　　　It is _____ foggy.

5 She goes swimming five days a week.　She _____ goes swimming.

C 다음 우리말과 같은 뜻이 되도록 주어진 단어를 배열하시오.

1 그들은 보통 주말에 외식을 한다. (usually / eat out / they / on weekends)

→ _____

2 당신은 얼마나 자주 프랑스 식당에 갑니까? (go to / do you / a French restaurant / how often)

→ _____

3 그는 절대 내게 화를 내지 않는다. (is / angry at me / never / he)

→ _____

4 나는 가끔 바쁘다. (am / busy / sometimes / I)

→ _____

5 Jenny는 아침에 항상 커피 한 잔을 마신다. (always / has / Jenny / in the morning / a cup of coffee)

→ _____

내신 FOCUS

A 다음 괄호 안의 빈도부사를 이용하여 문장을 다시 쓰시오.

1 She goes hiking. (sometimes) → _____.

2 He is tired. (never) → _____.

3 They are friendly. (always) → _____.

4 Susan has a party. (often) → _____.

B 다음 빈칸에 알맞은 말을 고르시오.

1 _____ often do you buy flowers?

ⓐ What ⓑ How ⓒ Where ⓓ Who

2 I have an allergy to cats. I _____ touch them.

ⓐ never ⓑ always ⓒ usually ⓓ sometimes

C 다음 중 어법상 옳지 않은 문장을 고르시오.

1 ⓐ How many time a week do you go swimming?

ⓑ Helen always loses her key.

ⓒ I never break a promise.

ⓓ We are usually at home after work.

2 ⓐ Does he sometimes buy his clothes on the Internet?

ⓑ Is she usually home at seven?

ⓒ Bill always is ready for a golf game.

ⓓ My friends are never rude to my parents.

D 다음 주어진 단어를 이용하여 문장을 완성하시오.

1 너는 그를 얼마나 자주 만나니? (you, meet, him)

→ _____

2 그들은 대개 구내 식당에서 점심을 먹는다. (they, have, lunch, in the cafeteria)

→ _____

3 나는 일주일에 세 번 우리 개를 산책시킨다. (I, walk my dog, a week)

→ _____

4 그는 항상 행복하다. (he, is, happy)

→ _____

비교/최상급의 의미와 형태

A 다음 중 가장 알맞은 것을 고르시오.

1 She dances better / well than he.

2 The apple tree is tall / taller than the cherry tree.

3 My teacher is the kind / kindest person in our school.

4 This car is the cheaper / cheapest in the store.

5 She looks thiner / thinner than last year.

6 Is New York the biggest / most big city in the USA?

7 Eric is heavy / heavier than Tom.

B 다음 주어진 단어를 이용하여 문장을 완성하시오.

1 I feel _____ (tired) than yesterday.

2 Foxes are _____ (clever) than rabbits.

3 She speaks English _____ (good) than he.

4 His father is the _____ (good) swimmer in his family.

5 You act _____ (funny) than Jim Carrey.

6 My new house has _____ (many) windows than my old house.

7 Donovan was the _____ (fast) runner in the world in 1996.

C 다음 우리말과 같은 뜻이 되도록 주어진 단어를 배열하시오.

1 Vatican은 세계에서 가장 작은 나라이다. (the smallest / the Vatican / in the world / is / country)

→ _____

2 당신의 건강이 돈보다 중요하다. (more important / money / your health / is / than)

→ _____

3 그녀는 합창단에서 가장 감미로운 목소리를 가지고 있다. (the sweetest, in the choir, voice, she, has)

→ _____

4 날씨가 어제보다 더 화창하다. (sunnier / the weather / than / is / yesterday)

→ _____

A 다음 형용사 또는 부사의 비교급과 최상급을 쓰시오.

1 cute - _____ - _____   **5** badly - _____ - _____   **9** short - _____ - _____

2 loud - _____ - _____   **6** old - _____ - _____   **10** famous - _____ - _____

3 busy - _____ - _____   **7** strong - _____ - _____   **11** well - _____ - _____

4 much - _____ - _____   **8** few - _____ - _____   **12** pretty - _____ - _____

B 다음 빈칸에 알맞은 말을 고르시오.

1 A cheetah is faster _____ a puma.

ⓐ that   ⓑ then   ⓒ than   ⓓ thin

2 She is _____ in my family.

ⓐ older   ⓑ the oldest   ⓒ old   ⓓ very old

C 다음 중 어법상 옳지 <u>않은</u> 문장을 고르시오.

1 ⓐ I am taller than he is.

ⓑ Do you want more coffee?

ⓒ It is hotter than yesterday.

ⓓ Is this ring the expensivest in your shop?

2 ⓐ He sings the song better than a rock star.

ⓑ This book is the more famous one in Korea.

ⓒ These people are the richest in this city.

ⓓ My sister is older than my brother.

D 다음 우리말과 같은 뜻이 되도록 주어진 단어를 배열하시오.

1 나의 선물은 그의 것보다 비싸다. (more costly / my gift / than / is / his)

→ _____

2 내 방은 우리 집에서 가장 크다. (the biggest / my room / in the house / is)

→ _____

3 날씨가 어제보다 좋지 않다. (worse / the weather / than / is / yesterday)

→ _____

4 이 건물이 우리 도시에서 가장 높다. (the tallest / this building / in our city / is)

→ _____

Unit 09

2 비교 표현

A 다음 중 가장 알맞은 것을 고르시오.

1 The movie is a lot / very more exciting than I expected.

2 I have as much money / more money as you.

3 David's cell phone is not as / as not new as mine.

4 The Alps is the highest / higher mountain chain in Western Europe.

5 Venice is more / most beautiful than any other city in Italy.

6 No other boy in my class is as handsome / more handsome as Brian.

7 The test is much / more easier than I thought.

B 다음 주어진 단어를 이용하여 문장을 완성하시오.

1 A: He is very good at swimming.

B: I know. He can swim _____ (fast) than any other person in Korea.

2 A: Why are you upset?

B: My math score is _____ (bad) than I expected.

3 A: How was your trip?

B: Well, no other place in the US is _____ (beautiful) Miami.

4 A: Her watch is 30 dollars. Mine is 30 dollars, too.

B: Then, her watch is _____ (expensive) yours.

C 다음 우리말과 같은 뜻이 되도록 주어진 단어를 배열하시오.

1 전자메일은 우편보다 훨씬 더 빠르다. (much / is / than / faster / an e-mail / postal mail)

→ _____

2 Picasso는 가장 유명한 화가 중 한 명이다. (the most / one of / Picasso / famous / painters / is)

→ _____

3 남극은 지구상의 다른 어떤 곳보다 춥다. (colder / any other place / than / is / the Antarctic / on earth)

→ _____

4 네 손은 내 손 만큼이나 더러워. (as / dirty / as mine / are / your hands)

→ _____

A 다음 빈칸에 알맞은 말을 쓰시오.

1 Mike is the most handsome guy in my class.

= Mike is _____ than any other guy in my class.

= No other guy in my class is _____ Mike.

2 Your bag is not as heavy as hers.

= Your bag is _____ than hers.

= Her bag is _____ than yours.

B 다음 빈칸에 알맞은 말을 고르시오.

1 The castle is _____ older than I thought.

ⓐ lot　　　　　　ⓑ very　　　　　　ⓒ many　　　　　　ⓓ much

2 The elephant is one of the _____.

ⓐ biggest animals　　ⓑ bigger animals　　ⓒ biggest animal　　ⓓ bigger animal

C 다음 중 어법상 옳지 않은 문장을 고르시오.

1 ⓐ Last summer was as not hot as this summer.

ⓑ The students finished their test much earlier than the teacher expected.

ⓒ He is kinder than any other guy in my neighborhood.

ⓓ This watch is as cheap as that one.

2 ⓐ His yard is as large as the soccer field.

ⓑ Bill Gates is one of the richer men in the world.

ⓒ The movie is much longer than I thought.

ⓓ No other country in the world is as large as Russia.

D 다음 우리말과 같은 뜻이 되도록 주어진 단어를 배열하시오.

1 너는 그녀보다 훨씬 더 똑똑해. (a lot / smarter / you / she / are / than)

→ _____

2 Kelly는 Tom만큼 영화를 좋아하지 않는다. (as much as / movies / Kelly / doesn't like / Tom)

→ _____

3 Jim은 우리 반에서 가장 키가 큰 소년들 중 하나이다. (the tallest boys / Jim / one of / in my class / is)

→ _____

Unit 10
1 목적어를 가지는 동사

A 다음 밑줄 친 동사에 목적어가 있으면 O, 없으면 X를 쓰시오.

1 The sun <u>shines</u> brightly. _____

2 The train <u>reached</u> the station at 8:30 a.m. _____

3 He <u>showed</u> me pictures of his family. _____

4 Kids <u>are singing</u> a Christmas carol for us. _____

5 They <u>sat</u> on the grass. _____

B 다음 주어진 문장을 목적어가 한 개 있는 문장으로 다시 쓰시오.

1 Tom brought me good news.

→ Tom _____.

2 My uncle made me a nice bed.

→ My uncle _____.

3 The teacher asked me a difficult question.

→ The teacher _____.

4 I got my parents two movie tickets.

→ I _____.

5 Aileen told me her secrets.

→ Aileen _____.

C 다음 우리말과 같은 뜻이 되도록 주어진 단어를 배열하시오.

1 그는 그의 아내에게 장미를 보냈다. (to his wife / he / sent / roses)

→ _____

2 Jenny는 종종 할머니에게 편지를 쓴다. (often / writes / Jenny / a letter / to her grandmother)

→ _____

3 Mark는 나무 아래에 서 있었다. (under / Mark / was standing / the tree)

→ _____

4 그들은 그들의 봄방학 여행을 계획하고 있다. (their spring break trip / they / are planning)

→ _____

5 Jim은 그녀에게 다이아몬드 반지를 사 주었다. (a diamond ring / her / bought / Jim)

→ _____

A 다음 문장의 목적어에 밑줄을 그으시오.

1 Mike makes Jenny happy.

2 She gave him a birthday gift.

3 He planted two apple trees yesterday.

4 I cook dinner for our family once a week.

B 다음 빈칸에 알맞은 말을 고르시오.

1 My brother ——————— me a nice kite.

ⓐ like   ⓑ know   ⓒ made   ⓓ has

2 She speaks ———————.

ⓐ me   ⓑ four languages   ⓒ him   ⓓ people

C 다음 중 어법상 옳지 않은 문장을 고르시오.

1 ⓐ Mary and James live Scotland.
  ⓑ The post office closes at 6 p.m.
  ⓒ I work for Walt Disney.
  ⓓ His father teaches students English.

2 ⓐ I spoke on the phone for two hours.
  ⓑ His friends prepared a surprise party for him.
  ⓒ She saw at the doctor yesterday.
  ⓓ The repairman fixed my TV.

D 다음 우리말과 같은 뜻이 되도록 주어진 단어를 배열하시오.

1 역사 수업은 아침 11시에 시작한다. (at 11 / in the morning / the history class / starts)
  → _____

2 그는 지난달에 그녀에게 소포를 보냈다. (a package / he / last month / her / sent)
  → _____

3 나는 연못에서 개구리들을 보았다. (I / in the pond / frogs / saw)
  → _____

4 그 학생은 그의 선생님에게 편지를 썼다. (the student / to his teacher / a letter / wrote)
  → _____

Unit 10

2 보어를 가지는 동사

A 다음 중 가장 알맞은 것을 고르시오.

1 The test was very difficult / very difficultly .

2 This cream soup smells great / greatly .

3 She named her cat Fluffy / Fluffy her cat .

4 Denim jeans became popular / popularly in the 1880's.

5 Jim Carrey always makes me laugh / laugh me .

6 I am going to be sick / sickly .

7 Her face turned very red / redly .

B 다음 주어진 단어를 이용하여 문장을 완성하시오.

1 Please _____. (keep, open, the door)

2 The little boy _____. (look, very healthy)

3 He _____. (her class, interesting, found)

4 I don't _____ for his failure. (sorry, feel)

5 My son never _____. (me, make, angry)

6 She _____. (seem, very friendly)

7 You _____ in the blue sweater. (nice, look)

C 다음 우리말과 같은 뜻이 되도록 주어진 단어를 배열하시오.

1 그는 그녀의 여자친구가 예쁘다고 믿는다. (believes / he / pretty / his girlfriend / is)

   → _____

2 그는 훌륭한 의사가 되었다. (a great doctor / became / he)

   → _____

3 그들은 매우 배가 고프다. (feel / they / very hungry)

   → _____

4 그녀는 그녀의 아들을 피아니스트로 만들었다. (a pianist / she / her son / made)

   → _____

A 다음 문장의 보어에 밑줄을 그으시오.

1 This armchair is comfortable.

2 I left the door open.

3 My brother calls me Piglet.

4 The news made her sad.

B 다음 빈칸에 알맞은 말을 고르시오.

1 She became _____.

ⓐ rich   ⓑ rich her   ⓒ richly   ⓓ her rich

2 The orange juice tastes _____.

ⓐ sourly   ⓑ sweet   ⓒ oranges   ⓓ deliciously

C 다음 중 어법상 옳지 않은 문장을 고르시오.

1 ⓐ My dog made me happy.
   ⓑ They are early birds.
   ⓒ You look wonderfully tonight.
   ⓓ Her face became red.

2 ⓐ Dad wants me for move the car.
   ⓑ The movie made us scared.
   ⓒ I am really wet from the rain.
   ⓓ The story seems strange to me.

D 다음 우리말과 같은 뜻이 되도록 주어진 단어를 배열하시오.

1 사람들은 그를 천재라 부른다. (people / him / a genius / call)
   → _____

2 그 케이크는 정말 달콤할 것 같아. (the cake / very sweet / seems)
   → _____

3 우리는 그를 우리의 지도자로 선택했다. (we / him / as our leader / chose)
   → _____

4 그들은 정말로 행복했다. (they / very happy / were)
   → _____

Unit 11

1 명령문

A 다음 중 가장 알맞은 것을 고르시오.

1 Is / Be a good boy.

2 Don't / Not eat too fast.

3 Get up now, or / and you will be late.

4 Practice hard, or / and you will win the game.

5 Let's have / has a surprise party for him.

6 Do / Does not enter this room.

7 Let's not / don't watch the movie.

B 다음 빈칸에 알맞은 말을 골라 문장을 완성하시오.

Word Bank	raise	take	go	be	turn	open

1 The airplane tickets are so expensive. Let's _____ by train.

2 I'm talking on the phone now. Please _____ down the volume.

3 Do you have any questions? Please _____ your hand.

4 I'm sorry to hear that, but don't _____ so sad.

5 _____ a taxi, and you will get there on time.

6 It's cold outside. Let's not _____ the door.

C 다음 주어진 단어들을 이용하여 문장을 완성하시오.

1 영문법을 공부합시다. (study, English grammar)

    → _____

2 저에게 전화하는 것 잊지 마세요. (forget, to call, me)

    → _____

3 콜라를 마시지 말자. (drink, Coke)

    → _____

4 오른쪽으로 돌면 은행이 보일 거야. (turn right, you, will see, the bank)

    → _____

5 조용히 해 주세요. (please, quiet)

    → _____

A 다음 밑줄 친 부분을 바르게 고친 후 문장을 다시 쓰시오.

1 <u>Drinks</u> lots of water. → _____

2 <u>Doesn't</u> make a noise. → _____

3 Let's <u>makes</u> plans for the next month. → _____

4 Let's <u>don't</u> go to a Japanese restaurant. → _____

5 <u>Do be</u> nice to your friends. → _____

B 다음 빈칸에 알맞은 말을 고르시오.

1 Walk. _____ run!

ⓐ Doesn't   ⓑ Don't   ⓒ Be not   ⓓ Be

2 Let's _____ lunch together.

ⓐ have   ⓑ has   ⓒ having   ⓓ to have

C 다음 중 어법상 옳지 <u>않은</u> 문장을 고르시오.

1 ⓐ Let's ask the teacher.
  ⓑ Please leave a message.
  ⓒ Don't be so nervous.
  ⓓ Go to bed now, and you will get up late.

2 ⓐ Be a good student.
  ⓑ Let's find a good restaurant.
  ⓒ Buy movie tickets now, or you cannot see the movie.
  ⓓ Not do waste your time.

D 다음 주어진 단어들을 이용하여 문장을 완성하시오.

1 질문에 대답해 주세요. (answer, the question, please)

  → _____

2 좀 쉬자. (take, a break)

  → _____

3 조심해! (careful)

  → _____

4 그 약을 먹어, 그러면 기분이 좀 나아질 거야. (take the pill, you, will, feel better)

  → _____

Unit 11

2 감탄문

A 다음 중 가장 알맞은 것을 고르시오.

1 What / How a sweet voice she has!

2 What / How interesting the movie was!

3 How a talkative man / talkative he is!

4 What small / a small fish it is!

5 What beautiful flowers / flower they are!

6 How exciting / excitingly the game is!

7 What a pretty / prettily doll you have!

B 다음 빈칸에 알맞은 말을 골라 문장을 완성하시오.

| Word Bank | boring | tall | expensive | kind |

1 A: I bought a watch yesterday. It was two hundred dollars.

   B: How _____ it is!

2 A: I saw a movie yesterday. I fell asleep during the movie.

   B: How _____!

3 A: I have a brother. He is 6 feet tall.

   B: What a _____ boy he is!

4 A: She always helps other people.

   B: What a _____ person!

C 다음 주어진 문장을 감탄문으로 고쳐 쓰시오.

1 The accident was very terrible.

   → How _____!

2 It was a very sweet dream.

   → What _____!

3 She has very beautiful eyes.

   → What _____!

4 My computer is very fast.

   → How _____!

A 다음 빈칸에 what 또는 how를 쓰시오.

1 _____ a good teacher she is!

2 _____ a nice present you got!

3 _____ dangerous it is!

4 _____ an amazing show!

5 _____ clever she is!

6 _____ happy he is!

7 _____ a silly mistake I made!

8 _____ generous he is!

B 다음 빈칸에 알맞은 말을 고르시오.

1 _____ a beautiful day it is!

ⓐ How   ⓑ That   ⓒ What   ⓓ Which

2 How _____ they are!

ⓐ friendly   ⓑ a friendly   ⓒ luckily   ⓓ a lucky couple

C 다음 중 어법상 옳지 <u>않은</u> 문장을 고르시오.

1 ⓐ What a good boy he is!
  ⓑ How clean your room is!
  ⓒ What a kind person she is!
  ⓓ What amazing the stories are!

2 ⓐ What a deep river!
  ⓑ How wise he is!
  ⓒ What a nice neighbors they are!
  ⓓ What a cold wind it is!

D 다음 주어진 단어를 이용하여 문장을 완성하시오.

1 넌 정말 좋은 언니를 두었구나! (a nice sister, you have)
  → _____

2 그것은 정말 슬픈 소식이구나! (sad news, it is)
  → _____

3 그것은 정말 재미있는 이야기구나! (a funny story, it is)
  → _____

4 그녀는 정말 아름답구나! (beautiful, she is)
  → _____

3 부가/선택의문문

A 다음 중 가장 알맞은 것을 고르시오.

1 Daniel and Dorothy couldn't make it, can't they / could they ?

2 Aileen won't be disappointed with me, will she / will Aileen ?

3 We are going to the park, are we / aren't we ?

4 She doesn't have a car, does she / doesn't she ?

5 What / Which is better for you, water or soda?

6 You were here yesterday, weren't you / were you ?

7 Who / Which is singing now, Toby Mac or his son?

B 다음 빈칸에 알맞은 말을 골라 문장을 완성하시오.

Word Bank	Who	Which	Where	Is	Did

1 _____ dessert do you prefer, cake or pie?

2 _____ plays golf better, Mr. Choi or Tiger Woods?

3 _____ you go there with Tina or Jenny?

4 _____ it good news or bad news?

5 _____ is his next visit, London or Paris?

C 다음 주어진 단어들을 이용하여 문장을 완성하시오.

1 너는 집으로 가는 길을 찾을 수 있지, 그렇지 않니? (you, can, find a way home)

→ _____

2 그는 감기에 걸린 게 아니지, 그렇지? (he, didn't, catch a cold)

→ _____

3 Billy는 그 시험에서 A를 받을 수가 없었지, 그렇지? (Billy, couldn't, get an A, on the test)

→ _____

4 복사기가 고장이 났지, 그렇지 않니? (the copy machine, is, out of order)

→ _____

SCORE: ▼

A 다음 빈칸에 알맞은 말을 쓰시오.

1 You can take pictures well, _____?

2 Jenny and Tommy will be here on time, _____?

3 William exercises every day, _____?

4 _____ is heavier, your bag or my bag?

B 다음 빈칸에 알맞은 말을 고르시오.

1 You broke the vase, _____?

ⓐ do you   ⓑ were you   ⓒ didn't you   ⓓ weren't you

2 _____ helped you, Jim or Dave?

ⓐ Which   ⓑ What   ⓒ Who   ⓓ When

C 다음 중 어법상 옳지 않은 문장을 고르시오.

1 ⓐ Which is longer, the Nile or the Amazon?

  ⓑ You have a headache, didn't you?

  ⓒ It is a lovely day, isn't it?

  ⓓ You were at the conference, weren't you?

2 ⓐ Ed wasn't at home, was he?

  ⓑ Which TV program do you watch, Lost and 24?

  ⓒ He doesn't wear a watch, does he?

  ⓓ You could catch the flight, couldn't you?

D 다음 우리말과 같은 뜻이 되도록 주어진 단어를 배열하시오.

1 나비와 벌 중에 어느 것이 빨리 날까? (which / a butterfly / or a bee / flies / faster)

  → _____

2 당신이 참치 샌드위치를 주문하셨죠, 그렇지 않나요? (didn't you / ordered / a tuna sandwich / you)

  → _____

3 Damon은 자전거를 탈 수 없지, 그렇지? (can he, cannot, ride a bike, Damon)

  → _____

4 Susan는 파티에 올 거죠, 그렇지 않나요? (won't she, come, to the party, will, Susan)

  → _____

1 명사적 쓰임

A 다음 중 가장 알맞은 것을 고르시오.

1 To see is | believe / to believe |.

2 My hobby is | to collect / to collects | coins.

3 I want | to have / having | a cat.

4 He doesn't mind | waiting / to wait | for a moment.

5 Did you finish | reading / to read | the newspaper?

6 We decided | to go / going | to India in May.

B 다음 주어진 문장을 to 부정사는 동명사로, 동명사는 to 부정사로 바꾸어 다시 쓰시오.

1 His hope is to be a pop singer.

→ His hope is _____.

2 I started studying French last year.

→ I started _____.

3 She loves reading cartoons.

→ She loves _____.

4 Getting up early is hard for me.

→ _____ is hard for me.

C 다음 우리말과 같은 뜻이 되도록 주어진 단어를 배열하시오.

1 그들은 산책하는 것을 좋아한다. (like / a walk / they / taking)

→ _____

2 그녀는 매일 일기 쓰는 것을 포기했다. (keeping a dairy / every day / gave up / she)

→ _____

3 내 꿈은 우주를 여행하는 것이다. (traveling / is / to space / my dream)

→ _____

4 그는 당신을 만나기를 원한다. (to meet / he / wants / you)

→ _____

5 그녀가 가장 좋아하는 것은 농구를 하는 것이다. (to play / favorite activity / her / basketball / is)

→ _____

A 다음 밑줄 친 부분을 알맞은 형태로 고치시오.

1 I love lie on the beach. → _____

2 He enjoys spend time with his pets. → _____

3 Their hope is buy a house with a big garden. → _____

4 Nancy needs put on weight. → _____

B 다음 빈칸에 알맞은 말을 고르시오.

1 She began _____ loudly.

ⓐ cry   ⓑ to crying   ⓒ to cry   ⓓ to crys

2 _____ mountains is very difficult.

ⓐ To climbing   ⓑ Climbing   ⓒ To climbs   ⓓ Climb

C 다음 중 어법상 옳지 <u>않은</u> 문장을 고르시오.

1 ⓐ I hate being late for work.
   ⓑ Skating is one of my hobbies.
   ⓒ We enjoy having parties.
   ⓓ My hope is enter Yale University.

2 ⓐ Their friends love to eat pizza.
   ⓑ He likes to walks his dog.
   ⓒ Setting the table is easy for me.
   ⓓ To water the lawn is difficult.

D 다음 주어진 단어를 이용하여 문장을 완성하시오.

1 나는 영화를 보는 것을 좋아한다. (I, like, see movies)
   → _____

2 그녀는 에세이 쓰는 것을 마쳤다. (she, finished, write an essay)
   → _____

3 Harry Potter를 읽는 것은 재미있다. (read, the Harry Potter books, is, exciting)
   → _____

4 너는 영화 배우가 되고 싶니? (do, you, want, be, a movie star)
   → _____

2 형용사적/부사적 쓰임

A 다음 중 가장 알맞은 것을 고르시오.

1 He goes jogging to be / being healthy.

2 I am very glad meeting / to meet you.

3 They saved money in order to / in order for buy a car.

4 She'll bring something to eat / eating .

5 Jenny is looking for some toys playing / to play with.

6 It's time to have / having lunch.

7 There is nothing doing / to do .

B 다음 빈칸에 알맞은 말을 골라 문장을 완성하시오.

Word Bank	stay	give	see	change	help	study

1 I was so excited to _____ the movie star.

2 We need to find a hotel to _____ in.

3 Angelina went to France to _____ art and design.

4 She has no time to _____ you a ride.

5 I called you to _____ the appointment.

6 They collected some money to _____ poor people.

C 다음 우리말과 같은 뜻이 되도록 주어진 단어를 배열하시오.

1 폐를 끼치게 되서 죄송합니다. (sorry / I / am / to / you / disturb)

→ _____

2 우리는 목요일에 치러야 하는 시험이 있다. (have / to take / on Thursday / we / a test)

→ _____

3 나는 이 클럽에 가입하기 위해서 여기에 왔다. (to join / came / this club / I / here)

→ _____

4 집에 갈 시간이다. (time / to / go / is / it / home)

→ _____

A   다음 밑줄 친 부분의 뜻을 쓰시오.

1 I have something to tell you.   _____

2 He went to the library to borrow some books.   _____

3 We are so sad to hear that.   _____

4 There are some clothes to wash in the basket.   _____

B   다음 빈칸에 알맞은 말을 고르시오.

1 Our school has seven rules _____.

   ⓐ to follow   ⓑ to following   ⓒ to follows   ⓓ following

2 It's time _____ your bed.

   ⓐ making   ⓑ to making   ⓒ to make   ⓓ to made

C   다음 중 어법상 옳지 않은 문장을 고르시오.

1 ⓐ I made a sandwich to eat.
   ⓑ There are no movies to rent in the store.
   ⓒ It was nice to seeing you.
   ⓓ They need some wood to make a fire.

2 ⓐ They are surfing the Internet to find some information.
   ⓑ She wants something to eat.
   ⓒ I'm disappointed to hear that.
   ⓓ Is there anything eating in the kitchen?

D   다음 주어진 단어를 이용하여 문장을 완성하시오.

1 난 마실 게 필요해. (need, something, drink)

   → _____

2 그는 그 소식을 듣고 놀랐다. (was surprised, hear the news)

   → _____

3 그녀는 빵을 좀 사기 위해 빵집에 갔다. (went to the bakery, buy some bread)

   → _____

4 이제 작별인사를 할 시간이야. (it's time, say good-bye)

   → _____

Unit 13

1 Unit 장소 전치사 1

A 다음 중 가장 알맞은 것을 고르시오.

1 The teddy bear is on the pillow.

→ The pillow is under / behind the teddy bear.

2 The garden is behind the house.

→ The house is next to / in front of the garden.

3 The drugstore is next to the bank.

→ The bank is beside / across from the drugstore.

4 The car is next to the tree. The car is beside the house.

→ The car is across from / between the tree and the house.

B 다음 빈칸에 알맞은 말을 골라 문장을 완성하시오.

Word Bank	under	in	behind	in front of	between

1 Toys are _____ the box. (상자 안에)

2 A ball was _____ the bed. (침대 밑에)

3 A bench is _____ the big tree. (나무 앞에)

4 James was _____ Jim and Tom. (Jim과 Tom 사이에)

5 A fan is _____ the table. (테이블 뒤에)

C 다음 우리말과 같은 뜻이 되도록 주어진 단어를 배열하시오.

1 내 차 열쇠는 서랍 안에 있다. (in / my car key / the drawer / is)

→ _____

2 역은 우체국 맞은 편에 있다. (across from / the station / the post office / is)

→ _____

3 당신의 겉옷이 소파 위에 있었다. (on / your jacket / the sofa / was)

→ _____

4 아이스크림 가게는 장난감 가게 옆에 있다. (next to / the ice cream shop / the toy store / is)

→ _____

A 다음 빈칸에 알맞은 말을 쓰시오.

1 책상 옆에 → _____ the desk

2 의자 위에 → _____ the chair

3 문 뒤에 → _____ the door

4 내 방과 화장실 사이에 → _____ my room and the bathroom

5 은행 맞은편에 → _____ the bank

6 소파 밑에 → _____ the sofa

7 TV 앞에 → _____ the TV

8 바구니 안에 → _____ the basket

B 다음 빈칸에 알맞지 <u>않은</u> 것을 고르시오.

1 Dolls were _____ the box.

ⓐ on   ⓑ in   ⓒ between   ⓓ next to

2 The post office is _____ the toy shop.

ⓐ over   ⓑ next to   ⓒ across from   ⓓ in front of

C 다음 중 어법상 옳지 <u>않은</u> 문장을 고르시오.

1 ⓐ Who are the women behind him?
   ⓑ A big tree is in front of the park.
   ⓒ A cat is under the bed.
   ⓓ His car was next the ambulance.

2 ⓐ The bus stop is across from the park.
   ⓑ Is my bike across the road?
   ⓒ My motorcycle is in front of the parking lot.
   ⓓ What is on the floor?

D 다음 주어진 단어를 이용하여 문장을 완성하시오.

1 치과는 은행 옆에 있다. (the dental clinic, the bank)

   → _____

2 내 고양이는 책상 밑에 있다. (my cat, the desk)

   → _____

3 서점은 도서관 맞은편에 있니? (the bookstore, the library)

   → _____

4 내 가방은 의자 뒤에 있어. (my bag, the chair)

   → _____

Unit 13

2 장소 전치사 2

A 다음 중 가장 알맞은 것을 고르시오.

1 The students are [on / at] the bus to the zoo.

2 My twin sister is [on / in] art class.

3 The nice picture is [on / in] the wall.

4 Mike was [on / at] home last weekend.

5 My grandparents are [in / at] Alaska.

6 Paul and Kate are [in / at] the bus stop.

B 다음 빈칸에 알맞은 말을 골라 문장을 완성하시오.

| **Word Bank** | on the flight | in the parking lot | on the roof | in the aquarium |

1 지붕 위에 검은 고양이가 있다.

 → The black cat is _____.

2 수족관에 세 마리의 상어가 있다.

 → Three sharks are _____.

3 Brian과 그의 아내는 비행기를 타고 있다.

 → Brian and his wife are _____.

4 빨간 차는 주차장에 있었다.

 → The red car was _____.

C 다음 우리말과 같은 뜻이 되도록 주어진 단어를 배열하시오.

1 그들은 회의 중이다. (at / they / are / the meeting)

 → _____

2 우리 오빠는 군대에 있다. (in / is / my brother / the army)

 → _____

3 Tim과 Joy는 길 위에 있다. (on / are / Tim and Joy / the street)

 → _____

4 너의 강아지가 문가에 있다. (at / your dog / the door / is)

 → _____

5 우리는 기차를 타고 있다. (on / we / the train / are)

 → _____

72

A 다음 빈칸에 알맞은 말을 쓰시오.

1 회의에 → _____ the meeting

2 길 위에 → _____ the street

3 박물관에 → _____ the museum

4 베이징에 → _____ Beijing

5 파티에 → _____ the party

6 3층에 → _____ the third floor

B 다음 빈칸에 알맞은 것을 고르시오.

1 My brother and sister were _____ the living room.

ⓐ at　　　ⓑ in　　　ⓒ on　　　ⓓ of

2 I am _____ the flight.

ⓐ at　　　ⓑ in front of　　　ⓒ on　　　ⓓ of

C 다음 중 어법상 옳지 않은 문장을 고르시오.

1 ⓐ Is your uncle in the army?
ⓑ Who is at the front door?
ⓒ Cats are in the roof.
ⓓ Paul and Diana are in Japan.

2 ⓐ They are at the airport.
ⓑ His car was in the parking lot.
ⓒ Two nice pictures are on the wall.
ⓓ Are you on the theater?

D 다음 주어진 단어를 이용하여 문장을 완성하시오.

1 그녀는 내 차 안에 있다. (in my car)
→ _____

2 그는 무대 위에 있다. (on the stage)
→ _____

3 그들은 버스 정류장에 있다. (at the bus stop)
→ _____

4 우리는 학교 버스에 있다. (on the school bus)
→ _____

Unit 13

3 There is/are

A 다음 중 가장 알맞은 것을 고르시오.

1 There / It are brushes in the box.

2 There was / were a mouse in the garage.

3 Is there / There is a mirror in the bathroom?

4 There are not / not are three candles on the table.

5 There is / are a zebra at the zoo.

6 There is / Is there a man in my room.

B 다음 주어진 조건에 맞게 고쳐 문장을 다시 쓰시오.

1 There are books on the desk. (부정문)

→ _____

2 There is a toilet in the store. (의문문)

→ _____

3 There was a restaurant on 5th Street 10 years ago. (부정문)

→ _____

4 There were frogs in the pond. (의문문)

→ _____

5 There are spoons on the table. (부정문)

→ _____

C 다음 우리말과 같은 뜻이 되도록 주어진 단어를 배열하시오.

1 우리 집에는 TV가 없다. (not / a TV / in / there is / my house)

→ _____

2 나무 밑에는 두 소년이 있다. (two boys / there are / the tree / under)

→ _____

3 박물관 맞은편에 공원이 있니? (across from / is there / the museum / a park)

→ _____

4 은행과 쇼핑 몰 사이에 영화관이 있다. (between the mall / there is / a cinema / and the bank)

→ _____

A 다음 문장을 괄호 안의 지시에 따라 바꾸시오.

1 There is a ball in the basket.

(의문문) → _____

2 There are students in the class.

(부정문) → _____

B 다음 빈칸에 알맞은 말을 고르시오.

1 _____ was a new bike in the yard.

ⓐ They ⓑ There ⓒ These ⓓ Those

2 There _____ four chairs at the table now.

ⓐ are not ⓑ is not ⓒ were not ⓓ not was

C 다음 중 어법상 옳지 <u>않은</u> 문장을 고르시오.

1 ⓐ There aren't any birds in the cage.

ⓑ Is there boys on the playground?

ⓒ There was a beautiful house on the hill.

ⓓ There is a movie on TV now.

2 ⓐ There is a yo-yo in the toy box.

ⓑ Are there crayons in the box?

ⓒ There were two boats on the water.

ⓓ There not is a sign on the window.

D 다음 우리말과 같은 뜻이 되도록 주어진 단어를 배열하시오.

1 집 앞에 차가 한 대 있다. (in front of / there / a car / is / the house)

→ _____

2 바닥에 축구공이 있니? (there / a soccer ball / is / on the floor)

→ _____

3 테이블 위에 선물 상자들이 있었다. (on the table / were / there / gift boxes)

→ _____

4 가게 옆에 우체국이 있다. (is / a post office / the store / there / next to)

→ _____

Unit 14

1 시간 전치사 1

A 다음 중 가장 알맞은 것을 고르시오.

1 She started her business at / on / in 2010.

2 I don't drive at / on / in a snowy day.

3 Black bears sleep at / on / in winter.

4 I was talking on the phone at / on / in that time.

5 We open gifts at / on / in Christmas morning.

6 At / On / In the end of the movie, I cried a lot.

7 He always has a cup of coffee at / on / in the morning.

B 다음 빈칸에 알맞은 말을 넣어 문장을 완성하시오.

1 A: When did you move into your apartment?

   B: I moved here _____ November.

2 A: Does the football game start _____ three?

   B: Yes, it does.

3 A: Do you enjoy watching TV _____ the evening?

   B: No, I don't.

4 A: When is Mother's Day in America?

   B: It is _____ the second Sunday of May.

C 다음 우리말과 같은 뜻이 되도록 주어진 단어를 배열하시오.

1 나는 금요일에는 수업이 없다. (on / any class / I / don't have / Fridays)

   → _____

2 Valentine's Day는 2월에 있다. (in / is / Valentine's Day / February)

   → _____

3 너는 점심시간에 무엇을 먹었니? (at / have / did you / lunchtime / what)

   → _____

4 우리는 추수감사절에 칠면조를 먹어. (on / a turkey / we / Thanksgiving Day / eat)

   → _____

A 다음 빈칸에 각각 공통으로 들어갈 알맞은 말을 쓰시오.

1 Sue is _____ class. School starts _____ September.

2 Linda called you _____ five. She was _____ the party.

3 We were _____ the train _____ Friday night.

B 다음 빈칸에 알맞은 말을 고르시오.

1 Don't eat anything _____ night.

ⓐ in   ⓑ on   ⓒ of   ⓓ at

2 They got married _____ 2012.

ⓐ in   ⓑ on   ⓒ of   ⓓ at

C 다음 중 어법상 옳지 <u>않은</u> 문장을 고르시오.

1 ⓐ She had an important meeting in October 3rd.

ⓑ He went to sleep at midnight yesterday.

ⓒ Strangely, this store opens at 3 a.m.

ⓓ We are always busy at this time of year.

2 ⓐ We are going to London in summer.

ⓑ They have science class in Monday afternoons.

ⓒ She ordered her lunch at 12.

ⓓ We go hiking on Saturdays.

D 다음 우리말과 같은 뜻이 되도록 주어진 단어를 배열하시오.

1 그는 겨울이면 항상 스키를 타러 간다. (in / goes skiing / he / winter / always)

→ _____

2 우리는 크리스마스 이브에 파티를 한다. (on / Christmas Eve / have / a party / we)

→ _____

3 너 점심시간에 어디 갔었니? (at / go / where / lunchtime / did you)

→ _____

4 그녀는 항상 오후에 차 한 잔을 마신다. (a cup of tea / always / she / has / in the afternoon)

→ _____

Unit 14

2 시간 전치사 2

A 다음 중 가장 알맞은 것을 고르시오.

1 They climbed the mountain [from / at] sunrise to sunset.

2 [Before / Around] the heavy snow, I got home safely.

3 He went on a trip [for / during] three months.

4 I don't eat anything [after / for] 8 p.m.

5 Were you nervous [on / during] the interview?

6 She usually has dinner [around / during] 7 p.m.

7 Kevin works from 9 [at / to] 6.

B 다음 빈칸에 알맞은 말을 골라 문장을 완성하시오.

Word Bank	before	after	around	for	from	during

1 I didn't meet him _____ graduation. (졸업 후에)

2 He stood under the hot sun _____ three hours. (3시간 동안)

3 She worked _____ lunchtime. (점심시간 동안)

4 They stayed with us _____ September to October. (9월부터 10월까지)

5 My sister went to bed _____ 12. (12시 경에)

6 Wash your hands _____ dinner. (저녁식사 전에)

C 다음 주어진 단어를 이용하여 문장을 완성하시오.

1 그는 4시부터 6시까지 그의 사무실에 없었다. (he, was not, in his office, four, six)

→ _____

2 콘서트는 5시쯤에 끝났어. (the concert, was over, five)

→ _____

3 우리 아빠는 저녁식사 후에 설거지를 하셨다. (my father, washed the dishes, dinner)

→ _____

4 나는 어제 2시간 동안 잔디를 깎았다. (I, mowed the lawn, two hours, yesterday)

→ _____

A 다음 빈칸에 알맞은 뜻을 쓰시오.

1 방과 후에 - _____ school

2 7일 동안 - _____ seven days

3 시험 전에 - _____ the test

4 방학 동안 - _____ the vacation

5 10시 경에 - _____ 10

6 3시부터 5시까지 - _____ 3 _____ 5

B 다음 빈칸에 알맞은 말을 고르시오.

1 Please don't make any noise _____ the class.

ⓐ for   ⓑ around   ⓒ during   ⓓ about

2 We took the same classes _____ 2012 to 2014.

ⓐ for   ⓑ from   ⓒ during   ⓓ before

C 다음 중 어법상 옳지 <u>않은</u> 문장을 고르시오.

1 ⓐ Let's clean our room before lunch.

   ⓑ Mary stayed in Paris from March to August.

   ⓒ I came home around 12.

   ⓓ My dog barked during three hours last night.

2 ⓐ The bus leaves before 9 a.m.

   ⓑ The speaker left at about 4.

   ⓒ She worked out in the gym during her lunch hour.

   ⓓ He was in Turkey for January to September.

D 다음 주어진 단어를 이용하여 문장을 완성하시오.

1 우리는 방과 후에 영화를 보러 갔다. (we, went to the movies, school)

   → _____

2 그녀는 2시부터 7시까지 수업이 있다. (she, has classes, two, seven)

   → _____

3 우리는 저녁식사 전에 숙제를 한다. (we, do our homework, dinner)

   → _____

4 그는 한 시간 동안 수영을 했다. (he, swam, one hour)

   → _____

Unit 14

3 기타 전치사

A 다음 중 가장 알맞은 것을 고르시오.

1 I cleaned the basement to / with / at my brother.

2 Did you hear the news about / to / without him?

3 I am always there for / to / by you.

4 We went to Seoul on / by / in train.

5 Mike is sitting between / among / in Tom and Jane.

6 We can't live with / without / for air, water, and sunlight.

7 It is very kind for / of / to you to help me.

B 다음 빈칸에 알맞은 말을 골라 문장을 완성하시오.

Word Bank	about	of	for	by	among	with

1 Her grandmother made a sweater _____ Amy. (Amy를 위해서)

2 Today we learned _____ the Bible. (성경에 대하여)

3 They came home _____ taxi. (택시로)

4 What is the title _____ the book? (그 책의)

5 Look at the boy _____ big eyes. (큰 눈을 가진)

6 She found him _____ many people. (많은 사람들 사이에서)

C 다음 우리말과 같은 뜻이 되도록 주어진 단어를 배열하시오.

1 그 영화는 Napoleon에 관한 것이다. (about / is / the movie / Napoleon)

→ _____

2 우리는 두 시험 시간 사이에 쉬는 시간을 가졌다. (between / had a break / two tests / we)

→ _____

3 나는 아무 도움 없이 내 침대를 옮겼다. (without / moved / my bed / any help / I)

→ _____

4 그녀는 종종 자전거로 학교에 간다. (by / goes to school / often / she / bike)

→ _____

5 George는 그의 부모님을 위해서 집을 지었다. (for / George / built / a house / his parents)

→ _____

A 다음 빈칸에 알맞은 전치사를 쓰시오.

> **Word Bank**   with   between   without   about   for   among

1 Will you go to the party _____ me?

2 This is _____ you and me.

3 What is this movie _____ ?

4 Happy birthday! This is _____ you.

5 Pick two cards _____ ten.

6 You can't enter _____ an ID.

B 다음 빈칸에 알맞은 말을 고르시오.

1 She is the most beautiful girl _____ them. (그들 사이에서)

ⓐ between   ⓑ among   ⓒ in   ⓓ without

2 She draws pictures only _____ a black pen. (검정색 펜으로)

ⓐ to   ⓑ of   ⓒ with   ⓓ for

C 다음 중 어법상 옳지 <u>않은</u> 문장을 고르시오.

1 ⓐ Did you paint your room without help?

   ⓑ He lost his book among the library books.

   ⓒ I always think to you.

   ⓓ They saw a documentary about a great artist.

2 ⓐ I'll pay by cash.

   ⓑ The children came without coats.

   ⓒ The secret is among us.

   ⓓ She reached the island by plane.

D 다음 주어진 단어를 이용하여 문장을 완성하시오.

1 나는 내 아내를 위해 크리스마스 선물을 샀다. (I, bought, a Christmas gift, my wife)

   → _____

2 그녀는 항상 그녀의 새 남자친구에 대해서 이야기 한다. (she, always, talks, her new boyfriend)

   → _____

3 그의 컴퓨터에 문제가 있어요. (there is, a problem, his computer)

   → _____

Unit 15

1 and/but/or/so

A 다음 중 가장 알맞은 것을 고르시오.

1 Andrew and / but / or Alfred are my cousins.

2 It began to rain, but / so / or I bought an umbrella.

3 Snow White and / or / but Cinderella are my favorite fairy tales.

4 Are they true stories or / so / but myths?

5 Tim is in class, but / so / or he can't go with us.

6 I had a nice cell phone, so / but / or I lost it.

7 Would you like to leave a message and / but / or call her back in one hour?

B 다음 빈칸에 알맞은 말을 골라 문장을 완성하시오.

Word Bank	or	and	but	so

1 It's already 9 p.m. You can go home _____ stay with us.

2 Last weekend, I invited my friends _____ had a barbecue party.

3 He saved my son's life, _____ my son called him "Superman."

4 She is a newcomer. Everybody likes her, _____ I don't.

C 다음 주어진 단어를 이용하여 하나의 문장으로 만드시오.

1 Would you like to have some apple pie? Would you like to have some cherry pie? (or)

→ _____

2 My grandfather is old. He is healthy. (but)

→ _____

3 They practiced hard. They won the football game. (so)

→ _____

4 My sister enjoys singing. My brother enjoys singing, too. (and)

→ _____

5 I hurried to go to the airport. I missed my flight. (but)

→ _____

82

A 다음 빈칸에 알맞은 접속사를 쓰시오. (and, but, or, so)

1 John _____ Debbie are my best friends.

2 I will leave today _____ tomorrow.

3 I found a dollar, _____ I bought some candy.

4 Matthew is lazy _____ smart.

B 다음 빈칸에 알맞은 말을 쓰시오.

1 He is smart _____ handsome.

ⓐ so   ⓑ and   ⓒ or   ⓓ but

2 You can go there by bus _____ by train.

ⓐ so   ⓑ and   ⓒ or   ⓓ but

C 다음 중 밑줄 친 부분이 어법상 옳지 않은 것을 고르시오.

1 ⓐ She is at work or at home.

ⓑ He won the race, but he wasn't happy.

ⓒ I went to the library or borrowed two books.

ⓓ It started raining, so my mom closed the window.

2 ⓐ I left him a message, but he didn't get it.

ⓑ My favorite colors are green and white.

ⓒ My cat was very sick, or I took it to the vet.

ⓓ This book or that book is fine for his gift.

D 다음 주어진 단어들을 이용하여 문장을 완성하시오.

1 그는 피곤해서 일찍 잠을 잤다. (he, was tired, he, went to bed, early)

→ _____

2 디저트로 아이스크림이나 푸딩을 사자. (let's, buy, ice cream, pudding, for dessert)

→ _____

3 나는 어제 수영하러 갔지만 내 동생은 가지 않았어. (I, went swimming, yesterday, my sister, didn't go)

→ _____

4 그녀는 햄버거와 오렌지 주스를 주문했다. (she, ordered, a hamburger, orange juice)

→ _____

2 기타 접속사

A 다음 중 가장 알맞은 것을 고르시오.

1 Since / When you see him, please give my regards to him.

2 If / Since she broke her glasses, she can't read well.

3 I called the police because / so I saw a thief.

4 Put on your coat before / after you go outside.

5 If / Before you help him, he can finish his homework easily.

6 After / Since you went out, your friend called you.

7 If / Before you read this book carefully, you will know the answer.

B 다음 빈칸에 알맞은 말을 골라 문장을 완성하시오.

Word Bank	because	if	when	after	before

1 _____ the game is over, let's have dinner together. (게임이 끝난 후에)

2 _____ he heard the news, he was surprised. (그가 뉴스를 들었을 때)

3 _____ you are free on Saturday, come to my party. (만약 토요일에 시간이 있다면)

4 Take an umbrella _____ it is raining. (비가 오고 있으니)

5 We always pray _____ we have meals. (우리는 식사를 하기 전에)

C 다음 주어진 단어를 이용하여 하나의 문장으로 완성하시오.

1 The train left at 4:00. We arrived at the station at 4:05. (before)

    → The train left _____ at the station.

2 The road was slippery. I slid down the road. (because)

    → I slid down the road _____.

3 We will walk to school. We will be late. (if)

    → _____, we will be late.

4 I was waiting for the bus. I saw them. (when)

    → I saw them _____ for the bus.

5 He has a bad cold. He stayed at home today. (since)

    → _____, he stayed at home today.

SCORE: ▼

A 다음 밑줄 친 부분을 우리말로 옮기시오.

1 I drink hot chocolate <u>when the weather is cold</u>. → _____

2 I graduated <u>after four years of college</u>. → _____

3 <u>If I get a ticket</u>, I will go to the concert. → _____

4 <u>Before you cross the street</u>, look both ways. → _____

5 <u>Since I didn't have lunch</u>, I was hungry. → _____

B 다음 빈칸에 알맞은 말을 고르시오.

1 _____ you need my help, let me know.

ⓐ After   ⓑ Since   ⓒ If   ⓓ Because

2 The sun appeared _____ the storm.

ⓐ because   ⓑ after   ⓒ if   ⓓ when

C 다음 중 밑줄 친 부분이 알맞지 <u>않은</u> 것을 고르시오.

1 ⓐ <u>After</u> we went hiking, I had pain in my knee.
  ⓑ <u>When</u> my sister feels great, she dances.
  ⓒ <u>If</u> you find the answer, you will be the winner.
  ⓓ <u>Before</u> it was raining, I didn't play outside.

2 ⓐ <u>If</u> you are sick, stay in bed.
  ⓑ <u>Since</u> he was tired, he didn't drive.
  ⓒ She will send the file <u>since</u> she finishes it.
  ⓓ The dog barked <u>because</u> the man was a stranger.

D 다음 주어진 단어들을 이용하여 문장을 완성하시오.

1 집에 도착하면 당신에게 전화할게요. (when, get home)

→ I'll call you _____.

2 더웠기 때문에 나는 창문을 열었다. (so, open, the window)

→ It was hot, _____.

3 그녀는 숙제를 끝낸 후 영화를 보러 갔다. (after, finish, her homework)

→ _____, she went to the movies.

4 날씨가 좋으면, 우리는 동물원에 갈 것이다. (if, the weather, nice)

→ _____, we'll go to the zoo this weekend.

The Grammar

Starter

Concise & Core Grammar
불필요하고 잘 사용하지 않는 문법은 배제하고
핵심적인 부분만을 간결하고 정확하게 예문
중심으로 이해할 수 있도록 구성

Sentence Expansion
기초 문법을 기반으로 문장을 완성, 확장해 가는
학습 방법 적용

A Variety of Question Types
문법 포인트 확인 · 기초 문법 문제 · 응용 문제 · 리뷰
테스트 · 문법 확장 문제 · 종합 문제

Preparation for School Tests
다양한 문제 유형을 통해 내신 대비는 물론 말하기
및 쓰기 실력 향상

Grammar Summary
배운 학습 내용을 차트 및 표로 정리하여 쉽게
암기할 수 있도록 구성

Workbook
내신 대비 및 서술형 평가 대비를 위한 충분한
분량의 문제가 수록된 워크북 제공

www.nexusEDU.kr
넥서스 초 · 중 · 고등 사이트

www.nexusbook.com
넥서스 홈페이지

	초1	초2	초3	초4	초5	초6	중1	중2	중3	고1	고2	고3

Writing

공감 영문법+쓰기
1~2

도전만점
중등내신 서술형 1~4

영어일기 영작패턴
1-A, B · 2-A, B

Smart Writing 1~2

Reading

Reading 101 1~3

Reading 공감 1~3

This Is Reading Starter 1~3

This Is Reading
전면 개정판 1~4

This Is Reading 1-1 ~ 3-2 (각 2권; 총 6권)

원서 술술 읽는
Smart Reading Basic 1~2

원서 술술 읽는
Smart Reading 1~2

[특급 단기 특강]
구문독해 · 독해유형

Listening

Listening 공감 1~3

The Listening 1~4

After School Listening
1~3

도전! 만점
중학 영어듣기 모의고사
1~3

만점 적중
수능 듣기 모의고사
20회 · 35회

TEPS

NEW TEPS 입문편 실전 250⁺
청해 · 문법 · 독해

NEW TEPS 기본편 실전 300⁺
청해 · 문법 · 독해

NEW TEPS 실력편 실전 400⁺
청해 · 문법 · 독해

NEW TEPS 마스터편 실전 500⁺
청해 · 문법 · 독해

이것이 THIS IS 시리즈다!

THIS IS GRAMMAR 시리즈

▷ 중 · 고등 내신에 꼭 등장하는 어법 포인트 분석 및 총정리

강남인강
강의교재

THIS IS READING 시리즈

▷ 다양한 소재의 지문으로 내신 및 수능 완벽 대비

강남인강
강의교재

THIS IS VOCABULARY 시리즈

▷ 주제별로 분류한 교육부 권장 어휘

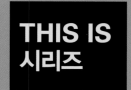